# THE GUIDE TO AUSTRALIAN USAGE AND PUNCTUATION

**Dr George Stern** was consultant lecturer in applied linguistics at the Australian National University for twenty-five years. He has a Diploma of English Studies from Cambridge University and other degree qualifications from Australian and US universities.

**Robert Bolitho** and **Russell Lutton** have between them over fifty years of practical experience in reporting the Australian Parliament. Both have occupied senior editorial positions in Federal Hansard and have been involved in establishing Hansard editorial policy and training in English usage.

# THE GUIDE TO AUSTRALIAN USAGE AND PUNCTUATION

George Stern  Robert Bolitho
Russell Lutton

**CollinsDove**
A Division of HarperCollins*Publishers*

Published by Collins Dove
A Division of HarperCollins*Publishers* (Australia) Pty Ltd
22–24 Joseph Street
North Blackburn, Victoria 3130

© Copyright George Stern, Robert Bolitho, Russell Lutton
All rights reserved. Except as provided by Australian copyright law, no part of this book may be reproduced without permission in writing from the publishers.

First published 1993
Designed by William Hung
Cover design by William Hung

Typeset in Australia by CollinsDove*Publishers*
Printed in Australia by Griffin Paperbacks, Adelaide

The National Library of Australia
Cataloguing-in-Publication Data:

Stern, George, 1930– .
 The guide to Australian usage and punctuation.

Includes index.
ISBN 0 86371 131 7.

 [1]. English language — Australia — Usage. 2. English language — Australia — Punctuation. I. Bolitho, Robert. II. Lutton, Russell. III. Title.

428.00994

## Acknowledgements
We gratefully acknowledge the following for their permission to use copyright material.
The estate of late Patrick White and publisher Johnathan Cape for extracts from *Voss*.
Kate Jennings, Helen Pitt and David O'Reilly for extracts from *The Bulletin with Newsweek*.

# Contents

Foreword ... vii
How to use this book ... ix

## PART I  Usage

1. Dogmatic myths about usage ... 1
2. Common problems of usage ... 8
3. Gender language and sexist language ... 19
4. Agreement of nominative and finite verb ... 30
5. Split infinitive verbs and split compound verbs ... 45
6. The subjunctive mood and conditional sentences ... 52
7. Numbers ... 71
8. The relative pronouns "who", "whom", "which", "that" ... 101
9. Parenthetic elements ... 116
10. Transforming direct speech into reported speech ... 127
11. Italic print and underlined roman print or writing ... 142
12. Capital letters and small letters ... 150

## PART II  Punctuation

13. Full stops ... 175
14. Exclamation marks ... 183
15. Question marks ... 189
16. Commas ... 197
17. Semicolons ... 226
18. Colons and dashes ... 236
19. Brackets ... 246

## Contents

| | | |
|---|---|---|
| 20. | Apostrophes | 250 |
| 21. | Hyphens | 265 |
| 22. | Slashes | 281 |
| 23. | Quotation marks | 284 |
| 24. | Ellipses | 301 |
| 25. | Asterisks and allied symbols | 310 |
| Glossary | | 314 |
| Index | | 337 |

# Foreword

Here is a problem in usage. Which of the following is it best to use?

1. This is the person that I work for.
2. This is the person for whom I work.
3. This is the person whom I work for.
4. This is the person I work for.

Now here is a problem in punctuation. Which of the following has the better punctuation?

1. They are cool, calm, and collected.
2. They are cool, calm and collected.

These are the sorts of problems that this book explores and that it gives you detailed guidance on. The book, though, is not a systematic manual of grammar, although grammar does come into the discussion. Neither does the book deal with problems such as whether you should use the spelling "fulfil" or "fulfill".

Rather, what this book does give you is guidelines on problems of usage and punctuation — the sorts of problems that all kinds of people encounter when they use, write or record spoken and written English. Among these people are authors and editors, students and teachers, public- and private sector executives, people who write correspondence and reports, Hansard reporters and minute takers, and other people who are interested in using the language in appropriate ways.

In writing this book we have given guidance on what we consider to be the best forms of usage and punctuation in various contexts. In doing so, we have sometimes found it necessary to enter the realm of grammar. But we have given only so much of the grammatical information as is needed for an understanding of our recommended practices. In these technical

# Foreword

excursions we have assumed no prior knowledge of grammar on your part, and we explain the technicalities as they arise in the text. At the back of the book we have also provided a glossary that you can turn to whenever you like.

We have based our explanations on the concepts and terminology of traditional grammar — verbs and nouns, singular and plural, subject and object, and the like. Our choice of traditional terminology for this book rests on two premises. One is that, if you, the reader, are familiar at all — even if only dimly so — with English grammar, then it is likely that your familiarity will be with traditional grammar. The other is that the terms and concepts of traditional grammar are the ones that are still most commonly used in dictionaries. So if you resort to a dictionary in association with this book, you will find both sources — this book and your dictionary — agreeing in their use of terminology.

But although we use traditional grammar as the basis for our explanations in this book, we are not dogmatic adherents of the kinds of rules of traditional grammar that you might have learned in your school days. Far from it. The main principle underlying this book is that the English language is not set in the concrete of traditional grammar but, rather, that it is a living and evolving system that allows variations and options at almost every turn. We show you what these variations and options are, and we leave it to you to choose among them.

By the way, if you have been wondering about the two sets of examples that we gave at the start of this foreword, then let us set your mind at ease. In the first set of examples you may, in varying circumstances, use any one of the given options. In the second set of examples you may punctuate the sentence either way. For a full understanding of the reasoning behind these solutions we invite you to turn the page and to read the prefatory chapter on how to use this book.

# How to use this book

At the foot of each alternate page of this book, you will find an identical set of footnotes. They are numbered from 1 to 6. In this preface we explain the meaning of the footnotes. In brief, the footnotes tell you the varying degrees of validity of the usages we present as examples. Before telling you what these degrees of validity are, though, we would like to tell you the logic behind our scheme of six usage categories.

In the bad old dogmatic days there were only two kinds of sentences — right and wrong. Authority figures of every kind used to reject whatever expressions contravened any particular rigid rule that they might have adopted. There was, after all, only one correct way to write things; and everything else was incorrect. Our view is that there is much more flexibility in English usage and punctuation, and that there is a much wider range of permissible styles and modes of expression. This does not mean that there are no standards at all. It means that we can make more subtle distinctions among a range of usages.

Our expanded range of usage categories, and what these categories mean, are as follows.

**1. STANDARD FORMAL: use this, and you can't go wrong in formal contexts.**
This usage is suitable for formal texts such as books and articles, business letters and essays. It agrees most nearly with what one might call textbook grammar. When we mark something as a usage of this type, we are suggesting that a deviation from it is old-fashioned (usage 4 below) or informal (usage 5 below) or nonstandard (usage 6 below).

> I wish they were here.[1]
> (As distinct from the old-fashioned: "Would that they were here."[4])
> It is I.[1]
> (As distinct from the standard informal: "It's me."[5])

## How to use this book

I did it.[1]
(As distinct from the nonstandard: "I done it."[6])

**2. STANDARD FORMAL WITH CONSISTENT OPTIONS: choose one and stick to it.**
Under this usage we always present two or more options — either (or any) of which is just as legitimate as usage 1 above. You may choose freely among the options but, once you have made your choice, you have to stick to it throughout the particular text you are writing. A clear example of this is the punctuation of a quotation. You may choose to enclose a quotation within single quotation marks or within double quotation marks. Both are equally correct in strict grammar but, once you have made the choice one way or the other, you cannot change it in that particular text.

They said, "We are happy."[2]
They said, 'We are happy.'[2]

**3. STANDARD FORMAL WITH FLEXIBLE OPTIONS: choose any one, any time.**
In usage 3 — as in usage 2 above — we always present two or more options, either (or any) of which is just as legitimate as usage 1 above. You may choose freely among the options, and it is not even necessary (as it is in usage 2 above) to remain consistent in your choice. You may opt for one way in one sentence and, in the very next sentence of the very same text, you may opt for another way. An example of usage 3 is the use or the omission of a comma after a phrase such as "Earlier this week" at the beginning of a sentence. Either is correct in strict grammar, and it doesn't matter two hoots which way you go.

Earlier this week I met an old friend.[3]
Earlier this week, I met an old friend.[3]

**4. OLD-FASHIONED: still all right, but fading from modern usage.**
This usage does not include such outright archaisms as "Whither art thou

---

1 Standard formal: *use this, and you can't go wrong in formal contexts.*
2 Standard formal with consistent options: *choose one and stick to it.*
3 Standard formal with flexible options: *choose any one, any time.*
4 Old-fashioned: *still all right, but fading from modern usage.*
5 Standard informal: *fine in conversation or in personal letters.*
6 Nonstandard: *you jez'gotta be kidding.*

# How to use this book

going?" — no one would use such language in normal prose anyway. What it does include are twentieth century usages that, though they are grammatically valid, are stodgy or outmoded.

Would that they were here.[4]
(More modern is: "I wish they were here."[1])
I met a Minister of the new Government.[4]
(More modern is: "I met a minister of the new government."[1])

**5. STANDARD INFORMAL: fine in conversation or in personal letters.**
This usage includes those forms of language that may not agree with the strictest canons of grammar, but that people use anyway in conversation or in informal contexts such as personal letters. Usage 5 is the language of people who are careful and sensitive in their use of language — when they use language in a relaxed or informal mode.

It's me.[5]
(As distinct from the standard formal but stilted: "It is I."[1])
Who are you looking for?[5]
(As distinct from the standard formal: "Whom are you looking for?"[1])

**6. NONSTANDARD: you jez' gotta be kidding.**
This usage includes language that would not be acceptable, say, in a newspaper article or in a book — unless enclosed by quotation marks. Most people would also not use such language in their normal conversation. It does have a validity, though, in jocular speech or in street argot.

They was happy.[6]
(As distinct from: "They were happy."[1])
I done it.[6]
(As distinct from: "I did it."[1])

For the rest of the book, whenever we give examples of usage and punctuation, we mark these examples with one of the numbers from 1 to 6. A glance at the numbers, and at the definitions of the numbers at the foot of any alternate page, will instantly tell you the status of the examples.

# PART I
# USAGE

|     |                                                        | Page |
| --- | ------------------------------------------------------ | ---- |
| 1.  | Dogmatic myths about usage                             | 1    |
| 2.  | Common problems of usage                               | 8    |
| 3.  | Gender language and sexist language                    | 19   |
| 4.  | Agreement of nominative and finite verb                | 30   |
| 5.  | Split infinitive verbs and split compound verbs        | 45   |
| 6.  | The subjunctive mood and conditional sentences         | 52   |
| 7.  | Numbers                                                | 71   |
| 8.  | The relative pronouns "who", "whom", "which", "that"   | 101  |
| 9.  | Parenthetic elements                                   | 116  |
| 10. | Transforming direct speech into reported speech        | 127  |
| 11. | Italic print and underlined roman print or writing     | 142  |
| 12. | Capital letters and small letters                      | 150  |

# CHAPTER 1
# Dogmatic myths about usage

## Overview

In this chapter we deal with five common myths about English usage. They are the sorts of myths that authority figures back up with dogmatic assertions such as: "You can't use that word here," or "You've got to use this word there." When you innocently inquire why you can't use this or you must use that, the triumphant explanation — also dogmatically asserted — is usually, "Because it isn't (or "Because it is") good usage." If you pressed the matter further and enquired what good usage was, you would probably get the answer that it's what some particular book, or some particular expert, said. And so we come full circle from one authority figure to another authority figure.

We don't hold with this attitude. The fact is that, in English-speaking countries, there is no central body — no academy of the English language, for example, or any other authority — that has the power to lay down firm rules on usage. Does this mean that anything goes; that one usage is as good as any other? No, it doesn't mean that at all. So what, then, is good usage?

Well, good usage is what good writers use. It's as simple as that. There is a sort of consensus among quality writers, quality publishing houses and quality periodicals as to what constitutes good usage. What these writers, publishers and periodicals use is what — in any given period — good usage is.

If you want to find out whether something is passable in English usage, don't blindly accept the authority of a self-appointed expert. Instead, go back to the original sources of good usage — the usage of quality writers, publishers and periodicals. You won't, for example, see them using expressions such as "We was ready" — except when they are quoting

## Usage

someone else's speech or if they are writing tongue in cheek. What you will see them use is what is consensually agreed to be good usage. And what is good enough for them is good enough for you and us. No strictures by authority figures can reverse that — any more than the authority of King Canute could reverse the tide.

There are five particular myths that we expose in this chapter.

### A. Never start a sentence with "and"
And we are still wondering why not.

### B. Never start a sentence with "but"
But many quality authors do just that.

### C. Never end a sentence with a preposition
As Churchill said of this myth, that is a piece of pedantry up with which we will not put.

### D. Never use the word "get" or any of its variant forms
We don't get the reason for this myth, because it has got no foundation.

### E. If you use "if" in the first part of a sentence, don't use "then" in the second part of the sentence
If that myth had any validity, then many reputable writers would be in trouble.

We discuss all these myths in the main part of the chapter, and we show — from the writings of reputable authors — that there is no validity to these myths.

### A. Never start a sentence with "and"
Of course, "and" is a conjunction (a joining word), and you will usually find it in the middle — rather than at the beginning — of a sentence. But that doesn't mean that you can never start a sentence, or even a paragraph,

---

1 Standard formal: *use this, and you can't go wrong in formal contexts.*
2 Standard formal with consistent options: *choose one and stick to it.*
3 Standard formal with flexible options: *choose any one, any time.*
4 Old-fashioned: *still all right, but fading from modern usage.*
5 Standard informal: *fine in conversation or in personal letters.*
6 Nonstandard: *you jez'gotta be kidding.*

### Dogmatic myths about usage

with this word. Here, to convince you that it is all right to do so, are some examples in which well-regarded writings have sentences that start with "and".

> ... Titan ... did hotly overlook them;
> Wishing Adonis and his team to guide,
> So he were like him and by Venus' side.
> **And** now Adonis ... cries, "Fie! no more of love ..."[1]
> William Shakespeare, *Venus and Adonis* (page 1076).

Shakespeare's language is now archaic, but his use of "and" at the beginning of a sentence is right up to date.

> She did, indeed, start. **And** she caught his wrist with both her hands.[1]
> Charles Dickens, *A Tale of Two Cities* (page 235).

> In the circumstances they would accept a hand or two. **And** Mr Voss had a strong wrist.[1]
> Patrick White, *Voss* (page 65).

> Listening to Richards, my heart leapt. **And** it continued to leap as woman after woman spoke from the podium or the floor.[1]
> *The Bulletin with Newsweek*, 4 August 1992 (page 33).

### B. Never start a sentence with "but"

Like the conjunction "and", the conjunction "but" usually occurs in the middle of a sentence. But this is no reason for asserting that you can never start a sentence or a new paragraph with the word. In fact, one of Shakespeare's sonnets starts with that very word, and other writers too have not hesitated to start sentences and paragraphs with "but". Here is the evidence.

> **But** wherefore do not you a mightier way
> Make war upon this bloody tyrant, Time?[1]
> William Shakespeare, "Sonnet XVI".

> Pride, contempt, defiance, stubbornness, submission, lamentation, succeeded one another ... **But** the face was in the main one face, and every head was prematurely white.[1]
> Charles Dickens, *A Tale of Two Cities* (page 224).

**Usage**

So he was proud for a little. **But** the rather delicate ornithologist remained humble.[1]
Patrick White, *Voss* (page 103).

International, constitutional and administrative law may also be changed. **But,** most importantly, the High Court decision underlines the need to come to some national compromise on the issue . . .[1]
*The Bulletin with Newsweek,* 4 August 1992 (page 24).

### C. Never end a sentence with a preposition

Prepositions are useful little words such as "for", "from", "with" and the like. If you couldn't put prepositions at the end of sentences, your language would be stilted and old-fashioned, rather than natural and modern.

"**What** do you want this **for**?"[1]
"**For what** do you want this?"[4]
"**Where** do you come **from**?"[1]
"**From where** do you come?"[4]

As you will see from the examples cited below, the stricture on not putting prepositions at the end of sentences is something that quality writers pay no attention to.

. . . The iron bit he crushes 'tween his teeth,
Controlling what he was controlled **with**.[1]
William Shakespeare, *Venus and Adonis* (page 1077).

. . . A mail journey from London in winter was an achievement to congratulate an adventurous traveller **upon**.[1]
Charles Dickens, *A Tale of Two Cities* (page 227).

. . . He is one of the superior ones, even though pitiable, those trousers that he has trodden **on**.[1]
Patrick White, *Voss* (page 17).

1 Standard formal: *use this, and you can't go wrong in formal contexts.*
2 Standard formal with consistent options: *choose one and stick to it.*
3 Standard formal with flexible options: *choose any one, any time.*
4 Old-fashioned: *still all right, but fading from modern usage.*
5 Standard informal: *fine in conversation or in personal letters.*
6 Nonstandard: *you jez'gotta be kidding.*

Right through the convention, runners delivered placards to each section, the messages on them coinciding with the personalities on the podium or the issues being dealt **with**.[1]
*The Bulletin with Newsweek*, 4 August 1992 (page 33).

## D. Never use the word "get" or any of its variant forms

The 1989 edition of *The Oxford English Dictionary* devotes ten pages to the useful little word "get", and it gives about three hundred definitions and subdefinitions for it. That same monumental work gives quotations incorporating the word "get" from scores of authors, including Geoffrey Chaucer, William Caxton, Alexander Pope, Jane Austen, Mark Twain, Alfred Lord Tennyson, George Bernard Shaw, Henry Miller and a host of other twentieth century writers.

By way of contrast, the dictionary devotes only one sixth of a page to the word "dogmatism" and one third of a page to the word "stupidity". Surely it is dogmatic and stupid to censor such a versatile and widely used word as "get". We are not saying that you have got to use the word in your writings: what we are saying is that, if you do use it in appropriate and legitimate contexts, you will be in the company of the best of writers — among them, those that we cite below.

> **Get** thee to a nunnery . . .[1]
> William Shakespeare, *Hamlet* (page 886).

> The passenger would then . . . lower the window to **get** the reality of mist and rain on his cheek.[1]
> Charles Dickens, *A Tale of Two Cities* (page 225).

> Harry Robarts, who had **got** there earliest after his leader, to be ignored, would have felt lost . . .[1]
> Patrick White, *Voss* (page 101).

> The government has talked at length of the need to educate and train workers to acquire skills necessary to **get** employment.[1]
> *The Bulletin with Newsweek*, 4 August 1992 (page 18).

Finally, we cannot resist quoting a verse from a poem by one of the greatest stylists of the English language.

**Usage**

>    ... Eaten by teeth of flame,
>    In a burning winding-sheet he lies,
>    And his grave has **got** no name.[1]
>    Oscar Wilde, *The Ballad of Reading Gaol* (page 860).

## E. If you use "if" in the first part of a sentence, don't use "then" in the second part of the sentence

As far as we can tell, no one has ever given a rational reason for this silly myth. Certainly, if a sentence starts with the word "if", there is no compelling need to have the word "then" in the continuation of the sentence. But that is not to say that there must be a ban on the word.

>    **If** ten of thine ten times refigur'd thee;
>    **Then** what could death do, if thou shouldst depart,
>    Leaving thee living in posterity?[1]
>    William Shakespeare, "Sonnet VI".

>    "... **If** his wife had implored the king, the queen, the clergy, for any tidings of him, and all quite in vain; **then** the history of your father would have been the history of this unfortunate gentleman ... "[1]
>    Charles Dickens, *A Tale of Two Cities* (page 235).

>    **If** I am lost, **then** who can be saved ... ?[1]
>    Patrick White, *Voss* (page 80).

>    ... **If** the skills of the unemployed can be increased, access will **then** be gained to middle-level jobs ...[1]
>    *The Bulletin with Newsweek*, 4 August 1992 (page 18).

The following schemata are said to have been set out by Chrysippus as indemonstrable:

1. **If** the first **then** the second; but the first; therefore the second;

2. **If** the first **then** the second; but not the first; therefore not the second ...[1]

---

1 Standard formal: *use this, and you can't go wrong in formal contexts.*
2 Standard formal with consistent options: *choose one and stick to it.*
3 Standard formal with flexible options: *choose any one, any time.*
4 Old-fashioned: *still all right, but fading from modern usage.*
5 Standard informal: *fine in conversation or in personal letters.*
6 Nonstandard: *you jez'gotta be kidding.*

**If** someone swears that he swears falsely, **then,** if he swears falsely, what he swears is not true . . . ; but **if** he does not swear falsely, **then** what he swears is true . . .[1]
*The New Encyclopaedia Britannica* (volume 23, pages 238 and 240).

In the above discussion we have cited seven sources. We could just as easily have cited seven hundred. The fact is that all writers and publishers ignore these myths. So can you, if you feel like it.

## Chronological bibliography for this chapter
William Shakespeare, *The Complete Works of William Shakespeare*. (London: Oxford University Press, 1954).

Charles Dickens, *A Christmas Carol, The Cricket on the Hearth, A Tale of Two Cities*. (London: Octopus Books Limited, 1980).

Oscar Wilde, *The Complete Works of Oscar Fingal O'Flahertie Wills Wilde: Stories, Plays, Poems, Essays*. (London: Collins, 1966).

Patrick White, *Voss*. (London: Eyre & Spottiswoode, 1957).

Philip W. Goetz (Editor-in-Chief), *The New Encyclopaedia Britannica*. (Chicago: University of Chicago, 1985).

J. A. Simpson and E. S. C. Weiner (editors), *The Oxford English Dictionary*, second edition. (Oxford: Clarendon Press, 1989).

*The Bulletin with Newsweek* (issue of 4 August 1992).

# CHAPTER 2
# Common problems of usage

## Overview
In this chapter we deal with a number of problems that don't deserve chapters of their own but that often stump people. Here is the array of topics we deal with.

### A. "Different from", "different to", or "different than"
All three are in use, and the problem is whether there is a preference for any one over the others.

### B. "I said" or "I said that"
Question: can you leave out the word "that" in a sentence such as "I said that it was getting late"?

### C. "I asked whether" or "I asked if"
Both expressions are in use. This section tells you the difference between them.

### D. "I only think it proper" or "I think it only proper"
The question here is the proper place for the word "only". The answer is determined by something called "the rule of proximity". You might only want to read this section of the chapter. Or should we say, "You might want to read only this section of the chapter"?

---

1 Standard formal: *use this, and you can't go wrong in formal contexts.*
2 Standard formal with consistent options: *choose one and stick to it.*
3 Standard formal with flexible options: *choose any one, any time.*
4 Old-fashioned: *still all right, but fading from modern usage.*
5 Standard informal: *fine in conversation or in personal letters.*
6 Nonstandard: *you jez' gotta be kidding.*

## Common problems of usage

### E. "Do like I say" or "Do as I say"
The experts have been getting purple in the face over this one. After you read this section, you too will be able to join the discussion in a knowledgeable way.

### F. "The minister and I", "the minister and me", or "the minister and myself"
How many times have you seen phrases like the ones above, and wondered which construction is correct? Read this section to find the answer.

### G. "Fewer" or "less"
Is it "There were less people at this week's meeting than at last week's", or "There were fewer people at this week's meeting than at last week's"? That's the topic of this section.

### H. "Shall" or "will"
Confused about whether to use "I shall" or "I will"? Remember some dim instructions from your school days about that? Well, be confused no more — just read this section of the chapter.


### A. "Different from", "different to", or "different than"
All three variants are in use. Their status is as follows:

    different from[1]
    different to[5]
    different than[6]

The common usage of good writers and quality publications has determined that "different from" is the way to go. A good way to remember which of the variants bears the designation 1 is to note that both words — "different" and "from" — contain the letter "f".

    They are **different from** us.[1]
    They are **different to** us.[5]
    They are **different than** us.[6]

## Usage

### B. "I said" or "I said that"
The guide in this, as in all questions of usage, is the common practice of quality books and publications. There you will find both forms used indiscriminately. Therefore both are equally valid.

    I **said that** it was getting late.[3]
    I **said** it was getting late.[3]
    I **told** them **that** it was getting late.[3]
    I **told** them it was getting late.[3]

What goes for "said" and "told" goes equally for "noted", "thought", "considered", "hoped", "foretold", "suppose", "know" and a host of similar verbs.

    I **thought that** they were happy.[3]
    I **thought** they were happy.[3]
    I **suppose that** they are returning.[3]
    I **suppose** they are returning.[3]

### C. "I asked whether" or "I asked if"
The first is standard formal; the second, despite its prevalence in conversational English, is standard informal.

    I **asked whether** they were ready.[1]
    I **asked if** they were ready.[5]

The conjunction "whether" is the standard formal way of introducing a reported question. The conjunction "if", though often used interchangeably with "whether" in speech and on other informal occasions, is really best suited to express a condition: "I will give you a reward **if** you do the job well."

What goes for "asked" goes equally for "inquired", "wondered", "doubted" and similar verbs.

---

1 Standard formal: *use this, and you can't go wrong in formal contexts.*
2 Standard formal with consistent options: *choose one and stick to it.*
3 Standard formal with flexible options: *choose any one, any time.*
4 Old-fashioned: *still all right, but fading from modern usage.*
5 Standard informal: *fine in conversation or in personal letters.*
6 Nonstandard: *you jez'gotta be kidding.*

> I **wonder whether** they are happy.¹
> I **wonder if** they are happy.⁵
> I do not **know whether** they agree.¹
> I do not **know if** they agree.⁵

A good reason for using "whether" rather than "if", in reported questions, is that the use of "if" may lead to ambiguity. "I will ask if they are ready" might mean either of two things: "I will ask whether they are ready", or "In the event that they are ready, I will ask them something."

## D. "I only think it proper" or "I think it only proper"

Here we are considering the position of the word "only" in a sentence. The means of deciding the matter is by what grammarians call the "rule of proximity". This is a fancy way of saying that, when concepts are closely linked, the words in a sentence that denote these concepts should stand as close to each other as possible. If they don't, the sentence may be ambiguous. Consider, for example, the following pair of sentences.

> I **only** ate one egg for breakfast.⁵
> I ate **only** one egg for breakfast.¹

The first sentence may mean either that you consumed no more than one egg, or that you only ate the egg — but didn't, say, throw it. The second sentence unambiguously denotes the consumption of a single egg.

The position of "only" in the following example also determines whether the sentence is ambiguous.

> I worked **only** one week last month.¹
> I **only** worked one week last month.⁵

The second sentence is ambiguous. It could mean either that I was unemployed for all but one week of last month; or it could mean that for one week last month I only worked, but had no time for play or sleep.

## E. "Do like I say" or "Do as I say"

The question here is whether you can use "like" as a conjunction. This is one of the most contentious questions in the field of usage. Before we answer it, let's look at the range of uses that this versatile word — "like" — has.

## Usage

I **like** their style.[1]
("Like" functions as a verb.)

We will never see her **like** again.[1]
("Like" functions as a noun.)

They worked **like** mad.[5]
("Like" functions as an adverb, qualifying the adjective "mad".)

It was a business**like** performance.[1]
("Like" functions as a suffix, transforming the noun "business" into the adjective "businesslike".)

**Like**, man, don't bug me.[6]
("Like" functions as a slang interjection.)

Their children look **like** them.[1]
("Like" functions as a preposition.)

None of these uses and none of their designations are contentious. But the use of "like" as a conjunction is contentious — at least, it seems to be nowadays. In days gone by, the most reputable writers had no hesitation in using "like" as a conjunction.

> Thou shalt come to thy grave in a full age, **like** as a shock of corn cometh in its season. (*Job*, 5:26)

> It always seemed to me that men wore their beards, **like** they wear their neckties, for show. (D. H. Lawrence, *Kangaroo*.)

Nowadays, though, many authorities — but by no means all — would prefer to use the pure conjunction "as" in the above contexts, rather than the disputed conjunction "like". Let us take a consensus of the authorities. *The Macquarie Dictionary* (1991) and *The Random House Dictionary of the English Language* (unabridged edition, 1987) list "like" as a conjunction; but *The Oxford English Dictionary* (1989) says that its use as such is "slovenly". Going back a little in time, we have Chambers (1901), who calls it "vulgar"; Treble and Vallins (1936), who say "'like' is certainly not

---

1 Standard formal: *use this, and you can't go wrong in formal contexts.*
2 Standard formal with consistent options: *choose one and stick to it.*
3 Standard formal with flexible options: *choose any one, any time.*
4 Old-fashioned: *still all right, but fading from modern usage.*
5 Standard informal: *fine in conversation or in personal letters.*
6 Nonstandard: *you jez'gotta be kidding.*

## Common problems of usage

a conjunction"; Fowler, as edited by Gowers (1965), who calls the use a "questionable construction"; and Strunk and White (1979), who put it down as "illiterate".

So what are we to do in the face of disagreement among the experts? Our recommendation is that, when you need a conjunction, you stick to "as" (or "as though" or "as if" or "not so ... as") in formal contexts but allow yourself the luxury of the conjunctive "like" whenever you relax into informality.

> It seems **as though** we have company.[1]
> It seems **like** we have company.[5]
> They should do **as** they are told.[1]
> They should do **like** they are told.[5]
> He is **not so** kind **as** you are.[1]
> He is **not** kind **like** you are.[5]

There is a good reason why we should preserve "as" as a formal conjunction and "like" as a formal preposition. If you blur the distinction, you can't tell the difference between the meanings of the following two sentences.

> **Like** a child, you behaved carelessly.[1]
> **As** a child, you behaved carelessly.[1]

The first means: "You behaved carelessly in the manner of a child." The second means: "When you were a child you behaved carelessly."

## F.  "The minister and I", "The minister and me", or "the minister and myself"

In official writing you will often see sentences such as these.

> The minister and **myself** will appear before the committee.[6]
> The committee will meet with the minister and **myself**.[6]
> The chairperson will question the minister and **myself**.[6]

The first sentence should have "I" instead of "myself", and the other two should have "me". How can you tell? Simply by omitting the words "the minister and".

## Usage

... **I** will appear before the committee.[1]
The minister and **I** will appear before the committee.[1]
The committee will meet with ... **me**.[1]
The committee will meet with the minister and **me**.[1]
The chairperson will question ... **me**.[1]
The chairperson will question the minister and **me**.[1]

So why do people use "myself" in officialese? For that matter, why do people use "myself" in business writing as well — with the substitution of "manager" for "minister"? The answer seems to be that people mistakenly believe that "myself" is somehow more dignified than "I" or "me". After all, "myself" has two syllables where "I" and "me" have only one apiece. In fact, though, the choice among these pronouns ("I", "me" and "myself") has nothing to do with dignity, but only with linguistic propriety.

We are not suggesting that "myself" (or any other pronoun ending in "-self" or "-selves") has no legitimate place in English sentences. It does indeed have its legitimacy: specifically in reflexive and in emphatic contexts.

A reflexive context is one in which the action denoted by the verb rebounds on the doer.

**I** wash **myself**.[1]
**I** know **myself**.[1]

An emphatic context is one in which you want to emphasise a pronoun or a noun.

**I myself** did it all.[1]
I spoke to the **minister himself**.[1]
I got it from the **artist herself**.[1]

---

1 Standard formal: *use this, and you can't go wrong in formal contexts.*
2 Standard formal with consistent options: *choose one and stick to it.*
3 Standard formal with flexible options: *choose any one, any time.*
4 Old-fashioned: *still all right, but fading from modern usage.*
5 Standard informal: *fine in conversation or in personal letters.*
6 Nonstandard: *you jez'gotta be kidding.*

Note that, in both the reflexive and the emphatic, the "-self" or "-selves" form goes together with a related noun ("**minister** himself") or pronoun ("**I** myself").

## G. "Fewer" or "less"

"Big", "bigger", "biggest" — the grammatical names for these degrees of the adjective are "positive", "comparative", "superlative". We see the same three degrees in "good", "better", "best" and in the following two series.

| POSITIVE | COMPARATIVE | SUPERLATIVE |
|---|---|---|
| little | less | least |
| few | fewer | fewest |

The word "little" in the above list has the sense of "not much" — rather than "not large". Bearing this in mind we can now see when "fewer" is appropriate and when "less" is appropriate.

"Fewer" (like "few" and "fewest") goes with any plural noun. "Less" (like "little" and "least") goes with any singular noun.

Here are two short lists of nouns with which you would use the two terms.

| Fewer: | Less: |
|---|---|
| people | discussion |
| dollars | money |
| hours | time |
| pages | paper |
| kilos | weight |

There were **fewer** people at this week's meeting than at last week's.[1]
There was **less** discussion at this week's meeting than at last week's.[1]

The distinction we have drawn between "fewer" and "less" allows us to distinguish the meanings of two such sentences as the following.

There are **less** wealthy people in this town.[1]
(There are people in this town who are not so wealthy.)
There are **fewer** wealthy people in this town.[1]
(There are not so many wealthy people in this town.)

## Usage

In some contexts, there are plural words that are taken in a singular sense. We mark this singular sense by the fact that we associate singular verbs such as "is" with them, rather than plural verbs such as "are".

> Fifty dollars **is** not much money.[1]
> Five minutes **is** not long to wait.[1]

In such contexts, you use "less" (rather than "fewer").

> It cost me **less** than $50.[1]
> It took me **less** than five minutes to get there.[1]

### H. "Shall" or "will"

Way back, around the middle of the century, school teachers throughout the English-speaking world drilled their students in the strict — and largely fallacious — rule that the future tense worked like this:

| | |
|---|---|
| I shall ... | we shall ... |
| you will ... | you will ... |
| he will ... | they will ... |
| she will ... | |
| it will ... | |

And if you wanted to express an emphatic future, it worked like this:

| | |
|---|---|
| I will ... | we will ... |
| you shall ... | you shall ... |
| he shall ... | they shall ... |
| she shall ... | |
| it shall ... | |

So, the story went, if you wanted to express an ordinary future tense, you would say (or write):

---

1 Standard formal: *use this, and you can't go wrong in formal contexts.*
2 Standard formal with consistent options: *choose one and stick to it.*
3 Standard formal with flexible options: *choose any one, any time.*
4 Old-fashioned: *still all right, but fading from modern usage.*
5 Standard informal: *fine in conversation or in personal letters.*
6 Nonstandard: *you jez'gotta be kidding.*

## Common problems of usage

I **shall** be going home tomorrow.[1]
**Will** you be staying long?[1]

But if you wanted to emphasise whatever action it was that you were talking about, you would say (or write):

I **will** not eat any more spinach![1]
They **shall** not pass.[1]

The truth is that the rule wasn't even entirely valid fifty years ago. Then, as now, "shall" and "will" were largely bound up with idiom and local usage. The story doesn't end there: over the past half century or so, there has been a progressive eroding of the distinction between "shall" and "will" — with "shall" pretty well losing out in usage to "will". Most people in the English-speaking world now generally prefer the use of "will" for most, if not all, cases of the future tense — plain or emphatic.

Thus, in the examples we have given so far, the options nowadays would be:

I **shall** be going home tomorrow.[3]
I **will** be going home tomorrow.[3]
**Will** you be staying long?[1]
I **shall** not eat any more spinach![3]
I **will** not eat any more spinach![3]
They **shall** not pass.[3]
They **will** not pass.[3]

Since idiom and local usage prevail in the matter, it is all but impossible to pin the use of "shall" and "will" down to an exact set of rules. But the following is a fair guide.

**a.** "Shall" is confined largely to certain idiomatic expressions — mainly in the question form and mainly (but not exclusively) with the pronoun "I" or "we" as the subject.

**Shall** we dance?[1]
**Shall** I bring it now?[1]

17

**Usage**

**b.** For other locutions in the future tense — whether plain or emphatic — use "shall" or "will" with "I" and with "we"; and use "will" with all other subjects.

> I **shall** tell you more later.[3]
> I **will** tell you more later.[3]
> They **will** not come after all.[1]

Beyond that, our advice on the use of "shall" and "will" boils down to the following:

**c.** if you are a native speaker of English, trust your own linguistic intuition and ignore the pedants' rules; otherwise,

**d.** if in doubt, use "will".

---

1 Standard formal: *use this, and you can't go wrong in formal contexts.*
2 Standard formal with consistent options: *choose one and stick to it.*
3 Standard formal with flexible options: *choose any one, any time.*
4 Old-fashioned: *still all right, but fading from modern usage.*
5 Standard informal: *fine in conversation or in personal letters.*
6 Nonstandard: *you jez'gotta be kidding.*

# CHAPTER 3
# Gender language and sexist language

## Overview

English grammar recognises four genders. The easiest way to grasp the concept of these genders is through examples.

MASCULINE GENDER:  he, him, his, himself, man, boy;
FEMININE GENDER:  she, her, herself, woman, girl;
NEUTER GENDER:  it, its, itself, book, table;
COMMON GENDER:  they, them, their, themselves, reporter, cousin.

Masculine gender words are usually associated with the male sex; feminine gender words with the female sex; neuter gender words with sexless things; and common gender words with any one or more of the other three. The association between grammatical gender and sex or sexlessness is not absolute. We can, for instance, speak of a ship as "she" or of a baby as "it". But the association is close enough for the practical purposes of this chapter.

Gender words are an integral part of the English language, which virtually guarantees that they serve a useful and legitimate function. And they do. It is perfectly legitimate, for example, to use gender-specific terms when you want to flag the sex of a person.

> Every patient in the obstetrics ward has **her** weight taken when **she** is admitted.[1]

> Anyone who is contemplating having a vasectomy should make sure that **he** won't regret **his** decision.[1]

In these two examples, the use of the grammatical genders is logical and unexceptionable. We call such legitimate uses of gender terms "gender language".

## Usage

Opposed to this is "sexist language", which involves the use of gender terms that, in their context, are exceptionable or irrelevant. Such a use may occur, for example, when in your speech or in your writing you really intend to refer to a member of either sex, but the term you use refers to a member of only one sex — usually the male sex. By way of example, here are two sentences from an article, published in *The Listener* in the 1970s, by Dame Mary Warnock, the British educationist and philosopher.

> School is for education, whatever the ability of the pupil or **his** age . . .[4]

> In the old days, a teacher's status and salary were allotted according to the age of **his** pupils . . .[4]

These sentences are sexist in the sense that, by using "his" when she is referring to "a pupil" and to "a teacher", the writer is suggesting — quite falsely, of course — that only boys are pupils and that only men are teachers. Such language is not only sexist but also old-fashioned. There is now a growing awareness of the need to reflect the equal status of females and males in language as well as in society.

The two sections of this chapter deal with how to avoid or eliminate sexist language.

### A. Gender identification in correspondence
Here we deal with problems associated with the use of official titles ("Dr", for instance) and courtesy titles ("Ms", for instance) in correspondence.

### B. Sexist language in prose
Dame Mary Warnock could have avoided sexist language by writing, for example:

> School is for education, whatever the ability of the pupils or **their** ages[1]

and

> In the old days, a teacher's status and salary were allotted according to the age of **his** or **her** pupils . . .[1]

---

1 Standard formal: *use this, and you can't go wrong in formal contexts.*
2 Standard formal with consistent options: *choose one and stick to it.*
3 Standard formal with flexible options: *choose any one, any time.*
4 Old-fashioned: *still all right, but fading from modern usage.*
5 Standard informal: *fine in conversation or in personal letters.*
6 Nonstandard: *you jez'gotta be kidding.*

## Gender language and sexist language

### A. Gender identification in correspondence

The problems we deal with in this section have to do with the use of official and courtesy titles, both when you know the name, gender and title of the person you are writing to, and when you don't know one or more of these factors.

**1. Correspondence with a person whose title, name and gender you know.**

**a.** If the person has a specific official title use it.

>   Dear **Dr** So-and-so[1]
>
>   Dear **Professor** So-and-so[1]

**b.** If the person does not have a specific official title, and the person is a man, use the courtesy title "Mr".

>   Dear **Mr** So-and- so[1]

**c.** If the person does not have a specific official title, and the person is a woman, use:

>   Dear **Mrs** So-and-so[2] (if you know that she prefers that courtesy title);
>
>   Dear **Miss** So-and-so[2] (if you know that she prefers that courtesy title);
>
>   Dear **Ms** So-and-so[2] (in all other cases).

**2. Correspondence with a person whose name you know, but whose gender and title you don't know.**

If you are writing a letter in reply to someone who has signed off as "J. So-and-so", you may not know whether the "J" stands for a masculine name ("John" or "James") or a feminine name ("Jennifer" or "Janice"). In this case use the coined courtesy title "M/-".

>   Dear **M/-** So-and-so[1]

**3. Correspondence with a person whose position you know, but whose name and gender you don't know.**

Use the title of the position, whatever it may be.

>   Dear **Director**[1]           Dear **Householder**[1]
>
>   Dear **Librarian**[1]          Dear **Personnel Officer**[1]

21

## Usage

**4. Correspondence with a person whose gender you know, but whose name and title you don't know.**
Use whichever of the following is suitable.

> Dear **Sir**[1]
> Dear **Madam**[1]

**5. Correspondence with a person whose title, name and gender you don't know.**
Choose from any of the following as appropriate, or make your own variation up.

> Dear **Madam/Sir**[3]
> Dear **Sir/Madam**[3]
> Dear **Madam or Sir**[3]
> Dear **Sir or Madam**[3]
> Dear **Colleague**[3]
> Dear **Friend**[3]

## B. Sexist language in prose
In this section we assume that the gender of the person or persons that you are referring to is irrelevant.

**6. Use both feminine and masculine.**
Replace a singular word such as "he" or "she" alone with a pair of words — "he/she" — in tandem.
**a.** Instead of using the singular "he" or "she" alone, use both words in tandem.

> Everyone knows what **he/she** wants.[3]
> Everyone knows what **she/he** wants.[3]
> Everyone knows what **he or she** wants.[3]
> Everyone knows what **she or he** wants.[3]

---

1 Standard formal: *use this, and you can't go wrong in formal contexts.*
2 Standard formal with consistent options: *choose one and stick to it.*
3 Standard formal with flexible options: *choose any one, any time.*
4 Old-fashioned: *still all right, but fading from modern usage.*
5 Standard informal: *fine in conversation or in personal letters.*
6 Nonstandard: *you jez'gotta be kidding.*

## Gender language and sexist language

There are another two options: one is the use of a plural personal pronoun; the other, the use of the singular coinage "s/he". Neither of these options is, as yet, standard formal.

> Everyone knows what **they** want.[5]
> Everyone knows what **s/he** wants.[5]

**b.** Instead of using "her" or "him" alone, use both words in tandem.

> Everyone should eat only what is good for **her/him**.[3]
> Everyone should eat only what is good for **him/her**.[3]
> Everyone should eat only what is good for **her or him**.[3]
> Everyone should eat only what is good for **him or her**.[3]

There are another two options: the use of the plural "them", and a new coinage, "hem". Neither of these options is, so far, standard formal.

> Everyone should eat only what is good for **them**.[5]
> Everyone should eat only what is good for **hem**.[6]

**c.** Instead of using the singular "his" or "her" alone, use both words in tandem.

> Everyone should be responsible for **his/her** own actions.[3]
> Everyone should be responsible for **her/his** own actions.[3]
> Everyone should be responsible for **his or her** own actions.[3]
> Everyone should be responsible for **her or his** own actions.[3]

Additional options are the use of the plural "their" and the singular coinage "hir". Neither option is, as yet, standard formal.

> Everyone should be responsible for **their** own actions.[5]
> Everyone should be responsible for **hir** own actions.[6]

**d.** Instead of using the singular "hers" or "his" alone, use both words in tandem.

> You look after your affairs; let everyone else look after **hers/his**.[3]
> You look after your affairs; let everyone else look after **his/hers**.[3]
> You look after your affairs; let everyone else look after **hers or his**.[3]
> You look after your affairs; let everyone else look after **his or hers**.[3]

## Usage

Two additional options are the use of the plural "theirs" and the singular coinage "hirs". Neither of these options is, to date, standard formal.

> You look after your affairs; let everyone else look after **theirs**.[5]
> You look after your affairs; let everyone else look after **hirs**.[6]

**e.** Instead of using the singular "himself" or "herself" alone, use both words in tandem.

> Everybody should be able to cook for **himself/herself**.[3]
> Everybody should be able to cook for **herself/himself**.[3]
> Everybody should be able to cook for **himself or herself**.[3]
> Everybody should be able to cook for **herself or himself**.[3]
> Everybody should be able to cook for **him-/herself**.[3]
> Everybody should be able to cook for **her-/himself**.[3]
> Everybody should be able to cook for **him- or herself**.[3]
> Everybody should be able to cook for **her- or himself**.[3]

Two additional options are the use of the plural "themselves" and the singular coinage "hermself". Neither option is, as yet, standard formal.

> Everybody should be able to cook for **themselves**.[5]
> Everybody should be able to cook for **hermself**.[6]

There are two things worth noting about the method we have just discussed.

**i.** When you use the two singular personal pronouns or adjectives in tandem, you should make a point of using the feminine gender word first about as often as the other way round.

**ii.** The method is all right if you use it sparingly — say, once in half a dozen or more pages of text. If you use it more frequently, it becomes tiresome or obtrusive. The same goes for the nonstandard options.

---

1 Standard formal: *use this, and you can't go wrong in formal contexts.*
2 Standard formal with consistent options: *choose one and stick to it.*
3 Standard formal with flexible options: *choose any one, any time.*
4 Old-fashioned: *still all right, but fading from modern usage.*
5 Standard informal: *fine in conversation or in personal letters.*
6 Nonstandard: *you jez'gotta be kidding.*

## Gender language and sexist language

Therefore, for a text in which you need to avoid or to eliminate a large number of sexist expressions, we recommend that you use one of the other methods listed below.

**7. Use a common-gender plural personal pronoun or adjective.**
This method entails replacing a singular word, such as "she" or "he" alone, with a plural word such as "they". You will need to take care, though, to ensure that you also make other associated changes from the singular to the plural in the same passage. For example, you may need to change "a person" into "persons", and "is" into "are". The range of possibilities under this head is as follows.

**a.** Instead of using the singular "he" or "she" alone, use the plural "they".

A **person** should know what **he** wants.[4]
**People** should know what **they** want.[1]

**b.** Instead of using the singular "her" or "him" alone, use the plural "them".

When you see **someone** in distress you should help **him**.[4]
When you see **people** in distress you should help **them**.[1]

**c.** Instead of using the singular "his" or "her" alone, use the plural "their".

A **person** likes to do **his** own thing.[4]
**People** like to do **their** own thing.[1]

**d.** Instead of using the singular "his" or "hers" alone, use the plural "theirs".

I mind my own business, and I expect **everyone** else to mind **his**.[4]
I mind my own business, and I expect **others** to mind **theirs**.[1]

**e.** Instead of using the singular "himself" or "herself" alone, use the plural "themselves".

A **child** should learn to look after **himself**.[4]
**Children** should learn to look after **themselves**.[1]

**8. Eliminate the singular masculine or singular feminine personal pronoun or adjective.**
You can do this by changes within the sentence.

## Usage

A hunter must **watch his step** so as not to frighten **his** prey.[4]

A hunter must **step warily** so as not to frighten **the** prey.[1]

**9. Use a common-gender noun.**

There are three ways in which English nouns show gender differences. For each of these ways there is a strategy for replacing gender-specific nouns with common-gender nouns.

**a.** Gender difference shown by a change of word:

| FEMININE GENDER | MASCULINE GENDER | COMMON GENDER |
|---|---|---|
| girl | boy | child |
| wife | husband | spouse |
| sister | brother | sibling |
| woman | man | person |

There have been both famous and infamous **kings** in history.[4]

There have been both famous and infamous **monarchs** in history.[1]

The limitation of this method is that not every masculine or feminine noun has a counterpart that is a common-gender noun. When you are writing about people for whom there is no choice but to use a gender-specific noun, you can avoid sexist language by using both the feminine and the masculine nouns together.

Young people usually enjoy the company of their **aunts and uncles**.[1]

---

1 Standard formal: *use this, and you can't go wrong in formal contexts.*
2 Standard formal with consistent options: *choose one and stick to it.*
3 Standard formal with flexible options: *choose any one, any time.*
4 Old-fashioned: *still all right, but fading from modern usage.*
5 Standard informal: *fine in conversation or in personal letters.*
6 Nonstandard: *you jez'gotta be kidding.*

**b.** Gender difference shown by a change of ending:

| MASCULINE GENDER | FEMININE GENDER | COMMON GENDER IN MODERN USAGE |
|---|---|---|
| author | authoress | author |
| comedian | comedienne | comedian |
| usher | usherette | usher |
| hero | heroine | hero |
| executor | executrix | executor |

Meredith Kinmont is an Australian **poetess**.[4]
Meredith Kinmont is an Australian **poet**.[1]

The limitation of this method is that, in some cases, words with gender endings are still standard formal (for example, "duchess" and "princess"). In such cases, simply write both the masculine and the feminine forms of the noun.

. The head of an abbey is called an **abbot**.[4]

The head of an abbey is called an **abbot** or an **abbess**.[1]

**c.** Gender difference shown by a word placed before or after the main word:

| FEMININE GENDER | MASCULINE GENDER | COMMON GENDER |
|---|---|---|
| female attorney | male attorney | attorney |
| policewoman | policeman | police officer |
| womankind | mankind | humanity |

The **chairman** called the meeting to order.[4]
The **chairperson** called the meeting to order.[3]
The **chair** called the meeting to order.[3]

The limitation of this method is that, for some words, there are no suitable common-gender terms. In such cases write both the feminine and the masculine forms.

There are specialist clothing shops for **brides and bridegrooms**.[1]

## Usage

**10. Use gender-free terms for things and for concepts that have no necessary relationship to gender.**

Eliminate terms such as "man-hours" and replace them with terms such as "working hours". Here is an indicative list of such expressions and of their gender-free equivalents:

| GENDER-SPECIFIC | GENDER-FREE |
|---|---|
| manpower[4] | work force[1] |
| man to man[4] | candid[1] |
| manhole[4] | utility hole[1] |

This is a **man-made** object.[4]   This is a **manufactured** object.[1]

(The element "man-" in words such as "manufacture" and "manual" comes from the Latin "manus", meaning "hand" — not from the English "man".)

**11. For gender-specific words that come in pairs, ensure that both members are on the same language level.**

Pair "women" with "men", for example, and "gentlemen" with "ladies" — but not "men" with "ladies".

**Bob** and **Mrs** So-and-so[4]
**Hazel** and **Bob** So-and-so[3]
**Mr** and **Mrs** So-and-so[3]

We recommend the practice of putting the feminine member of each pair in front of the masculine member about as often as the other way round.

**12. Avoid singling out women or men in a group for identification.**

There were twelve people in the room **including three women**.[4]
There were twelve people in the room.[1]

---

1 Standard formal: *use this, and you can't go wrong in formal contexts.*
2 Standard formal with consistent options: *choose one and stick to it.*
3 Standard formal with flexible options: *choose any one, any time.*
4 Old-fashioned: *still all right, but fading from modern usage.*
5 Standard informal: *fine in conversation or in personal letters.*
6 Nonstandard: *you jez'gotta be kidding.*

## Gender language and sexist language

If there is some special reason for mentioning gender, we recommend that you mention the gender of both groups.

There were twelve people in the room: **nine men and three women**.[1]

# CHAPTER 4
# Agreement of nominative and finite verb

## Overview
We begin this overview by explaining the concepts that underlie the three terms used in the chapter heading: "agreement", "nominative", "finite verb" — though not in that order — and an additional term, "subject".

**a.** Agreement.
Look at the following two sentences.

> It is here.
> They are here.

Why do we use "is" in the first sentence and "are" in the second? The answer is that, in the first sentence, the word "it" is singular, so we use the singular "is" with that word. In the second sentence, the word "they" is plural, so we use the plural "are" with that word. In the first sentence we have agreement between the two singulars, "it" and "is"; in the second sentence, between the two plurals, "they" and "are".

**b.** Finite verb.
A finite verb is a verb that can inflect — that is, change its form — to accommodate, among other things, a change in number. We have already seen, in our sentences under **a.** above, that the verb "to be" inflects from "is" to "are" in order to accommodate a change from singular to plural.

Nearly all finite verbs — "can" and "must" are among the handful of exceptions — inflect in the present tense between third person singular and all the rest. Here are two examples of inflected finite verbs.

---

1 Standard formal: *use this, and you can't go wrong in formal contexts.*
2 Standard formal with consistent options: *choose one and stick to it.*
3 Standard formal with flexible options: *choose any one, any time.*
4 Old-fashioned: *still all right, but fading from modern usage.*
5 Standard informal: *fine in conversation or in personal letters.*
6 Nonstandard: *you jez'gotta be kidding.*

## Agreement of nominative and finite verb

THIRD PERSON SINGULAR   ALL THE REST
He / she / it **goes**    I / you / we / they **go**
He / she / it **plays**   I / you / we / they **play**

Some verbs are compound — that is, they consist of more than one verb. In "She has been working", for example, "has", "been" and "working" are all verbs; and these verbs together make up a compound verb ("has been working"). If we change "she" into "they", only one verb in the compound changes its form — "They **have** been working". "Has" and "have", in the above examples, are finite; "been" and "working" are nonfinite.

**c.** Subject.
The subject is that part of a sentence that tells us who or what the agent (or "doer") of the finite verb is. A subject can be simple (consisting of one word only), or compound (consisting of more than one word).

SIMPLE SUBJECTS
**It** broke.
**They** waited.

COMPOUND SUBJECTS
**Ten thousand people expecting to buy tickets** waited.
**The vase handed down through generations** broke.

**d.** Nominative.
The nominative is the word or words in the subject that cause the present tense finite verb to inflect for the singular or the plural. Among the examples we have considered so far, we have had some nominatives that have been coextensive with the subject ("she", "he", "it", "they"). We have also had nominatives that have been buried somewhere in longer subjects ("vase", "people"); but these buried nominatives were easy to spot too. Sometimes, though, it is not so easy to determine which word in a subject is the nominative. Consider the following subjects.

A team of players . . .
Either they or she . . .
We and he . . .
A number of people . . .

## Usage

Each of these compound subjects contains a singular and a plural noun. We need some method of determining which word — or words — in each subject constitutes the nominative. Once we have found the nominative, we will be able to decide how to inflect the finite verb that goes with it — "is" or "are", for example; or "play" or "plays".

This chapter deals with the agreement of nominatives and finite verbs, both the easy and the not so easy. For the sake of simplicity, we will mostly be using "is" as our example of a singular finite verb, and "are" as our example of a plural one. Remember, though, that what goes for these two finite verbs goes for any of the tens of thousands of finite verbs in the English language — "play/plays", "go/goes", "eat/eats" and so on.

We deal with the topic of the chapter under two headings.

### A. Simple subjects
These are the subjects in which the nominative is the only reasonable candidate noun around. "The big bad wolf . . ." has the singular "wolf" as its nominative. A singular finite verb therefore agrees with the nominative.

### B. Compound subjects
These are the subjects in which there isn't a single unmistakable nominative. Examples of such compound subjects are: "My friend and companion . . .", "Either she or they . . .", "A fistful of dollars . . ." In this section we examine the methods for identifying the nominative, and for deciding when to use singular and when to use plural finite verbs with these nominatives.

### A. Simple subjects
In the majority of cases, the choice of finite verb for a simple subject presents no problem. If the nominative is singular, the finite verb will be singular too; if the nominative is plural, the finite verb will be plural too: "child" goes with "is", and "children" goes with "are". That's what agreement is all about.

---

1 Standard formal: *use this, and you can't go wrong in formal contexts.*
2 Standard formal with consistent options: *choose one and stick to it.*
3 Standard formal with flexible options: *choose any one, any time.*
4 Old-fashioned: *still all right, but fading from modern usage.*
5 Standard informal: *fine in conversation or in personal letters.*
6 Nonstandard: *you jez'gotta be kidding.*

## Agreement of nominative and finite verb

But there are cases that aren't as easy as "child is" and "children are". For example, what about "a team" or "politics" or "two dollars"? Do we follow these nominatives with "is" or with "are"? It is these harder cases that take up the bulk of our discussion in this section. First, though, come the easy cases.

**1. The standard case: "A person is"; "Persons are".**
**a.** The choice of finite verb is clear: a singular nominative takes a singular finite verb, and a plural nominative takes a plural finite verb.

**She is** happy.[1]

**They are** happy.[1]

**b.** The word "you", even when you use it to refer to a single person, takes "are" as its finite verb.

**You are** happy.[1]

**c.** "I am" presents no problem in a positive statement. But what about the negative? Here the options begin.

**I am not** happy.[1]
**I'm not** happy.[5]
**I ain't** happy.[6]

In a negative question the options are as follows.

**Am I not** a clever fellow?[1]
**Aren't I** a clever fellow?[5]
**Ain't I** a clever fellow?[6]

**d.** The mysterious case of "he were", "she were" and "it were".
This looks like a case of a singular nominative with a plural finite verb, but it isn't. It's something altogether different — the subjunctive mood. We use this special mood of the verb to talk (or write) about something that isn't the case in the present.

If only **she were** here now.[1]
(This means that, in fact, she's somewhere else.)

**Usage**

> I wish **it were** raining.[1]
> (This means that it isn't raining.)

Contrast these two wishful sentences above with the following factual ones.

> If **she was** there, she probably spotted you.[1]
> (This leaves open the question of whether she was or wasn't there.)
> **It was** raining last night.[1]
> (This is a simple statement of fact.)

We deal more fully with the subjunctive in chapter 6.

**2. Words ending in "-ics".**
These are words that denote fields of human activity or knowledge.
**a.** Some take a singular or a plural finite verb, depending on the context.

> **Politics is** a demanding occupation.[1]
> Your **politics are** different from mine.[1]
> **Demographics is** about human populations.[1]
> The **demographics** of this shire **are** different from the demographics of that one.[1]

**b.** Others take only singular finite verbs.

> **Physics is** an elective subject at this college.[1]
> **Semantics is** about meaning.[1]

**3. "News", "series" and "species".**
**a.** Long ago — until about the middle of the sixteenth century — "news" was a plural nominative. Nowadays it's singular.

> The **news is** good.[1]
> The **news are** good.[6]

---

1 Standard formal: *use this, and you can't go wrong in formal contexts.*
2 Standard formal with consistent options: *choose one and stick to it.*
3 Standard formal with flexible options: *choose any one, any time.*
4 Old-fashioned: *still all right, but fading from modern usage.*
5 Standard informal: *fine in conversation or in personal letters.*
6 Nonstandard: *you jez'gotta be kidding.*

## Agreement of nominative and finite verb

**b.** "Series" and "species" serve both as the singular and as the plural forms of the words. Therefore only the context can tell you whether they go with singular or with plural finite verbs.

>One comedy **series is** over, but another **two series are** commencing.[1]
>
>There **is one species** of this tree in Alaska and there **are** another **two species** in Oregon.[1]

**4. Words with Greek or Latin singular and plural endings.**
**a.** "Agendum" was the Latin — and, until a few decades ago, the English — singular; "agenda", the plural. Today, "agenda" is singular.

>The **agenda is** ready.[1]
>
>The **agendas are** ready.[1]

**b.** "Datum" and "medium" have, as their Latin (and English) plurals, "data" and "media" respectively. You can't go wrong, therefore, if you use "data" and "media" with plural finite verbs. It is, however, becoming increasingly standard usage, though still a tinge informal, to use "data" and "media" as singular nouns.

>The **data** on this matter **are** inconclusive.[1]
>
>The **data** on this matter **is** inconclusive.[5]
>
>Our news **media are** not state controlled.[1]
>
>Our news **media is** not state controlled.[5]

As a further complication, engineers and surveyors favour the plural form "datums". In the arts, or when you are referring to people who claim to communicate with the spirit world, "mediums" is an accepted plural form.

>Here **are** the **datums** on the tensile properties of steel.[1]
>
>There **are** three **mediums** at the table-rapping session.[1]
>
>Some **mediums** in art **are** harder to handle than others.[2]
>
>Some **media** in art **are** harder to handle than others.[2]

**c.** "Phenomena" and "criteria" are the Greek (and also the English) plural forms of "phenomenon" and "criterion" respectively.

**Usage**

These **phenomena are** most interesting.[1]
This **phenomenon is** most interesting.[1]
This **phenomena is** most interesting.[6]

**5. Adjectives used as nouns.**
**a.** Take this sentence: "The young person has lots of energy." "Young" is an adjective. But you can also use the word "young" as a noun standing for a collection of people with that particular attribute. When you do, it properly goes with a plural finite verb.

The **young are** energetic.[1]

What goes for "young" goes also for other adjectives used as nouns: "the poor", "the noble", "the artistic" and so on.

**b.** Certain adjectives can stand for ideas rather than for a collection of people. In such cases, they go with singular finite verbs.

The **good is** what the gods desire.[1]
("Good" stands for an idea.)

Notice the difference between the above example and the following one.

The **good are** deserving of praise.[1]
("Good" stands for people.)

**6. Collective nouns.**
Collective nouns ("group", "team" "staff", "government") are singular in form but they contain the idea of collections of individuals. So how are we to treat them: as singular or as plural? The answer depends on the context — and on convention.

**a.** If the context suggests that you are dealing with the collection as a whole, a singular finite verb is always suitable.

The **orchestra is** in good form.[1]
The firefighting **team is** on its way.[1]

---

1 Standard formal: *use this, and you can't go wrong in formal contexts.*
2 Standard formal with consistent options: *choose one and stick to it.*
3 Standard formal with flexible options: *choose any one, any time.*
4 Old-fashioned: *still all right, but fading from modern usage.*
5 Standard informal: *fine in conversation or in personal letters.*
6 Nonstandard: *you jez'gotta be kidding.*

## Agreement of nominative and finite verb

**b.** If the context suggests that you are dealing with the individuals of the group, rather than with the group as a whole, you can opt between singular and plural finite verbs.

> The **staff is** expressing different views on the subject.[2]
> The **staff are** expressing different views on the subject.[2]
> The **squad is** putting on blue uniforms.[2]
> The **squad are** putting on blue uniforms.[2]

**c.** For words denoting teams in sporting events you can choose between the singular and the plural.

> **England is** all out for 278, and **New Zealand is** coming in to bat.[2]
> **England are** all out for 278, and **New Zealand are** coming in to bat.[2]

### 7. Plural units of measure.

"Three kilos" and "five dollars" are the kinds of measures we are dealing with here. Technically, of course, "kilos" and "dollars" are plural; but the choice of finite verb depends on the context.

> Two **dollars is** a small sum of money.[1]
> Two **dollars are** rattling around in my pocket.[1]

### 8. Plural titles of singular things.

Confusing, isn't it? But simple enough, really. You treat them as singular nominatives.

> *Blue Poles* **is** a painting by Jackson Pollock.[1]
> *The Times* **is** published in London.[1]

### 9. "None is" or "none are".

The difficulty in deciding whether it should be singular or plural is well illustrated by two passages in an issue of *TIME International*. On page 56 (16 October 1990) we find this.

> Engineers fired shrapnel . . . at the iridium casings. **None was** pierced.

On the next page we find this.

37

**Usage**

Of the four daughters she bore in Paris . . . **none were** [married].

What are we to make of this: that both are right, or that one is wrong? The answer is this: "none" is an alternative way of saying "not one", which is a singular nominative. It therefore takes a singular finite verb in standard formal usage. But a plural finite verb is all right too, in standard informal usage.

Of all my friends, **none is** better than you.[1]

Of all my friends, **none are** better than you.[5]

I invited several people, but **none is** here yet.[1]

I invited several people, but **none are** here yet.[5]

### B. Compound subjects

Compound subjects are those that have — or seem to have — more than a single term in the nominative.

| | |
|---|---|
| He, together with his son | One of them |
| Either they or I | Jack and Jill |
| A number of people | Law and order |
| Neither he nor she | Two plus three |

In order to determine what finite verbs to use with such subjects we first have to sort out what the nominatives are.

### 10. Compound subjects featuring the conjunctions "and", "both . . . and".

**a.** These conjunctions add together the terms that go with them. If the terms denote separate individuals or items, they give us a plural nominative and take a plural finite verb.

**He and she are** happy.[1]

**Both she and he are** happy.[1]

---

1 Standard formal: *use this, and you can't go wrong in formal contexts.*
2 Standard formal with consistent options: *choose one and stick to it.*
3 Standard formal with flexible options: *choose any one, any time.*
4 Old-fashioned: *still all right, but fading from modern usage.*
5 Standard informal: *fine in conversation or in personal letters.*
6 Nonstandard: *you jez'gotta be kidding.*

**b.** If the terms refer to a single individual or item, they take a singular finite verb.

My **friend and confidant** is a reliable person.[1]

The **chief cook and bottle-washer is** on strike.[1]

**c.** In some cases the terms denote separate individuals or items, but ones that are so closely related that you treat them as one.

The **hue and cry is** raised.[1]

**Drinking and driving is** dangerous.[1]

**d.** In yet other cases, the terms denote separate items that are less closely connected. Then the choice of whether to use a singular or a plural finite verb is up to you.

**Research and development is** important.[2]
**Research and development are** important.[2]

**Law and order is** strictly maintained.[2]
**Law and order are** strictly maintained.[2]

**e.** Sometimes, with such connected terms, the context tells you that you need to use a plural finite verb.

**Research and development are** separately funded.[1]

**Law and order are** administered by different departments.[1]

**f.** When you use "and" in a mathematical sense, the choice of finite verb is yours; but the choice has to be a consistent one.

**Two and two is** four.[2]
**Two and two are** four.[2]

## 11. Compound subjects with "plus".

"Plus" is a preposition (like "in", "with", "by" and so on) — not a conjunction (like "and"). So here is how it works.

**a.** With numbers alone, you can opt for a singular or for a plural finite verb, as long as you opt consistently.

## Usage

Two plus two **is** four.[2]
Two plus two **are** four.[2]

**b.** If you add singular nouns to the numbers, you have two options.

One **brick plus** one **brick is** two bricks.[2]
One **brick plus** one **brick are** two bricks.[2]

**c.** With plural nouns there is only one way.

Two **bricks plus** two **bricks are** four bricks.[1]

**12. "As well as", "in addition to", "with" "along with", "together with".**
The terms that go with these expressions aren't even part of the subject: they are part of the predicate. Therefore they have no effect on the finite verb.

He **is** up the hill **together with his friend.**[1]
She **is** travelling abroad **along with her sister.**[1]

This remains the case even if you bring that part of the predicate up front with the subject.

He, **together with his friend, is** up the hill.[1]
She, **along with her sister, is** travelling abroad.[1]

**13. "And not", "but not", "rather than", "let alone", "not to mention".**
All these expressions specifically exclude the terms that follow them. Those terms therefore don't figure in the nominative and don't affect the finite verbs.

She **but not they is** arriving on the next bus.[1]
He, **let alone she, is** ready for anything.[1]
She, **rather than they, is** already there.[1]

---

1 Standard formal: *use this, and you can't go wrong in formal contexts.*
2 Standard formal with consistent options: *choose one and stick to it.*
3 Standard formal with flexible options: *choose any one, any time.*
4 Old-fashioned: *still all right, but fading from modern usage.*
5 Standard informal: *fine in conversation or in personal letters.*
6 Nonstandard: *you jez'gotta be kidding.*

### Agreement of nominative and finite verb

**14. Compound subjects featuring the conjunctions "or", "nor", "either" ... or", "neither ... nor".**
**a.** These conjunctions have a disjunctive function: that is, they separate rather than connect the terms with which they are associated. Therefore, if the terms are singular, so too is any finite verb that goes with them.

**She or he is** coming with me.[1]

**Is** neither he nor she going away?[1]

**b.** Things get really tough when one of the terms is singular and the other plural, as in "either he or they". The question is: which of the two terms ("he" or "they") do we take as the nominative? The answer to that question is a simple one: we take the term that is nearer to the finite verb.

Either she or **they are** to report to me.[1]

There **is** either **one person** or several persons in that shed.[1]

**Is** neither **he** nor they going?[1]

His friends or **he is** arriving at any moment.[1]

**15. A compound subject with a singular and a plural noun separated by "of".**
Look at the following subjects.

| | |
|---|---|
| Portions of cake | A bunch of flowers |
| Sacks of flour | The flock of birds |
| Words of wisdom | A set of tools |

Each of the left-hand set of examples has a plural noun before "of", and a singular noun after "of"; each of the right-hand set has a singular noun before "of", and a plural noun after "of". The question is: which noun (the one before or after "of") is the nominative? The answer is that, technically speaking, it's always the word before "of", and that you can therefore nearly always make the finite verb agree with that word. We show how this works under four subheadings.
**a.** The word before "of" is plural; the word after "of" is singular.
No problem — the finite verb is plural.

# Usage

The **buckets** of water **are** there.[1]

The **bars** of gold **are** heavy.[1]

Their **words** of wisdom **are** welcome.[1]

The **sheets** of paper **are** yellow.[1]

It makes no difference that "water", "gold", "wisdom", "paper" are singular. The nominatives are the plural "buckets", "bars", "words", "sheets"; so the finite verb in each case is "are".

**b.** The word before "of" is singular; the word after "of" is plural.
In many cases there is no problem. Since it is the word before "of" that counts as the nominative, the finite verb should be singular.

The **bag** of coins **is** heavy.[1]

The **bunch** of flowers **is** on the table.[1]

The **book** of poems **is** a gift.[1]

The **bowl** of nuts **is** there.[1]

It doesn't matter that "coins", "flowers", "poems", "nuts" are all plural. In each case we still use "is", because "bag", "bunch", "book" and "bowl" are singular nominatives.

**c.** The word before "of" is a singular collective noun; the word after "of" is a plural noun.
We have already seen, in item **6** above, that we can sometimes hitch a singular collective noun to a singular finite verb ("The **group is** flying home"), and sometimes to a plural finite verb ("The **committee are** of different minds"). It all depends on the context. The same goes for compound subjects with "of".

**i.** Sometimes the context tells you specifically whether you should use a singular or a plural finite verb.

---

1 Standard formal: *use this, and you can't go wrong in formal contexts.*
2 Standard formal with consistent options: *choose one and stick to it.*
3 Standard formal with flexible options: *choose any one, any time.*
4 Old-fashioned: *still all right, but fading from modern usage.*
5 Standard informal: *fine in conversation or in personal letters.*
6 Nonstandard: *you jez'gotta be kidding.*

## Agreement of nominative and finite verb

The **number** of patients **is** growing.[1]
(The "number" is growing.)

A number of **patients are** improving.[1]
(The "patients" are improving.)

The **crowd** of spectators **is** large.[1]
(The "crowd" is large.)

The crowd of **spectators are** cheering.[1]
(The "spectators" are cheering.)

**ii.** Sometimes the context is not so obligingly clear. In those cases, matching the finite verb with the singular nominative is standard formal; matching it with the plural noun is standard informal.

**None of them** is ready.[1]
**None of them** are ready.[5]

A **group of people** is there.[1]
A **group of people** are there.[5]

The **remainder of the tickets** is unsold.[1]
The **remainder of the tickets** are unsold.[5]

**d.** "A lot of" or "a couple of" followed by a plural noun.
Strictly speaking, "lot" and "couple" are singular nouns. But anything other than plural finite verbs to go with these structures is nowadays nonstandard.

A **lot of them are** happy.[1]
A **lot of them is** happy.[6]

A **couple of my friends are** here.[1]
A **couple of my friends is** here.[6]

**16. "Who" relating to a compound subject.**
"Who" — like "whom", "which", "that" and a few other words — is a relative pronoun. To determine whether you follow "who" with a singular or with a plural finite verb, you first have to identify the noun or the pronoun to which it relates. In most cases this is simple.

I would like you to meet my mother, **who is** just back from overseas.

**Usage**

"Who", in the above example, relates to the singular noun "mother", so it takes the singular finite verb "is".

I would like you to meet my parents, **who are** just back from overseas.[1]

"Who" relates to the plural "parents", so it takes the plural finite verb "are".

But it is not always so easy, because "who" may just as well relate to a compound subject as to a simple one.

My colleague is **one of those people who** (is/are) . . .

In this sentence, does "who" relate to "one" (which takes "is"), or does it relate to "people" (which takes "are")?

To find the answer to this question we need to transform the sentence with "who" into two sentences without "who".

SENTENCE WITH "WHO"

My colleague is one of those people **who (is/are)** always complaining.

TRANSFORMED WITHOUT "WHO"

My colleague is one of those people. Such **people are** always complaining.

The second of the transformed sentences (without "who") clearly shows that "who" relates to the plural "people". Therefore, "who" takes a plural finite verb in standard formal usage.

My colleague is one of those people **who are** always complaining.[1]
My colleague is one of those people **who is** always complaining.[5]

---

1 Standard formal: *use this, and you can't go wrong in formal contexts.*
2 Standard formal with consistent options: *choose one and stick to it.*
3 Standard formal with flexible options: *choose any one, any time.*
4 Old-fashioned: *still all right, but fading from modern usage.*
5 Standard informal: *fine in conversation or in personal letters.*
6 Nonstandard: *you jez'gotta be kidding.*

# CHAPTER 5
# Split infinitive verbs and split compound verbs

## Overview

Let us begin by defining our terms.

Infinitive verbs are base-form verbs preceded by "to".

> to go  to understand
> to run  to accept

To split such infinitive verbs means putting one or more words between the word "to" and the base form of the verb.

> to **never** go  to **clearly and thoroughly** understand
> to **quickly** run  to **gladly and gratefully** accept

You may instinctively feel that the examples of split infinitive verbs given above are slightly odd. If so, your instinct for language is in good shape. Split infinitive verbs have something of a bad name among some grammarians because, they argue, the bond between "to" and the associated verb is too intimate to allow for splitting. The fact is, though, that split infinitives are quite convenient and workable for informal occasions — in speech, for example, or in personal letters. What's more, many eminent writers have used them in their literary works from time to time, though other equally eminent writers have fastidiously avoided them.

So what are non-eminent workaday writers to do about split infinitive verbs? We suggest that using them is something like entering a posh establishment in crumpled jeans. You can get away with it if you are a millionaire. Similarly, you can get away with splitting infinitive verbs if you are an eminent author. But if you are an ordinary diner going to a posh

## Usage

establishment, you would show up in neat and tidy clothes. Similarly, if you are a workaday writer, we suggest that you avoid splitting infinitive verbs in formal contexts.

We turn now to compound verbs. These are clusters of words all the members of which are verbs:

    have gone                        would be understood
    will have been running      does accept

Note that, in compound verbs, only the last member of each cluster carries the meaning of the compound: "... gone", "... running", "... under- stood", "... accept". The members that carry the meaning are called notional verbs. The other members of the compounds ("have ...", "will have been ...", "would be ...", "does ...") fulfil grammatical functions but carry no meaning. These other members are called auxiliary verbs.

To split compound verbs means putting one or more additional words among the member verbs of the compounds. These additional words may come between two auxiliary verbs or between an auxiliary and a notional verb.

    have **never ever** gone        would be **clearly** understood
    will **soon** have been running   does **not by any means** accept

If your instinct for language tells you that there is nothing odd about these examples, your instinct is holding up well. There is, in fact, nothing in the slightest odd about the examples; and grammarians as well as practitioners of the language will unhesitatingly split compound verbs in the way we have shown in the examples.

In this chapter we deal with these topics in two sections.

---

1  Standard formal: *use this, and you can't go wrong in formal contexts.*
2  Standard formal with consistent options: *choose one and stick to it.*
3  Standard formal with flexible options: *choose any one, any time.*
4  Old-fashioned: *still all right, but fading from modern usage.*
5  Standard informal: *fine in conversation or in personal letters.*
6  Nonstandard: *you jez'gotta be kidding.*

## Split infinitive, split compound verbs

### A. Infinitive verbs without objects and with objects
This section covers every sin that you can commit with split infinitive verbs, and it shows you how you can avoid splitting them — if you feel so inclined.

### B. Split compound verbs
This section tells you the degree to which you may — indeed, sometimes must — split compound verbs.

### A. Infinitive verbs without objects and with objects
Before we launch into the section, let us begin by defining the key concept — object. An object is that part of a sentence that denotes the person or thing at which the action of the verb is directed. An object, in other words, is the target of the verb.

Some infinitive verbs in English are not followed by objects.

>They want **to sleep**.[1]

Other infinitive verbs are followed by objects, and these objects may be short or long.

>I have **to see** them.[1]
>I would like **to hear** what they said at the meeting last night.[1]

### 1. Infinitive verbs without objects.
If you have a split infinitive verb without an object, there are standard informal and standard formal options.
**a.** Let the split infinitive verb stand.

>I would like you **to** quickly **run** there.[5]

**b.** Reposition the word or words that split the infinitive verb.

>I would like you **quickly** to run there.[3]
>I would like you to run there **quickly**.[3]

### 2. Infinitive verbs with short objects.
If you have a split infinitive verb, and that verb is followed by a short object, there are standard informal and standard formal options.
**a.** Let the split infinitive verb stand.

**Usage**

> I would like **to** once again **borrow** your book.[5]

**b.** Reposition the word or words that split the infinitive verb.

> I would like **once again** to borrow your book.[3]
> I would like to borrow your book **once again**.[3]

**c.** One option that is not available in standard English is to reposition the word or words between the infinitive verb and its object.

> I would like **to borrow** once again **your book**.[6]

This option is unavailable because the bond between a verb and its object is even more intimate than that between the two parts of the infinitive verb. It is, therefore, better to split an infinitive than to separate the infinitive from its object.

**3. Infinitive verbs with long objects.**
In point **2.b.** above, we saw that if the infinitive has a short object it is possible to unsplit the infinitive by putting the intervening word or words after the object. But this option does not work if the object is long. The resultant sentence simply does not read well.

> I would like to borrow **the book that you lent me last week and that you recommended so heartily after reading it several times yourself** once again.[6]

By the time we get to "once again" at the end of this sentence, we're not quite sure what it was that occurred — or will occur — once again.

Nevertheless, in such cases there are still several options available.
**a.** Let the split infinitive verb stand.

> They decided **to** immediately **accept** the challenge issued by their rivals.[5]

---

1 Standard formal: *use this, and you can't go wrong in formal contexts.*
2 Standard formal with consistent options: *choose one and stick to it.*
3 Standard formal with flexible options: *choose any one, any time.*
4 Old-fashioned: *still all right, but fading from modern usage.*
5 Standard informal: *fine in conversation or in personal letters.*
6 Nonstandard: *you jez'gotta be kidding.*

**b.** Reposition the word or words that split the infinitive before the infinitive.

> They decided immediately **to accept** the challenge issued by their rivals.[3]

**c.** Recast the sentence so that the infinitive verb changes into a noun. That way there is no infinitive to split!

> They decided on an immediate **acceptance** of the challenge issued by their rivals.[3]

**4. Infinitive verbs and parentheses.**
**a.** One case when you need not be shy about splitting an infinitive verb is when the splitting word or words are parenthetical — that is, when the word or words act as an aside. But then you have to set the parenthesis off with commas, dashes or round brackets.

> They decided to, **notwithstanding my protest,** do what they wanted.[3]
> They decided to — **notwithstanding my protest** — do what they wanted.[3]
> They decided to (**notwithstanding my protest**) do what they wanted.[3]

The split in the infinitive verb works here because, by parenthesising the splitting words, you are in a sense telling the reader to ignore them.

**b.** Of course you may also opt to reposition the parenthesis elsewhere in the sentence.

> **Notwithstanding my protest,** they decided to do what they wanted.[3]
> They decided to do what they wanted — **notwithstanding my protest**.[3]
> They decided (**notwithstanding my protest**) to do what they wanted.[3]

## B. Split compound verbs

While there is some lingering inhibition about splitting infinitive verbs, there is absolutely none about splitting compound verbs. Indeed, compound verbs are there for the splitting. In this section we show you some of the options available to you.

## Usage

**5. Split compound verbs in the negative and in the interrogative.**
When you cast a verb in the interrogative (that is, the question form) or in the negative (with "not"), you can't help splitting the compound verb.

> They **did** not **rest**.[1]
> **Will** they **return**?[1]

The same goes for compound verbs in the negative-interrogative (that is, a question with "not").

> **Did** they not **rest**?[1]
> **Will** they not **return**?[1]

**6. Compound verbs and adverbs of frequency.**
**a.** Adverbs of frequency are adverbs such as "never", "seldom", "often", "frequently" and the like. The natural place for such adverbs is in the middle of compound verbs.

> I **have** never **seen** such a thing.[3]
> We **have** often **heard** that story.[3]

**b.** The alternative is to put the adverbs of frequency elsewhere in the sentences.

> **Never** have I seen such a thing.[3]
> **Often** have we heard that story.[3]
> We have heard that story **often**.[3]

**7. Compound verbs and other adverbs (or adverb phrases).**
**a.** Adverbs other than adverbs of frequency, and adverb phrases (that is, groups of words that together act as adverbs), can also nestle comfortably and legitimately in the middle of compound verbs.

---

1 Standard formal: *use this, and you can't go wrong in formal contexts.*
2 Standard formal with consistent options: *choose one and stick to it.*
3 Standard formal with flexible options: *choose any one, any time.*
4 Old-fashioned: *still all right, but fading from modern usage.*
5 Standard informal: *fine in conversation or in personal letters.*
6 Nonstandard: *you jez'gotta be kidding.*

They **have** vehemently **denied** it.³

I **am** at last **living** comfortably.³

**b.** But such adverbs can also come in other positions in the sentence.

They have denied it **vehemently**.³

**At last** I am living comfortably.³

I am living comfortably **at last**.³

**8. Compound verbs and parentheses.**
**a.** You may, if you wish, put a great big parenthesis smack in the middle of a compound verb.

They have, **to the best of my knowledge and belief and as far as I can tell from the documents,** behaved in a proper way.³

They have — **to the best of my knowledge and belief and as far as I can tell from the documents** — behaved in a proper way.³

They have (**to the best of my knowledge and belief and as far as I can tell from the documents**) behaved in a proper way.³

**b.** Of course, you may also opt to put these words outside of the compound verb — for example at the beginning or at the end of the sentence.

**To the best of my knowledge and belief and as far as I can tell from the documents,** they have behaved in a proper way.³

They have behaved in a proper way — **to the best of my knowledge and belief and as far as I can tell from the documents.**³

# CHAPTER 6
# The subjunctive mood and conditional sentences

## Overview

"Subjunctive mood" and "conditional sentences" are technical terms that grammarians use to denote structures that you have been using almost since you started talking in sentences. A few simple examples and a bit of explanation, and the concepts lurking behind the terminology will become clear.

**a.** Moods.

"Mood" is a grammatical term that means the mode or manner of expression that a verb conveys in a sentence and that, consequently, the sentence as a whole conveys. We can see what a grammatical mood is by looking at three sentences that are slightly different in structure, and that express different moods.

    **i.** God saves the Queen.
    **ii.** God, save the Queen!
    **iii.** God save the Queen.

If you look closely at the three example sentences, you will see minor differences among them. These differences are conveyed by the verbs, the structures and/or by the punctuation, and they account for the differences in mood in the sentences.

    **i.** The indicative mood.

"God saves the Queen" is a statement of fact. The statement may be true or false. That doesn't matter. What does matter is that the verb ("saves"),

---

1 Standard formal: *use this, and you can't go wrong in formal contexts.*
2 Standard formal with consistent options: *choose one and stick to it.*
3 Standard formal with flexible options: *choose any one, any time.*
4 Old-fashioned: *still all right, but fading from modern usage.*
5 Standard informal: *fine in conversation or in personal letters.*
6 Nonstandard: *you jez'gotta be kidding.*

## Subjunctives and conditionals

and the way that the sentence is structured and punctuated, indicate that the sentence deals with the realm of reality, the realm of fact. When this is the case, the verb and the sentence are in the indicative mood. Over ninety per cent of the sentences we use in daily life (from "I'm tired" to "Kant was a transcendental philosopher") are in the indicative mood.

**ii.** The imperative mood.

"God, save the Queen!" is not a statement of fact. The verb, the punctuation, the sentence structure — all of these tell us that the sentence expresses a command. Verbs and sentences of this kind are in the imperative mood. We use such sentences quite often in daily life to convey orders. "Ready, set, go!" and "Don't do that, please" are examples of imperatives.

**iii.** The subjunctive mood.

"God save the Queen" is neither a statement of fact nor a command. It is an expression of wishful thinking or hope. Verbs and sentences of this kind are in the subjunctive mood. "If only I were rich!" and "I wish that they would help me" are examples of subjunctives.

**b.** Conditional sentences.

Conditional sentences (or just "conditionals") are sentences that come in two parts: a condition and a consequence.

| CONDITION | CONSEQUENCE |
|---|---|
| If you come home now, | I will forgive you. |
| If he were to work harder, | he might succeed. |
| If I had known he was coming, | I would have prepared a welcome. |

Often — as in the second and third examples above — you use the subjunctive mood in conditional sentences.

In this chapter we explore subjunctives and conditional sentences in three sections.

## A. How to express the subjunctive mood

The major means of expressing the subjunctive mood is through verbs. In this section we look at how verbs operate in the subjunctive.

## Usage

### B. Uses of the subjunctive mood
Under this head we list different, though allied, uses of the subjunctive mood. The uses range from the practical ("I propose that we adjourn") to the poetic ("If music be the food of love . . .").

### C. Conditional sentences
Here we show how one expresses conditions, often with the use of subjunctive structures. An example: "Had I known they were in need, I would have helped them."

### A. How to express the subjunctive mood
Differences in structure and in meaning set the subjunctive apart from other moods.

#### 1. The subjunctive "were".
A feature of the subjunctive mood is that it uses verbs that normally pass for indicative verbs, but it uses them in a specialised way. The most obvious case of this is the verb "were", which functions one way in the indicative mood and a different way in the subjunctive mood.

> **i.** In the indicative mood, "were" denotes an actual state or event relating to a plural subject in the past.
>
> **They were** here last week.[1]
>
> (The sentence asserts a fact — that they were here last week.)
>
> **ii.** In the subjunctive mood, "were" denotes a hypothetical or imaginary state or event relating either to a singular or to a plural subject in the present or in the future.
>
> If only **they were** here![1]
>
> (This suggests that they are not actually here now.)
>
> I wish **she were** here.[1]
>
> (This sentence suggests that she is in fact not here now.)

---

1 Standard formal: *use this, and you can't go wrong in formal contexts.*
2 Standard formal with consistent options: *choose one and stick to it.*
3 Standard formal with flexible options: *choose any one, any time.*
4 Old-fashioned: *still all right, but fading from modern usage.*
5 Standard informal: *fine in conversation or in personal letters.*
6 Nonstandard: *you jez'gotta be kidding.*

## Subjunctives and conditionals

In the subjunctive, "was" with a singular subject is nonstandard.

I wish **she was** here.[6]

**2. The modal auxiliaries "would", "should", "could", "may", "might", "must", "ought".**

The verbs listed in the heading, and a handful of others, often crop up in the subjunctive mood. For this reason (among others) grammarians have coined a special name for them — "modal auxiliaries". Each of the modal auxiliaries — like "were" in point 1 above — has a dual role: indicative (which suggests that we are dealing with the realm of fact), and subjunctive (which suggests we are dealing with the possible or the hypothetical). We now look at how they function in sentences in each of their two roles.

**a. i.** "Would" used in the indicative mood.

When I was a child, I decided that I **would be** a pilot.[1]
("Would be" refers to something that was going to take place later on, after the moment of decision.)

**ii.** "Would" used in the subjunctive mood.

I **would be** sorry to see you leave.[1]
("Would be" refers to a possibility in the present or in the future.)

**b. i.** "Should" used in the indicative mood.

You **should come** at noon.[1]
("Should come" refers to an actual obligation.)

**ii.** "Should" used in the subjunctive mood.

If they **should come**, it would surprise me.[1]
("Should come" refers to a remote possibility.)

**c. i.** "Could" used in the indicative mood.

When I was young I **could jump** over that fence.[1]
("Could jump" refers to something that was actually the case in the past.)

## Usage

**ii.** "Could" used in the subjunctive mood.

I don't quite believe what they said: they **could be** wrong.[1]
("Could be" indicates a degree of doubt about something in the present.)

**d. i.** "May" used in the indicative mood.

You **may enter** the room without knocking.[1]
("May enter" refers to something that is actually allowed in the present.)

**ii.** "May" used in the subjunctive mood.

I have not yet made my mind up, but I **may enter** later.[1]
("May enter" indicates a state of indecision about the future.)

**e. i.** "Might" used in the indicative mood.

I told them that they **might do** whatever they felt like doing.[1]
("Might do" refers to permission that was actually granted in the past.)

**ii.** "Might" used in the subjunctive mood.

I am not too sure about it, but I **might do** it tomorrow.[1]
("Might do" denotes a doubtful state of mind about what might happen in the future.)

**f. i.** "Must" used in the indicative mood.

The law says that I **must pay** income tax.[1]
("Must pay" refers to an actual obligation.)

**ii.** "Must" used in the subjunctive mood.

They came through the door: I **must have left** it unlocked.[1]
("Must have left" indicates a supposition or hypothesis.)

---

1 Standard formal: *use this, and you can't go wrong in formal contexts.*
2 Standard formal with consistent options: *choose one and stick to it.*
3 Standard formal with flexible options: *choose any one, any time.*
4 Old-fashioned: *still all right, but fading from modern usage.*
5 Standard informal: *fine in conversation or in personal letters.*
6 Nonstandard: *you jez'gotta be kidding.*

## Subjunctives and conditionals

**g. i.** "Ought" used in the indicative mood.

They **ought to wait** their turn, just like everybody else.[1]
("Ought to wait" indicates an actual obligation.)

**ii.** "Ought" used in the subjunctive mood.

They said they wrote a week ago: I **ought to get** the letter soon.[1]
("Ought to get" indicates a hope or expectation for the future.)

**3. Other verbs and verb forms used indicatively and subjunctively.**
Verbs and verb forms other than those involving modal auxiliaries (for which see point 2 above) also have this dual role — indicative and subjunctive.

**a. i.** The base form of a verb used in the indicative mood.

I will **be** there tomorrow.[1]
("Be" refers to an actual state of affairs in the future.)

**ii.** The base form of a verb used in the subjunctive mood.

**Be** that as it may, I will not change my mind.[1]
("Be" indicates a doubtful state of affairs in the present.)

**b. i.** The past simple form of a verb used in the indicative mood.

Last week he **took** my advice.[1]
("Took" indicates something that he did last week.)

**ii.** The past simple form of a verb used in the subjunctive mood.

If he **took** my advice it would turn out well.[1]
("Took" indicates an action that may or may not come about in the present or in the future.)

**c. i.** The past perfect form of a verb used in the indicative mood.

They said that they **had been** on holiday.[1]
("Had been" refers to an actual state in the past.)

**Usage**

**ii.** The past perfect form of a verb used in the subjunctive mood.

I wish I **had been** there to see it.[1]

("Had been" refers to something that was not the case in the past.)

## B. Uses of the subjunctive mood

In this section we look at the uses to which you can put the subjunctive mood. It is often possible to express the subjunctive in several different ways. Sometimes it is even possible to express it through the indicative mood. In order to flag the structural and other differences between the subjunctive and the other moods, we will add an example sentence in one of the other moods (in brackets) to every set of subjunctive examples — except where you can use the indicative to stand in for the subjunctive. The bracketed sentences are not intended to have the same meaning as the example sentences. They are there only to highlight the peculiarities of the subjunctive.

**4. The subjunctive mood used to express a wishful command.**
The subjunctive wishful command has more of the wish to it than of the command. A typical example is: "May all your troubles be little ones." Its characteristics are that it has a subject ("your troubles") and that you can formulate it either in the second or in the third person. By way of contrast, a full blown command (in the imperative mood) has no subject, and you always formulate it in the second person. A typical example is: "Behave yourself." Now for some examples of the subjunctive wishful command.
**a.** In the second person, with the modal auxiliary "may".

**May** you **get** well soon.[1]

(Imperative mood: "**Get** well soon.")

**May** you **not suffer** any more.[1]

(Imperative mood: "**Don't suffer** any more.")

**b.** In the third person, with the modal auxiliary "may"; or with the base form of the verb.

---

1 Standard formal: *use this, and you can't go wrong in formal contexts.*
2 Standard formal with consistent options: *choose one and stick to it.*
3 Standard formal with flexible options: *choose any one, any time.*
4 Old-fashioned: *still all right, but fading from modern usage.*
5 Standard informal: *fine in conversation or in personal letters.*
6 Nonstandard: *you jez'gotta be kidding.*

## Subjunctives and conditionals

May heaven **help** us.[3]
Heaven **help** us.[3]
(Indicative mood: "Heaven helps us.")

**May** your kingdom come.[3]
Your kingdom **come**.[3]
(Indicative mood: "Your kingdom **comes**.")

**5. The subjunctive mood used to express a wish about the future, the present or the past.**
Characteristically, the way to express such a wish in the subjunctive is to prefix it with the words "I wish" or "I wish that" or "If only". There is another way — prefixing it with "Would that" — but this is old-fashioned.
**a.** Wishes relating to the future, using the modal auxiliary "would".

I wish he **would come**.[3]
I wish that he **would come**.[3]
If only he **would come**.[3]
**Would** that he **would come**.[4]
(Indicative mood: "I expect that he **will come**.")
I wish she **would answer**.[3]
I wish that she **would answer**.[3]
If only she **would answer**.[3]
**Would** that she **would answer**.[4]
(Indicative mood: "I hope that she **will answer**.")

**b. i.** Wishes relating to the present, using the modal auxiliary "were".

I wish she **were** here.[3]
I wish that she **were** here.[3]
If only she **were** here.[3]
**Would** that she **were** here.[4]
(Indicative mood: "She **is** here.")

**ii.** Wishes relating to the present, using any past simple form of the verb.

## Usage

> I wish I **knew** the answer.[3]
> I wish that I **knew** the answer.[3]
> If only I **knew** the answer.[3]
> **Would** that I **knew** the answer.[4]
> (Indicative mood: "I **know** the answer.")

**c.** Wishes relating to the past, using the past perfect form of the verb with or without the modal auxiliary "would".

> I wish I **had done** it better.[3]
> I wish that I **had done** it better.[3]
> If only I **had done** it better.[3]
> **Would** that I **had done** it better.[4]
> (Indicative mood: "I **did** it better.")
> I wish I **had known** about it sooner.[3]
> I wish that I **had known** about it sooner.[3]
> If only I **had known** about it sooner.[3]
> **Would** that I **had known** about it sooner.[4]
> (Indicative mood: "I **knew** about it sooner.")

**6. The subjunctive mood used to express unlikely or failed hypotheses about the future, the present or the past.**

Characteristically, you introduce such hypotheses with the words "as if" or "as though". The introductory wording is optional, and we show it as such in the examples that follow. We also show a range of modal auxiliaries and other verbs that can come into play in this use of the subjunctive mood.

**a.** Hypotheses relating to the future, using modal auxiliaries.

> It appears as if it **might rain** tomorrow.[3]
> It appears as though it **might rain** tomorrow.[3]
> It appears as if it **could rain** tomorrow.[3]

---

1 Standard formal: *use this, and you can't go wrong in formal contexts.*
2 Standard formal with consistent options: *choose one and stick to it.*
3 Standard formal with flexible options: *choose any one, any time.*
4 Old-fashioned: *still all right, but fading from modern usage.*
5 Standard informal: *fine in conversation or in personal letters.*
6 Nonstandard: *you jez'gotta be kidding.*

### Subjunctives and conditionals

It appears as though it **could rain** tomorrow.³
It appears as if it **should rain** tomorrow.³
It appears as though it **should rain** tomorrow.³
(Indicative mood: "It appears that it **will rain** tomorrow.")

**b.** Unlikely or failed hypotheses relating to the present, using modal auxiliaries or the past simple form of the verb.

You look as if you **might know** the truth.³
You look as though you **might know** the truth.³
You look as if you **could know** the truth.³
You look as though you **could know** the truth.³
You look as if you **knew** the truth.³
You look as though you **knew** the truth.³
(Indicative mood: "I think you **know** the truth.")

**c.** Unlikely or failed hypotheses relating to the past, using modal auxiliaries or the past perfect form of the verb.

It seemed as if they **might** never **have tried**.³
It seemed as though they **might** never **have tried**.³
It seemed as if they **could** never **have tried**.³
It seemed as though they **could** never **have tried**.³
It seemed as if they **had** never **tried**.³
It seemed as though they **had** never **tried**.³
(Indicative mood: "It seemed that they never **tried**.")

**7. The subjunctive mood used to express an intention, suggestion, wish or request, after a preliminary clause followed by "that".**
A typical example is, "I move that the meeting be adjourned." Another example, this time in the negative subjunctive: "I move that the meeting not be adjourned." There are optional ways of expressing such intentions, hopes and the like. We look at these options below, first in the positive and then in the negative.
**a.** In the positive, there are two different forms of the subjunctive that you may use: one without and one with the modal subjunctive "should". As a third option, you may also use the indicative. This last option is becoming increasingly popular in modern usage.

61

# Usage

I request that he **go**.[3]
I request that he **should go**.[3]
I request that he **goes**.[3] (Indicative mood.)
I suggest that she **be given** a hearing.[3]
I suggest that she **should be given** a hearing.[3]
I suggest that she **is given** a hearing.[3] (Indicative mood.)

**b.** In the negative, the same three options hold.

The meeting resolves that the member **not be heard**.[3]
The meeting resolves that the member **should not be heard**.[3]
The meeting resolves that the member **is not heard**.[3] (Indicative mood.)

There is another word order that you sometimes see, but it is not standard English.

The meeting resolves that the member **be not heard**.[6]

In the above examples, we have used the preliminary clauses "I move that", "I request that", "I suggest that", "The meeting resolves that". Other typical preliminary clauses followed by the same options are —

I demand that
The sentence is that
I ask that
I recommend that

I insist that
I propose that
It is important that
I desire that

## 8. The subjunctive mood used in stock expressions.

The subjunctive mood had a much wider currency in older varieties of English than it has in current English. In current English, some of the subjunctives from earlier times, both literary and popular, survive as stock expressions. They are all slightly quaint, though they serve useful, if somewhat specialised, purposes. As in the rest of this section, the

---

1 Standard formal: *use this, and you can't go wrong in formal contexts.*
2 Standard formal with consistent options: *choose one and stick to it.*
3 Standard formal with flexible options: *choose any one, any time.*
4 Old-fashioned: *still all right, but fading from modern usage.*
5 Standard informal: *fine in conversation or in personal letters.*
6 Nonstandard: *you jez'gotta be kidding.*

## Subjunctives and conditionals

bracketed words don't have the same meaning as the subjunctives. We put them there to highlight the peculiar features of the subjunctives.

Be that as it **may** . . .[1]  
(That's how it is . . .)  
Lest we **forget**[1]  
(Let us not forget . . .)  
**May** it **please** the court . . .[1]  
(It pleases the court . . .)  
**Come** the revolution . . .[1]  
(When the revolution comes . . .)  
**Come** what **may** . . .[1]  
(Whatever happens . . .)  
**Should** auld acquaintance **be forgot** . . .[1]  
(If old acquaintance is forgotten . . .)

So **be** it[1]  
(It is so)  
**Would** that it **were** so[1]  
(It isn't so)  
**Suffice** it to say . . .[1]  
(It is enough to say . . .)  
Far **be** it from me[1]  
(It is far from me . . .)  
. . . as it **were**.[1]  
( . . . as it was.)

### C. Conditional sentences

Conditional sentences consist of two clauses: a condition clause ("If I had the time . . .") and a consequence clause (". . . I would take a vacation"). Conditional sentences are very complex linguistic devices. To introduce them, therefore, we start with a simplified outline, and we follow this up with a more detailed examination. But first, a sketch of the four basic types of conditional sentences.

**a.** Type A conditional sentences: the possible indefinite time.

If you **help** me I **will help** you.[3]  
I will **help** you if you **help** me.[3]

This type of conditional sentence most usually refers (in both its parts) to acts or states that may come about in the future. Because the acts or states are possible — even likely — the verbs in both clauses are in the indicative mood. Typically, the verb in the condition clause is in a present tense form, while the verb in the consequence clause is in a future tense form.

**b.** Type B conditional sentences: the counterfactual present or future.

## Usage

If I **were** a bird I **would** fly away.³
I **would fly** away if I **were** a bird.³
**Were** I a bird I **would fly** away.³
I **would fly** away **were** I a bird.³

In this type of conditional sentence both clauses refer to an act or a state that is not the case in the present. Indeed, the case is the direct opposite of what the words say — I'm not a bird, so I can't fly away. The verbs in both parts of such conditional sentences are in the subjunctive mood. Typically the verb in the condition clause is a past simple tense form, while the verb in the consequence clause consists of the modal auxiliary "would" followed by a verb in the base form. This is called the future in the past simple form.

   **c.** Type C conditional sentences: the failed past.

If you **had come** earlier you **would have met** them.³
**Had** you **come** earlier you **would have met** them.³
You **would have met** them if you **had come** earlier.³
You **would have met** them **had** you **come** earlier.³

In this type of conditional sentence both clauses refer to an act or a state that failed to come about in the past. Indeed, what actually happened was the opposite of what the words say — you didn't come earlier, so you didn't meet them. The verbs in both parts of such conditional clauses are in the subjunctive mood. Typically the verb in the condition clause is in the past perfect tense form, while the verb in the consequence clause consists of the modal auxiliary "would" + "have" + a past participle verb. This is called the future in the past perfect form.

   **d.** Type D conditional sentences: mixed conditionals.

If you **had come** late I **would be** upset.³
**Had** you **come** late I **would be** upset.³
I **would be** upset if you **had come** late.³
I **would be** upset **had** you **come** late.³

---

1 Standard formal: *use this, and you can't go wrong in formal contexts.*
2 Standard formal with consistent options: *choose one and stick to it.*
3 Standard formal with flexible options: *choose any one, any time.*
4 Old-fashioned: *still all right, but fading from modern usage.*
5 Standard informal: *fine in conversation or in personal letters.*
6 Nonstandard: *you jez' gotta be kidding.*

## Subjunctives and conditionals

Here we have a type C condition yoked to a type B consequence: the condition failed to materialise in the past, therefore the consequence does not hold in the present — you didn't come late, so I'm not upset. The verbs in both parts of the sentence are in the subjunctive mood.

Now let us look at three features of conditional sentences. The first feature is that, in conditional sentences, it is always as legitimate to start the sentence with the condition clause as it is to start it with the consequence clause. We have illustrated this feature in each of the conditional sentence types from A to D inclusive.

The second feature is that, while condition clauses characteristically start with the conjunction "if", it is also possible in some cases to dispense with that conjunction. We have illustrated this in some of the example sentences in types B, C and D.

The third feature is not illustrated in any of the above example sentences. It is that, apart from the conjunction "if", condition clauses can start with a whole range of conjunctions including the following.

| | |
|---|---|
| unless | in case |
| as long as | supposing that |
| provided | on condition that |
| providing | assuming that |

It is worth keeping these three features in mind as you read the more detailed treatment of conditional sentences that follows. But in that treatment we will, for the sake of simplicity, start each example sentence with the condition clause and — if we use any conjunction at all — we will use the conjunction "if". For type B, C and D conditional sentences we also give (in brackets) the meaning of each example sentence.

### 9. Type A conditional sentences: the possible indefinite time.

Sentences of this type deal with real or possible acts or states. The sentences therefore feature verbs in moods other than the subjunctive.

**a.** The most common pattern is an indicative present tense verb in the condition clause, and an indicative future tense verb in the consequence clause.

If you **write** me a letter I **will answer**.[1]
If you **are working** now I **will not disturb** you.[1]

# Usage

**b.** A variation is to have an imperative verb in the consequence clause.

If you **are feeling** unwell **see** a doctor.[1]
If you **know** the end of the story **don't give** it away.[1]

**c.** You get an expanded range of variations by matching any of the verb types in the left-hand column with any of the verb types in the right-hand column.

| CONDITION CLAUSE | CONSEQUENCE CLAUSE |
| --- | --- |
| Indicative present tense | Indicative present tense |
| Indicative past tense | Indicative past tense |
| Indicative future tense | Indicative future tense |
|  | Imperative mood |

If you **want** my help just **give** me a call.[1]
If she **promised** to come she **will** come.[1]
If you **will** only **be** patient you **will** soon **see** the result.[1]
If he **was** in the burning building he **was** lucky to escape.[1]
If you **have done** the work, **show** it to me.[1]
If he **doesn't arrive** on the next bus then he probably **missed** it.[1]

The patterns and the examples we have given will have made it clear why we call conditional sentences of this type "indefinite time" conditionals. Some of our examples refer to the past, some to the present, some to the future.

## 10. Type B conditional sentences: the counterfactual present or future.

Conditional sentences of this type typically deal with acts or states that don't exist in the present or that won't come about in the future — hence the descriptive name "counterfactual". The moods of the verbs in such sentences are subjunctive.

---

1 Standard formal: *use this, and you can't go wrong in formal contexts.*
2 Standard formal with consistent options: *choose one and stick to it.*
3 Standard formal with flexible options: *choose any one, any time.*
4 Old-fashioned: *still all right, but fading from modern usage.*
5 Standard informal: *fine in conversation or in personal letters.*
6 Nonstandard: *you jez'gotta be kidding.*

## Subjunctives and conditionals

**a.** The most common pattern is a past simple tense form in the condition clause, and a future in the past simple tense form in the consequence clause.

If I **knew** the answer I **would reveal** it.[1]
(As I don't know the answer, I can't reveal it.)
If I **were** not so busy I **would help** you.[1]
(As I am busy, I can't help you.)

**b.** You can obtain an expanded range of type B conditional sentences by matching any of the verb forms in the left-hand column with any in the right-hand column.

| CONDITION CLAUSE | CONSEQUENCE CLAUSE |
|---|---|
| Indicative past simple or past continuous tense | Modal auxiliary "should", "would", "could" or "might" followed by a base-form verb |
| Modal auxiliary "should", "would", "could" or "might" followed by a base-form verb | Imperative mood |
| "Were" followed by an infinitive-form verb | |

If I **were anticipating** an inspection I **would have** everything ready.[3]
**Were** I **anticipating** an inspection I **would have** everything ready.[3]
(I'm not anticipating an inspection, so I haven't got everything ready.)
If I **should fail** I **could try** again.[3]
**Should** I **fail** I **could try** again.[3]
(I don't think I'll fail, so I probably won't need to try again.)
If they **were to come** early we **might not be** ready.[3]
**Were** they **to come** early we **might not be** ready.[3]
(I doubt that they'll come early, so we probably will be ready.)
If I **were** in your place I **would not do** that.[3]
**Were** I in your place I **would not do** that.[3]
(I'm not in your place, so the possibility of my doing that doesn't arise.)

## Usage

If they **could come** it **would make** my day.[3]
**Could** they but **come** it **would make** my day.[3]
(It's probable that they can't come, so my day won't be made.)
"If I **should die, think** only this of me . . . "[3] (Rupert Brooke)
**Should** I **die, think** only this of me . . .[3]
If I **were to die, think** only this of me . . .[3]
(I'm not dead just yet, so you don't actually have to think it.)

**11. Type C conditional sentences: the failed past.**
Conditional sentences of this type deal with acts or states that failed to come about in the past. Consequently, the moods of the verbs in such sentences are subjunctive.

**a.** The most common pattern is a past perfect tense form in the condition clause, with a modal auxiliary "would" + "have" + a past participle verb in the consequence clause.

If you **had worked** faster you **would have finished** the job.[3]
**Had** you **worked** faster you **would have finished** the job.[3]
(You didn't work faster, so you didn't finish the job.)
If I **had found** the mistake I **would have corrected** it.[3]
**Had** I **found** the mistake I **would have corrected** it.[3]
(I didn't find the mistake, so I didn't correct it.)

**b.** You obtain an expanded range of type C conditional sentences by matching any of the verb forms in the left-hand column with any of the verb forms in the right-hand column.

| CONDITION CLAUSE | CONSEQUENCE CLAUSE |
|---|---|
| Past perfect tense form | "would" + "have" + a past participle verb |
| Past perfect continuous tense form | "should" + "have" + a past participle verb |
| | "could" + "have" + a past participle verb |
| | "might" + "have" + a past participle verb |

---

1  Standard formal: *use this, and you can't go wrong in formal contexts.*
2  Standard formal with consistent options: *choose one and stick to it.*
3  Standard formal with flexible options: *choose any one, any time.*
4  Old-fashioned: *still all right, but fading from modern usage.*
5  Standard informal: *fine in conversation or in personal letters.*
6  Nonstandard: *you jez'gotta be kidding.*

If you **had come** earlier you **would not have missed** the show.[3]
**Had** you **come** earlier you **would not have missed** the show.[3]
(You didn't come earlier, so you missed the show.)

If you **had done** your work properly I **should not have rebuked** you.[3]
**Had** you **done** your work properly I **should not have rebuked** you.[3]
(You didn't do your work properly, so I rebuked you.)

If I **had known** about it earlier I **could have done** something about it.[3]
**Had** I **known** about it earlier I **could have done** something about it.[3]
(I didn't know about it earlier, so there was nothing I could do about it)

If you **had been keeping** watch you **might have spotted** them.[3]
**Had** you **been keeping** watch you **might have spotted** them.[3]
(You weren't keeping watch, so you failed to spot them.)

**12. Type D conditional sentences: mixed conditionals.**
The beauty and the flexibility of the English language are such that it is possible to match one type of condition clause with a different type of consequence clause. This gives you a mixed conditional sentence. For example, if something failed to occur in the past and this has a counterfactual consequence in the present, you get a type C condition clause with a type B consequence clause. This is our first example below, and we follow it with other examples of mixed conditional sentences.

C–B: If they **had kept** their word yesterday I **would not be** so angry now.[3]
**Had** they **kept** their word yesterday I **would not be** so angry now.[3]
(They didn't keep their word yesterday, so I am angry now.)

B–C: If I **were** really angry with you I **would not have come** to visit you.[3]
**Were** I really angry with you I **would not have come** to visit you.[3]
(I'm not really angry with you, so I came to visit you.)

## Usage

B–A: If you **should fail** the test this time, **take** it again.[3]
Should you **fail** the test this time, **take** it again.[3]
(You probably won't fail the test, but take it again if you do.)

The actual number of possible type D structures — never mind sentences, of which there is an infinity — runs into the hundreds. But enough is enough!

1 Standard formal: *use this, and you can't go wrong in formal contexts.*
2 Standard formal with consistent options: *choose one and stick to it.*
3 Standard formal with flexible options: *choose any one, any time.*
4 Old-fashioned: *still all right, but fading from modern usage.*
5 Standard informal: *fine in conversation or in personal letters.*
6 Nonstandard: *you jez'gotta be kidding.*

CHAPTER 7
# Numbers

## Overview
This chapter is about writing numbers in ordinary prose — numbers of people and things. We also deal with how you write numbers when you are dealing with such elements as time, money and measures. But specialised topics such as numbers in mathematics or in science are outside the ambit of this book.

The following are the sections of the chapter.

### A. When to write numbers as digits and when to write numbers as words
Should you write "There were 23 people at the party" or "There were twenty-three people at the party"? Read this section for the answers.

### B. How to write cardinal numbers
Cardinal numbers come in digits ("23") and in words ("twenty-three"). They also come in combinations of digits and words ("23 million"). Here we deal with all the variations — and with their associated punctuation.

### C. How to write ordinal numbers
In digits, the ordinal numbers are "1st", "2nd", "3rd"; in words, "first", "second", "third". This section shows how one writes ordinal numbers as digits and as words.

### D. How to write fractions
We examine two types of fractions: common fractions such as "½" ("a half"), and decimal fractions such as "0.5" ("nought point five").

### E. How to write roman numerals
If only the practical Romans had had the practicality to invent a decimal numbering system, you would have been spared reading about how to

**Usage**

express "24" (Arabic style) as "XXIV" or "xxiv" (Roman style). As it is, this section tells you how to handle Roman numbers — at least up to certain practical limits.

## F. How to write dates, clock times, money sums and sporting scores

Among other things in this section, we show you twenty different ways to write Christmas Day 1994, using digits or words or a combination of digits and words.

## A. When to write numbers as digits and when to write numbers as words

In ordinary prose you sometimes express numbers in digits and sometimes in words. There is no uniform code, no set of rules, to tell you when to opt for words and when to opt for digits. Various journals and various publishing houses follow different practices — some more consistently, some less so. In this section we present our own system for handling this problem. We think — but who knows? — that this system has the virtues of consistency and rationality.

### 1. For general quantification — numbers of people or of things.

**a.** Write the numbers in words if you can express the numbers in one or two words each.

> They had **nine** dogs.[1]
>
> There are **a hundred** things to do.[1]
>
> There were **fifty-eight** plants in the greenhouse.[1]
>
> There were **two thousand** fans at the game.[1]

**b.** Write the numbers as digits if it would take more than two words to express each number. The rational principle here is that, if it takes more than two words to express a number, it's easier to read and to understand in digit form.

---

1 Standard formal: *use this, and you can't go wrong in formal contexts.*
2 Standard formal with consistent options: *choose one and stick to it.*
3 Standard formal with flexible options: *choose any one, any time.*
4 Old-fashioned: *still all right, but fading from modern usage.*
5 Standard informal: *fine in conversation or in personal letters.*
6 Nonstandard: *you jez'gotta be kidding.*

There were **148** sheep in the flock.[1]
The carpark can hold **2314** vehicles.[1]

**2. Expressing a number in words, even if it takes more than two words.**
**a.** If a sentence starts with a number, express the number in words, even if it takes more than two words to express. Alternatively, recast the sentence so that it doesn't start with the number.

**One hundred and forty-eight** sheep were in the flock.[3]
There were **148** sheep in the flock.[3]

**b.** For some stock expressions you may use words even for a number that requires more than two words.

I have told you this **a hundred and one** times.[1]
It's like an adventure from **a thousand and one** nights.[1]

**3. Expressing a number in digits, even if takes one or two words.**
Use digits in the following cases.
**a.** When a sentence contains mixed types of numbers — those expressible in up to two words, and those expressible in more words.

I have **80** tapes and **124** CDs.[1]

**b.** When you want the numbers to stand out for the sake of comparison.

Last year the council built **90** flats; this year, **100** flats.[1]

**c.** When you write a passage rich in numbers.

On their farm they have **3** cows, **120** chickens and **20** goats.[1]

**4. Numbers combined with standard units of weights and measures.**
**a.** Use digits if you use the abbreviation for the standard unit; words, if you express the standard unit fully.

| 3cm[2] | $10[2] | 50%[2] |
|---|---|---|
| three centimetres[2] | ten dollars[2] | fifty per cent[2] |

**b.** If the number that goes with the standard unit takes three or more words to write, use digits.

**Usage**

147cm[2]

147 centimetres[2]

**5. The use of digits and words to avoid ambiguity.**
When two numbers occur consecutively, express one as a word and one as a digit. Express the longer number as a digit.

> I had **three 45-metre** lengths of pipe.[1]
> I had **45 three-metre** lengths of pipe.[1]

If there is no distinction in length, spell out the first number.

> I had **two 2-metre** lengths of pipe.[1]

## B. How to write cardinal numbers

Cardinal numbers are positive whole numbers — including, in this section, the number "0" (or "zero"). There are two ways of writing cardinal numbers: as digits ("1", "2", "3"), and as words ("one", "two", "three"). Here we are on more solid ground than we were in section A — there are conventions governing the writing of these numbers. We begin the section by listing these conventions.

**a.** Numbers in digits.

> **i.** If the number consists of four digits, write it unspaced or with a comma or a space before the last three digits.

2,400[2]

2 400[2]

2400[2]

> **ii.** If the number consists of more than four digits, group the digits — from the right — in groups of three, and separate each group with a comma or a space.

42,300,000[2]

42 300 000[2]

---

1 Standard formal: *use this, and you can't go wrong in formal contexts.*
2 Standard formal with consistent options: *choose one and stick to it.*
3 Standard formal with flexible options: *choose any one, any time.*
4 Old-fashioned: *still all right, but fading from modern usage.*
5 Standard informal: *fine in conversation or in personal letters.*
6 Nonstandard: *you jez'gotta be kidding.*

# Numbers

**b.** Numbers in words.

**i.** Put a comma after the word that corresponds with the digit that could be followed by a comma — if a multiple of a hundred follows the comma.

eighteen thousand, four hundred[1]      (18,400)
forty million, eight hundred thousand[1]      (40,800,000)

**ii.** If a smaller-order number than hundreds (other than nil) follows the word where you could put a comma in digits, use the word "and" instead of a comma.

eighteen thousand and thirty[1]      (18,030)
forty million and twenty[1]      (40,000,020)

**iii.** Put the word "and" after the word "hundred" — if a whole number other than zero follows the "hundred".

six hundred **and** fifty[1]      (650)
eight hundred **and** five thousand, two hundred[1]      (805,200)

**iv.** Hyphenate the tens with the immediately following units — for all tens and units except teens.

**twenty-seven**[1]      (27)
**fifty-one** thousand[1]      (51,000)

**v.** Teens you write as single (unhyphenated) words.

**thirteen**[1]      (13)
**eighteen**[1]      (18)

The above rules cover just about every contingency, but — if you want to check in detail how to express numbers from one to sixteen or more digits — read on.

## Usage

**6. The number "0".**

0[1]
nil[2]
zero[2]
nought[2]
oh[5]

**7. Other one-digit numbers.**

4[1]
four[1]

**8. Two-digit numbers expressing ten, teens or multiples of ten.**

10[1]          18[1]            60[1]
ten[1]         eighteen[1]      sixty[1]

**9. Two-digit numbers expressing tens and units.**

21[1]                    43[1]
twenty-one[1]            forty-three[1]

**10. Three-digit numbers expressing multiples of a hundred.**

100[1]                   400[1]
a hundred[2]             four hundred[1]
one hundred[2]

**11. Three-digit numbers expressing multiples of a hundred together with numbers of a lower order of magnitude.**

112[1]                              876[1]
a hundred and twelve[2]             eight hundred and seventy-six[1]
one hundred and twelve[2]

---

1 Standard formal: *use this, and you can't go wrong in formal contexts.*
2 Standard formal with consistent options: *choose one and stick to it.*
3 Standard formal with flexible options: *choose any one, any time.*
4 Old-fashioned: *still all right, but fading from modern usage.*
5 Standard informal: *fine in conversation or in personal letters.*
6 Nonstandard: *you jez'gotta be kidding.*

# Numbers

12. **Four-digit numbers expressing multiples of a thousand.**

$1000^2$                  $6000^2$
$1,000^2$               $6,000^2$
$1\ 000^2$               $6\ 000^2$
a thousand$^2$        six thousand[1]
one thousand$^2$

13. **Four-digit numbers expressing multiples of a thousand together with multiples of a hundred.**

$4300^2$
$4,300^2$
$4\ 300^2$
forty-three hundred$^2$
four thousand, three hundred$^2$

14. **Four-digit numbers expressing multiples of a thousand together with numbers of a lower order of magnitude other than, or in addition to, multiples of a hundred.**

$2010^2$
$2,010^2$
$2\ 010^2$
two thousand and ten[1]
$4862^2$
$4,862^2$
$4\ 862^2$
forty-eight hundred and sixty-two$^2$
four thousand, eight hundred and sixty-two$^2$

15. **Five-digit numbers.**

$50,000^2$
$50\ 000^2$
fifty thousand[1]
$96,500^2$
$96\ 500^2$
ninety-six thousand, five hundred$^2$

77

## Usage

ninety-six and a half thousand[2]
76,835[2]
76 835[2]
seventy-six thousand, eight hundred and thirty-five[1]

**16. Six-digit numbers expressing multiples of a hundred thousand.**

100,000[2]           500,000[2]
100 000[2]           500 000[2]
0.1 million[2]           0.5 million[2]
0.1m[2]           0.5m[2]
a hundred thousand[2]           five hundred thousand[2]
one hundred thousand[2]           half a million[2]
point one of a million[2]           point five of a million[2]

**17. Six-digit numbers expressing multiples of a hundred thousand together with numbers of a lower order of magnitude.**

300,900[2]
300 900[2]
three hundred thousand, nine hundred[1]
723,826[2]
723 826[2]
seven hundred and twenty-three thousand, eight hundred and twenty-six[1]
480,050[2]
480 050[2]
four hundred and eighty thousand and fifty[1]

At least some six-digit numbers you can also express as fractions of a million.

---

1 Standard formal: *use this, and you can't go wrong in formal contexts.*
2 Standard formal with consistent options: *choose one and stick to it.*
3 Standard formal with flexible options: *choose any one, any time.*
4 Old-fashioned: *still all right, but fading from modern usage.*
5 Standard informal: *fine in conversation or in personal letters.*
6 Nonstandard: *you jez'gotta be kidding.*

Numbers

a quarter of a million[2]             (250,000)
point two five of a million[2]
three quarters of a million[2]           (750,000)
point seven five of a million[2]

(See also "half a million" in point **16** above.)

**18. Seven-digit numbers expressing multiples of a million.**

1,000,000[2]              4,000,000[2]
1 000 000[2]              4 000 000[2]
1 million[2]                4 million[2]
1m[2]                        4m[2]
a million[2]                four million[1]
one million[2]

**19. Seven-digit numbers expressing multiples of a million together with numbers of a lower order of magnitude than a million.**

2,500,000[2]
2 500 000[2]
2.5 million[2]
2½ million[2]
2.5m[2]
2½m[2]
two million, five hundred thousand[2]
two and a half million[2]
two point five million[2]
3,350,428[2]
3 350 428[2]
three million, three hundred and fifty thousand, four hundred and twenty-eight[1]
4,000,090[2]
4 000 090[2]
four million and ninety[1]

# Usage

**20. Numbers consisting of eight or nine digits, expressing teens, tens and hundreds of millions.**

58,000,000[2]
58 000 000[2]
58 million[2]
58m[2]
fifty-eight million[1]
66,500,000[2]
66 500 000[2]
66.5 million[2]
66.5m[2]
66½ million[2]
66½m[2]
sixty-six million, five hundred thousand[2]
sixty-six and a half million[2]
sixty-six point five million[2]
123,420,052[2]
123 420 052[2]
a hundred and twenty-three million, four hundred and twenty thousand and fifty-two[2]
one hundred and twenty-three million, four hundred and twenty thousand and fifty-two[2]

**21. Numbers consisting of ten, eleven or twelve digits, expressing thousands of millions.**

For numbers in these three orders of magnitude there is variable terminology: in most English speaking countries, these numbers are called "billions"; in Britain they are called "milliards". But even in Britain "milliards" is beginning to sound somewhat old-fashioned and is giving way to "billions". As a substitute for both these terms — the more

---

1 Standard formal: *use this, and you can't go wrong in formal contexts.*
2 Standard formal with consistent options: *choose one and stick to it.*
3 Standard formal with flexible options: *choose any one, any time.*
4 Old-fashioned: *still all right, but fading from modern usage.*
5 Standard informal: *fine in conversation or in personal letters.*
6 Nonstandard: *you jez'gotta be kidding.*

# Numbers

common "billions" and the ageing British "milliards" — it is possible to substitute the unambiguous and uniformly acceptable "thousands of millions".

1,000,000,000[2]
1 000 000 000[2]
1,000 million[2]
1000 million[2]
1 000m[2]
1 billion[2]
1b[2]
1 milliard[4]   (UK)
a billion[2]
one billion[2]
a thousand million[2]
one thousand million[2]
a milliard[4]   (UK)
one milliard[4]   (UK)
25,500,000,000[2]
25 500 000 000[2]
25,500 million[2]
25 500 million[2]
25.5 billion[2]
25.5b[2]
25½ billion[2]
25½b[2]
25.5 milliard[4]   (UK)
25½ milliard[4]   (UK)
twenty-five billion, five hundred million[2]
twenty-five and a half billion[2]
twenty-five point five billion[2]
twenty-five and a half thousand million[2]
twenty-five point five thousand million[2]
twenty-five milliard, five hundred million[4]   (UK)
twenty-five and a half milliard[4]   (UK)
twenty-five point five milliard[4]   (UK)

## Usage

300,200,500,001[2]
300 200 500 001[2]

three hundred billion, two hundred million, five hundred thousand and one[1]

three hundred milliard, two hundred million, five hundred thousand and one[4]   (UK)

**22. Numbers consisting of thirteen, fourteen and fifteen digits.**
Numbers in this range are called "trillions" in most English speaking countries; "billions", in the by now old-fashioned English terminology. It is, perhaps, not very practical to handle such large numbers either in digit form or in word form — except in round figures. Nevertheless, you will occasionally come across such numbers as, for example, in the 10 September 1990 issue of *TIME International*, which reported that the US debt had reached $3,214,512,688,472.82. In round figures you would say that the sum was:

$3.2 trillion[2]
three point two trillion dollars[2]
over three million million dollars[2]
over three trillion dollars[2]
over three thousand billion dollars[2]
$3.2 billion[4]   (UK)
three point two billion dollars[4]   (UK)
over three billion dollars[4]   (UK)

**23. Numbers consisting of sixteen digits or more.**
Here we are dealing with "quadrillions", "quintillions", and numbers of higher orders of magnitude. They are useful mainly in fields such as mathematics and science, and workers in these fields have their own ways of dealing with them.

---

1 Standard formal: *use this, and you can't go wrong in formal contexts.*
2 Standard formal with consistent options: *choose one and stick to it.*
3 Standard formal with flexible options: *choose any one, any time.*
4 Old-fashioned: *still all right, but fading from modern usage.*
5 Standard informal: *fine in conversation or in personal letters.*
6 Nonstandard: *you jez'gotta be kidding.*

# Numbers

## C. How to write ordinal numbers

Ordinal numbers express certain kinds of relationships among items — most commonly, but not exclusively, the order of the numbered item or items in a series. Ordinal numbers come in three grammatical forms.

**a.** As nouns.

It was a **first** for them.[1]
This shop sells only **seconds**.[1]

**b.** As adjectives.

I was **first** in line.[1]
This is the **second** time you have done this.[1]

**c.** As adverbs.

**First**, close the door; **second**, lock it.[1]

There are four things to note about the writing of ordinal numbers.

**i.** Ordinal numbers have characteristic endings —

as digits — "**1st**", "**2nd**", "**3rd**", "**4th**" and so on;
as words — "**first**", "**second**", "**third**", "**fourth**" and so on.

**ii.** In all respects other than **i.** above, the guidelines on the use of commas, hyphens, spaces and the word "and" in cardinal numbers apply also to ordinal numbers. This is so both for ordinal numbers written as digits and for ordinal numbers written as words.

**iii.** In many cases, when an ordinal number is used as an adjective you use the word "the" in front of the ordinal number.

This is **the hundredth** time I've told you this.[1]
He is **the 345th** customer today.[1]

**iv.** In other cases, you don't use "the". In this section, for the sake of simplicity, we omit the word "the".

This is her **tenth** birthday.[1]
It's a **twentieth** anniversary present.[1]

The above rules cover most cases. If you want to check how to handle a specific ordinal number from one to thirteen or more digits, read on.

**Usage**

**24. One digit numbers expressing units.**

1st[1]                5th[1]                9th[1]
first[1]              fifth[1]              ninth[1]

**25. Two-digit numbers expressing ten, teens and multiples of ten.**

10th[1]               18th[1]               60th[1]
tenth[1]              eighteenth[1]         sixtieth[1]

**26. Two-digit numbers expressing tens and units.**

21st[1]               43rd[1]               75th[1]
twenty-first[1]       forty-third[1]        seventy-fifth[1]

**27. Three-digit numbers expressing multiples of a hundred.**

100th[1]                          900th[1]
hundredth[2]                      nine hundredth[1]
one hundredth[2]

**28. Three-digit numbers expressing multiples of a hundred together with numbers of a lower order of magnitude.**

103rd[1]
hundred and third[1]
352nd[1]
three hundred and fifty-second[1]
870th[1]
eight hundred and seventieth[1]

---

1 Standard formal: *use this, and you can't go wrong in formal contexts.*
2 Standard formal with consistent options: *choose one and stick to it.*
3 Standard formal with flexible options: *choose any one, any time.*
4 Old-fashioned: *still all right, but fading from modern usage.*
5 Standard informal: *fine in conversation or in personal letters.*
6 Nonstandard: *you jez'gotta be kidding.*

# Numbers

**29. Four digit numbers expressing multiples of a thousand.**

7000th[2]
7,000th[2]
7 000th[2]
seven thousandth[1]

**30. Four-digit numbers expressing multiples of a thousand together with multiples of a hundred.**

4300th[2]
4,300th[2]
4 300th[2]
forty-three hundredth[2]
four thousand, three hundredth[2]

**31. Four-digit numbers expressing multiples of a thousand together with numbers of a lower order of magnitude other than, or in addition to, multiples of a hundred.**

2001st[2]
2,001st[2]
2 001st[2]
two thousand and first[1]
4844th[2]
4,844th[2]
4 844th[2]
four thousand, eight hundred and forty-fourth[1]
6500th[2]
6,500th[2]
6 500th[2]
sixty-five hundredth[2]
six thousand, five hundredth[2]

## Usage

**32. Five-digit numbers.**

96,500th[2]
96 500th[2]
ninety-six thousand, five hundredth[1]
77,835th[2]
77 835th[2]
seventy-seven thousand, eight hundred and thirty-fifth[1]

**33. Six-digit numbers expressing multiples of a hundred thousand.**

100,000th[2]
100 000th[2]
hundred thousandth[2]
one hundred thousandth[2]
500,000th[2]
500 000th[2]
0.5 millionth[2]
0.5mth[2]
½ millionth[2]
½ mth[2]
five hundred thousandth[2]
nought point five millionth[2]
zero point five millionth[2]
half millionth[2]

**34. Six-digit numbers expressing multiples of a hundred thousand together with numbers of a lower order of magnitude.**

300,900th[2]
300 900th[2]
three hundred thousand, nine hundredth[1]

---

1 Standard formal: *use this, and you can't go wrong in formal contexts.*
2 Standard formal with consistent options: *choose one and stick to it.*
3 Standard formal with flexible options: *choose any one, any time.*
4 Old-fashioned: *still all right, but fading from modern usage.*
5 Standard informal: *fine in conversation or in personal letters.*
6 Nonstandard: *you jez'gotta be kidding.*

480,050th[2]
480 050th[2]
four hundred and eighty thousand and fiftieth[1]
250,000th[2]
250 000th[2]
0.25 millionth[2]
0.25mth[2]
¼ millionth[2]
¼ mth[2]
two hundred and fifty thousandth[2]
quarter millionth[2]
nought point two five millionth[2]
zero point two five millionth[2]

**35. Seven-digit numbers expressing multiples of a million.**

3,000,000th[2]
3 000 000th[2]
3 millionth[2]
3mth[2]
three millionth[1]

**36. Seven-digit numbers expressing multiples of a million together with numbers of a lower order of magnitude than a million.**

3,500,000th[2]
3 500 000th[2]
3.5 millionth[2]
3.5mth[2]
3½ mth[2]
3½ millionth[2]
three million, five hundred thousandth[2]
three and a half millionth[2]
three point five millionth[2]
2,000,001st[2]
2 000 001st[2]
two million and first[1]

## Usage

**37. Numbers consisting of eight or nine digits expressing teens, tens and hundreds of millions.**

11,000,000th[2]
11 000 000th[2]
11 millionth[2]
11mth[2]
eleven millionth[1]
50,000,000th[2]
50 000 000th[2]
50 millionth[2]
50mth[2]
fifty millionth[1]
222,000,000th[2]
222 000 000th[2]
222 millionth[2]
222mth[2]
two hundred and twenty-two millionth[1]

**38. Numbers consisting of ten to twelve digits expressing thousands of millions, with or without lower order numbers.**

4,000,000,000th[2]
4 000 000 000th[2]
4,000 millionth[2]
4000 millionth[2]
4 000 millionth[2]
4 billionth[2]
4bth[2]
4 milliardth[4]   (UK)
four billionth[2]

---

1 Standard formal: *use this, and you can't go wrong in formal contexts.*
2 Standard formal with consistent options: *choose one and stick to it.*
3 Standard formal with flexible options: *choose any one, any time.*
4 Old-fashioned: *still all right, but fading from modern usage.*
5 Standard informal: *fine in conversation or in personal letters.*
6 Nonstandard: *you jez'gotta be kidding.*

four thousand millionth[2]
four milliardth[4]  (UK)
300,000,000,001st[2]
300 000 000 001st[2]
three hundred billion and first[1]
three hundred milliard and first[4]  (UK)

**39. Numbers consisting of thirteen or more digits.**
There is very little call for ordinal numbers of this order of magnitude. Still, if you like, you can play around with expressions such as the following.

In 1990, the US debt exceeded its **$3 trillionth**.[2]
In 1990, the US debt exceeded its **three trillionth dollar**.[2]
In 1990, the US debt exceeded its **three billionth dollar**.[4]  (UK)

## D. How to write fractions

We examine two kinds of fractions—

**a.** decimal fractions, the denominator of which is a power of ten, and which you write as a number or numbers to the right of a decimal point; and

**b.** common fractions (also called "vulgar fractions"), which you write with a numerator above a horizontal bar (or to the left of a diagonal bar) and a denominator below a horizontal bar (or to the right of a diagonal bar). In this section we will be using only the diagonal bar — but the horizontal bar is just as legitimate.

**40. Decimal numbers.**
**a.** In digits.

 **i.** If the number consists of a decimal number alone, write a "0" to the left of the decimal point, and the decimal number or numbers to the right of the decimal point.

0.5[1]
0.48356[1]

 **ii.** If the number consists of a whole number together with a decimal number, write the whole number to the left of the decimal point, and the decimal number to the right of the decimal point.

## Usage

3.5[1]
18,300.4835[2]
18 300.4835[2]

By convention, you don't separate the digits of a long decimal number with commas or spaces.

**b.** In words.

**i.** If the number consists of a decimal number alone, write the word "zero" (or a synonym of "zero") before the word "point", and express the decimal number in terms of cardinal units.

zero point five[2] (0.5)
nought point five[2]
nil point five[2]
oh point five[5]

zero point four eight three five[2] (0.4835)
nought point four eight three five[2]
nil point four eight three five[2]
oh point four eight three five[5]

For some common expressions you can omit the word "zero" or its synonyms.

a point two-two calibre rifle[1] (.22)
a blood alcohol level of point one[1] (.1)

**ii.** If the number consists of a whole number together with a decimal number, write the whole number before the word "point", and the decimal number (expressed in terms of cardinal units) after the word "point".

three point five[1] (3.5)
eighteen thousand, three hundred, point four eight three five[1]
(18,300.4835)

---

1 Standard formal: *use this, and you can't go wrong in formal contexts.*
2 Standard formal with consistent options: *choose one and stick to it.*
3 Standard formal with flexible options: *choose any one, any time.*
4 Old-fashioned: *still all right, but fading from modern usage.*
5 Standard informal: *fine in conversation or in personal letters.*
6 Nonstandard: *you jez'gotta be kidding.*

# Numbers

**41. Common or vulgar fractions.**
**a.** When you write common fractions as digits, separate the numerator from the denominator either with a horizontal or with a diagonal bar. (In this section, we have chosen to use the diagonal bar throughout.) In all other respects, the guidelines that we set down for cardinal numbers in section **B** above apply just as well to the digits of these fractions.

2/3[1]
7/1000[2]
7/1,000[2]
7/1 000[2]

**b.** When you write common fractions in words, there is a distinction between how you express the numerator and the denominator. You express the numerator in terms of cardinal numbers (for which see section **B** above). You express the denominator in either of two ways.

**i.** One way is to express the denominator in the same terms as the cardinal numbers. When you do this, you precede the number with the word "over".

| | |
|---|---|
| one over two[1] | (1/2) |
| two over three[1] | (2/3) |
| seventeen over two hundred and seventy-eight[1] | (17/278) |
| thirteen over a million and one[1] | (13/1,000,001) |

**ii.** The other way is more complex. It involves using terms similar to those used in writing ordinal numbers as words — for example, "a tenth" and "one twenty-first" — but with the following distinctions.

If the denominator is "2", "3" or "4", express the common fractions as follows.

| | |
|---|---|
| a half[2] | (1/2) |
| one half[2] | |
| a third[2] | (1/3) |
| one third[2] | |
| two thirds[1] | (2/3) |

91

**Usage**

| | |
|---|---|
| a quarter[2] | (1/4) |
| one quarter[2] | |
| a fourth[2] | |
| one fourth[2] | |
| three quarters[2] | (3/4) |
| three fourths[2] | |

Express the denominator of all other fractions that have "1" as their numerator in the same way as ordinal numbers (see section C above) — and use the word "a" or "one" to express the numerator.

| | |
|---|---|
| an eighth[2] | (1/8) |
| one eighth[2] | |
| a hundredth[2] | (1/100) |
| one hundredth[2] | |
| a thousand, two hundred and forty-second[2] | (1/1242) |
| one thousand, two hundred and forty-second[2] | |

For common fractions that have a numerator greater than "1", express the numerator in the same way as a cardinal number, and the denominator in the same way as an ordinal number — but with the addition of a plural "s".

| | |
|---|---|
| three fifths[1] | (3/5) |
| two seventeenths[1] | (2/17) |
| two hundred and thirteen thousandths[1] | (213/1000) |
| twenty-seven millionths[1] | (27/1,000,000) |

If you write a fraction in words and you use it as an attributive adjective — that is, before the noun it modifies — hyphenate the fraction.

I have a **two-thirds share** in this business.[1]
This is a **three-quarters full barrel**.[1]

---

1 Standard formal: *use this, and you can't go wrong in formal contexts.*
2 Standard formal with consistent options: *choose one and stick to it.*
3 Standard formal with flexible options: *choose any one, any time.*
4 Old-fashioned: *still all right, but fading from modern usage.*
5 Standard informal: *fine in conversation or in personal letters.*
6 Nonstandard: *you jez'gotta be kidding.*

Used predicatively — after the noun it modifies — the hyphen is optional.

My share in this business is **two-thirds**.[1]
My share in this business is **two thirds**.[2]

## E. How to write roman numerals

The Romans, for all their vaunted practicality, didn't manage to think up a numbers system that changed the values of numbers by powers of ten, with a shift in the position of the numbers. That practical system we inherited from the Arabs. The Romans — and their medieval Latinist successors — had to mess around with letters of the alphabet standing in for numbers.

Today people still use roman numerals, but only in limited contexts. We list these contexts in number **44** below. First, though, we show you how to write the roman numerals.

**42. Single-digit roman numerals.**
**a.** Numerals, expressed by roman letters, have the same values whether you write them in the upper or in the lower case.

| | | | | | | |
|---|---|---|---|---|---|---|
| $I^2$ | $i^2$ | = 1 | $C^2$ | $c^2$ | = | 100 |
| $V^2$ | $v^2$ | = 5 | $D^2$ | $d^2$ | = | 500 |
| $X^2$ | $x^2$ | = 10 | $M^2$ | $m^2$ | = | 1000 |
| $L^2$ | $l^2$ | = 50 | | | | |

**b.** A bar above a roman numeral multiplies its value by 1000.

$\overline{I}^2$     $\overline{i}^2$     = 1000
$\overline{X}^2$     $\overline{x}^2$     = 10,000
$\overline{M}^2$     $\overline{m}^2$     = 1 million

**43. Multi-digit roman numerals.**
The general principle governing the writing of such numbers is the principle of greatest economy: you write any given multi-digit number with the fewest possible numerals.

## Usage

**a.** Repeat the roman numerals two or three times to obtain a multiple value.

$III^2$  $iii^2$ = 3  $CCC^2$  $ccc^2$ = 300
$XX^2$  $xx^2$ = 20  $MM^2$  $mm^2$ = 2000

**b.** To avoid a greater than threefold repetition, you resort to the following techniques.

**i.** Subtract the numbers of lesser value from the numbers of higher value to their right.

$IX^2$  ix = 9
$XIX^2$  $IXX^2$  $xix^2$  $ixx^2$ = 19
$VL^2$  $vl^2$ = 45
$XC^2$  $xc^2$ = 90

**ii.** Add the numbers of lesser value to the numbers of higher value to their left.

$XII^2$  $xii^2$ = 12
$LVI^2$  $lvi^2$ = 56
$DCLVIII^2$  $dclviii^2$ = 658

**iii.** You can combine methods **i.** and **ii.** above. Write the numeral of greatest value in the middle; subtract from it the value of any numeral(s) to its left; add to it the value of any numeral(s) to its right.

$CMX^2$  $cmx^2$ = 910
$XLIV^2$  $XLIV^2$ = 44
$MCMXCIII^2$  $mcmxciii^2$ = 1993

---

1 Standard formal: *use this, and you can't go wrong in formal contexts.*
2 Standard formal with consistent options: *choose one and stick to it.*
3 Standard formal with flexible options: *choose any one, any time.*
4 Old-fashioned: *still all right, but fading from modern usage.*
5 Standard informal: *fine in conversation or in personal letters.*
6 Nonstandard: *you jez'gotta be kidding.*

# Numbers

**44. The uses of roman numerals.**

**a.** Capital roman numerals after the names of people.

Queen Elizabeth II[1]
Pope John XXIII[1]

**b.** Capital roman numerals or Arabic numerals for historical events.

World War II[4]
World War 2[1]

**c.** Capital roman numerals as an alternative to other forms of numbers in chapter headings.

Chapter VII[4]
Chapter 7[2]
Chapter seven[2]
Chapter Seven[2]

**d.** Lower case roman numerals or Arabic numerals for the pagination of introductory pages of a book or a report.

| i | 1 |
| ii | 2 |
| iii[2] | 3[2] |

**e.** Roman numerals as an alternative to other methods of itemisation. (We use lower case roman numerals in this book for some items, but only after we run out of Arabic numerals and letters.)

The Big Five after WW2 were:

I. the United States
II. Great Britain
III. the Soviet Union
IV. China
V. France[4]

**Usage**

The Big Five after WW2 were:

i. the United States
ii. Great Britain
iii. the Soviet Union
iv. China
v. France²

The Big Five after WW2 were:

1. the United States
2. Great Britain
3. the Soviet Union
4. China
5. France²

The Big Five after WW2 were:

a. the United States
b. Great Britain
c. the Soviet Union
d. China
e. France²

## F. How to write dates, clock times, money sums and sporting scores

In this section we deal with how to write these numbers in digits, words, and a mix of digits and words. We also give guidelines on when you might use the various methods of writing such numbers.

### 45. Writing dates in digits.

For all everyday purposes write dates either in digits alone, or in a mixture of digits and words — with the names of the months written as words. For legal documents, you may need to spell out the whole date in words.

---

1 Standard formal: *use this, and you can't go wrong in formal contexts.*
2 Standard formal with consistent options: *choose one and stick to it.*
3 Standard formal with flexible options: *choose any one, any time.*
4 Old-fashioned: *still all right, but fading from modern usage.*
5 Standard informal: *fine in conversation or in personal letters.*
6 Nonstandard: *you jez'gotta be kidding.*

# Numbers

There are rival systems for the sequence of elements in a date. (For all the examples below, we use Christmas Day 1994.)

**a.** The British (UK) and allied system — which is common also in Australia — is to write a date in the sequence of day, month, year. The US and allied system is to write a date in the sequence of month, day, year. The system recommended by the International Organisation for Standards (IOS) is the sequence of year, month, day.

| | |
|---|---|
| 25.12.1994[2] | (UK) |
| 12.25.1994[2] | (US) |
| 1994.12.25[2] | (IOS) |

**b.** An alternative method of writing dates in digits (in the UK and the US systems) is to give only the last two digits of the year.

| | |
|---|---|
| 25.12.94[2] | (UK) |
| 12.25.94[2] | (US) |

**c.** Instead of the full stops between the dates you may use colons, slashes or hyphens; but these are old-fashioned.

| | |
|---|---|
| 25:12:94[4] | (UK) |
| 25/12/94[4] | (UK) |
| 25-12-94[4] | (UK) |

**d.** Dates with the months written as words.

| | |
|---|---|
| 25 December 1994[2] | (UK) |
| 25 Dec 1994[2] | (UK) |
| December 25, 1994[2] | (US) |
| Dec 25, 1994[2] | (US) |

Writing the day with an ordinal ending is old-fashioned.

| | |
|---|---|
| 25th December 1994[4] | (UK) |
| December 25th, 1994[4] | (US) |

## Usage

**e.** The whole date expressed in words.

Christmas Day, nineteen ninety-four[2]
twenty-fifth of December, nineteen ninety-four[2]    (UK)
the twenty-fifth of December, nineteen ninety-four[2]    (UK)
twenty-five December, nineteen ninety-four[2]    (UK)
December twenty-fifth, nineteen ninety-four[2]    (US)
December twenty-five, nineteen ninety-four[2]    (US)

### 46. Clock time.

For all everyday purposes you write clock time in digits alone. You may, for the sake of precision or in a legal document, want to write the clock time in a mix of digits and words or in words alone.

**a.** Whole hours.

   **i.** On a twelve-hour basis.

8am[2]
8.00am[2]
8 o'clock[2]
eight o'clock[2]

   **ii.** On a twenty-four-hour basis.

0800 hours[2]
eight hundred hours[2]
zero eight hundred hours[2]
oh eight hundred hours[5]

**b.** Hours and fractions of hours.

   **i.** On a twelve-hour basis.

8.15am[2]
eight fifteen a m[2]
eight fifteen in the morning[2]
a quarter past eight in the morning[2]

---

1 Standard formal: *use this, and you can't go wrong in formal contexts.*
2 Standard formal with consistent options: *choose one and stick to it.*
3 Standard formal with flexible options: *choose any one, any time.*
4 Old-fashioned: *still all right, but fading from modern usage.*
5 Standard informal: *fine in conversation or in personal letters.*
6 Nonstandard: *you jez'gotta be kidding.*

**ii.** On a twenty-four-hour basis.

0815 hours[2]
eight hundred and fifteen hours[2]
zero eight fifteen hundred hours[2]
oh eight fifteen hundred hours[5]

**c.** Hours and minutes.

**i.** On a twelve-hour basis.

8.17am[2]
eight seventeen a m[2]
eight seventeen in the morning[2]
seventeen past eight in the morning[2]

**ii.** On a twenty-four-hour basis.

0817 hours[2]
eight hundred and seventeen hours[2]
zero eight hundred and seventeen hours[2]
oh eight hundred and seventeen hours[5]

**47. Money sums in digits, in words, and in digits and words.**
For all everyday purposes you write money sums in digits. For the sake of precision, though, or when you are writing money sums on cheques or in contracts, you may want to write the sums in words as well as in digits.

**a. i.** In digits — for whole dollars

$250.00[2]
$250[2]

**ii.** In words for whole dollars.

two hundred and fifty dollars[1]

**b. i.** In digits — for dollars and cents.

$250.05[1]

**Usage**

    **ii.** In words and digits for dollars and cents.

        two hundred and fifty dollars, 05c[2]
        two hundred and fifty dollars and 05c[2]

**48. Sporting scores.**
Use words or digits.

        We beat them **three-two**.[2]
        We beat them **3-2**.[2]

---

1 Standard formal: *use this, and you can't go wrong in formal contexts.*
2 Standard formal with consistent options: *choose one and stick to it.*
3 Standard formal with flexible options: *choose any one, any time.*
4 Old-fashioned: *still all right, but fading from modern usage.*
5 Standard informal: *fine in conversation or in personal letters.*
6 Nonstandard: *you jez'gotta be kidding.*

100

# CHAPTER 8
# The relative pronouns "who", "whom", "which", "that"

## Overview
To begin with, here are two example sentences to show what relative pronouns are and how they work.

> My parents, **who** have just come back from overseas, phoned me last night.[1]

> Please return the books **that** you borrowed from me a month ago.[1]

The words "who" and "that" are called relative pronouns because they relate to other words. In the above two examples, they relate to the nouns "parents" and "books" respectively. So far so simple. But the use of these simple relative pronouns can involve quite considerable complexities. To understand these complexities we first have to consider some of the concepts and to define some of the terms that accompany their use. We look at these under six subheadings.

    **a.** Personal pronouns and relative pronouns.
    **b.** Antecedents.
    **c.** Antecedent clauses and relative clauses.
    **d.** Subjects and objects.
    **e.** Defining, nondefining and situational relative clauses.
    **f.** The punctuation of relative clauses.

**a.** Personal pronouns and relative pronouns.
In a loose sense, all pronouns serve as replacements or substitutes for nouns. Let us consider two classes of pronouns that fulfil this function in different ways.

    **i.** One is the class of personal pronouns that includes the pronouns "I", "me", "you", "he", "him", "she", "her" and some others.

## Usage

I have a cousin. **She** is visiting me today.[1]
(The personal pronoun "she", in the second of the above two sentences, substitutes for "cousin".)

**ii.** Another is the class of relative pronouns that includes the pronouns "who", "whom", "which", "that" and some others.

I have a cousin, **who** is visiting me today.[1]
(The relative pronoun "who", in the second part of the above sentence, substitutes for "cousin".)

**b.** Antecedents.
Antecedents are the words or groups of words that the relative pronouns relate to.

**They have all gone**, which makes me rather sad.[1]
("They have all gone" is the antecedent of "which".)

My eldest **child**, whom you've never met, is coming here tonight.[1]
("Child" is the antecedent of "whom".)

Here are the **papers** that you wanted.[1]
("Papers" is the antecedent of "that".)

The above examples show that antecedents can relate to people, things or situations.

**c.** Antecedent clauses and relative clauses.
The antecedent clauses are those that contain the antecedents; the relative clauses, those that contain the relative pronouns. The example sentences we have considered so far split up into these two kinds of clauses as follows.

---

1 Standard formal: *use this, and you can't go wrong in formal contexts.*
2 Standard formal with consistent options: *choose one and stick to it.*
3 Standard formal with flexible options: *choose any one, any time.*
4 Old-fashioned: *still all right, but fading from modern usage.*
5 Standard informal: *fine in conversation or in personal letters.*
6 Nonstandard: *you jez'gotta be kidding.*

## "Who", "whom", "which", "that"

| ANTECEDENT CLAUSES | RELATIVE CLAUSES |
|---|---|
| My **parents** phoned me last night | **who** have just come back from overseas |
| Please return the **books** | **that** you borrowed from me a month ago |
| I have a **cousin** | **who** is visiting me today |
| **They have all gone** | **which** makes me rather sad |
| My eldest **child** is coming tonight | **whom** you've never met |
| Here are the **papers** | **that** you wanted |

The relative clause should come as close as possible to its antecedent, even if this means inserting the relative clause in the middle of the antecedent clause.

> My friend, **whom I have been expecting**, has arrived.[1]
> My friend has arrived, **whom I have been expecting**.[5]

**d.** Subjects and objects.
Take two simple English sentences.

> **They** watched **us**.[1]
>
> **The bug-eyed monsters from outer space** have been watching **everything going on down here**.[1]

Central to each sentence is the verb: "watched" in the first sentence; "have been watching" in the second sentence. The word in front of the verb in the first sentence, and all the words in front of the verb in the second sentence, tell us who the agent or doer of each verb is. Such an agent — whether it consists of one word or more — is the grammatical subject of the verb.

"Us" in the first sentence, and "everything going on down here" in the second sentence, tell us the target of the verb — that is, whom the action of the verb is directed at. Such a target — whether it consists of one word or more — is the grammatical object of the verb.

Prepositions also have objects. Loosely speaking, prepositions are words that express some kind of relationship between people or between things. "In", "on", "with", "by", "for" and "among" are some sample prepositions. The following sentence has one subject and two objects.

## Usage

**They** took **a book** from **us**.[1]

**i.** "They" is the subject of the verb "took";
**ii.** "a book" is the object of the verb "took";
**iii.** "us" is the object of the preposition "from".

The matter of subjects and objects is important for our discussion, because the functions of the relative pronouns (as subjects or as objects) may determine the choice of relative pronouns.

I'd like you to meet my parents, **who** have just arrived from overseas.[1]
("Who" is the subject of the verb "have arrived".)

I'd like you to meet my parents, **whom** you know only from photographs.[1]
("Whom" is the object of the verb "know".)

I'd like you to meet my parents, about **whom** we've often spoken.[1]
("Whom" is the object of the preposition "about".)

There is a simple test to establish which function — subject or object — a relative pronoun performs in a relative clause. The test is to transform the relative clause into an independent sentence, and to substitute a personal pronoun for the relative pronoun.

I'd like you to meet my parents, **who** have just arrived from overseas.[3]
I'd like you to meet my parents. **They** have just arrived from overseas.[3]
("They", like "who", is the subject of the verb "have arrived".)

I'd like you to meet my parents, **whom** you know only from photo- graphs.[3]
I'd like you to meet my parents. You know **them** only from photo- graphs.[3]
("Them", like "whom", is the object of the verb "know".)

---

1 Standard formal: *use this, and you can't go wrong in formal contexts.*
2 Standard formal with consistent options: *choose one and stick to it.*
3 Standard formal with flexible options: *choose any one, any time.*
4 Old-fashioned: *still all right, but fading from modern usage.*
5 Standard informal: *fine in conversation or in personal letters.*
6 Nonstandard: *you jez'gotta be kidding.*

# "Who", "whom", "which", "that"

I'd like you to meet my parents, about **whom** we've often spoken.[3]
I'd like you to meet my parents. We've often spoken about **them**.[3]
("Them", like "whom", is the object of the preposition "about".)

In the above examples, the subject "who" equates with the subject "they"; and the object "whom" with the object "them". Of course, this equating of pronouns works not only with these sample pronouns, but with a range of pronouns.

**i.** "Who" equates with the subject pronouns "I", "you", "he", "she", "we", "they".

**ii.** "Whom" equates with the object pronouns "me", "you", "him", "her", "us", "them".

**e.** Defining, nondefining and situational relative clauses.
There are three kinds of relative clauses.

**i.** A situational relative clause relates to the situation denoted by the whole of the antecedent clause.

They worked hard, **which was just what I expected**.[1]

They arrived early, **which somewhat embarrassed me**.[1]

In each of the above two examples, the relative clause relates to the situation denoted by the whole of the antecedent clause: "They worked hard" and "They arrived early" respectively.

**ii.** A defining relative clause serves to define — or identify — a noun in the antecedent clause.

A roof **that leaks** isn't much good.[1]
("That leaks" defines what kind of "roof" the sentence is about.)

Parents **who help their children** are good parents.[1]
("Who help their children" defines the kind of "parents" the sentence is about.)

**iii.** A nondefining relative clause serves to add some information about an already defined (or identified) noun in the antecedent clause.

The roof of my house, **which never leaks**, is good.[1]
("Which never leaks" adds some information about the already identified "roof" — namely, the roof of my house.)

## Usage

My parents, **who live just around the corner**, are good parents.[1]
("Who live just around the corner" adds some information about the already identified "parents" — namely, my parents.)

Here is a simple procedure to help you distinguish between defining and nondefining relative clauses. Omit the relative clause from the sentence, and see whether the sentence makes sense without it. Take, for example, the four sentences we've just given above, and omit the relative clause in each one.

A roof . . . isn't much good.[6]
Parents . . . are good parents.[6]
The roof of my house . . . is good.[1]
My parents . . . are good parents.[1]

The first two sentences seem incomplete: we need the defining relative clauses to tell us what kind of (or which particular) roof, and what kind of (or which particular) parents we're talking about. The last two sentences are all right as they stand, even without the relative clauses. So the distinction between the two types of relative clauses is that a defining relative clause is necessary to the meaning of the sentence in which it occurs; a nondefining relative clause is unnecessary in this sense.

**f.** The punctuation of relative clauses.
The guidelines for punctuating relative clauses are simple and invariable.

**i.** Separate situational relative clauses from their antecedent clauses with commas.

They are glad, **which made me glad too**.[1]
They recovered quickly, **which allowed them to return to work**.[1]

**ii.** Don't separate defining relative clauses from their antecedent clauses with commas.

I need a car **that is reliable**.[1]
Any parents **who care about their children** will help them.[1]

---

1 Standard formal: *use this, and you can't go wrong in formal contexts.*
2 Standard formal with consistent options: *choose one and stick to it.*
3 Standard formal with flexible options: *choose any one, any time.*
4 Old-fashioned: *still all right, but fading from modern usage.*
5 Standard informal: *fine in conversation or in personal letters.*
6 Nonstandard: *you jez'gotta be kidding.*

# "Who", "whom", "which", "that"

**iii.** Separate nondefining relative clauses from their antecedent clauses with commas.

I have had my present car, **which is pretty reliable**, for four years.[1]
My parents, **who care about their children**, will help me.[1]

If you look back at some of the earlier example sentences in this overview, you will see more instances of these guidelines on punctuation.

Our chapter on relative pronouns has two sections.

## A. Relative pronouns that relate to antecedent things or situations

Things (to borrow a few examples from the poem by Lewis Carroll) include "shoes" and "ships" and "sealing wax" and "cabbages". Situations — to quote from two of our examples — are denoted by clauses such as "They are glad" and "They recovered quickly".

## B. Relative pronouns that relate to antecedent persons

Antecedents coming under this heading include "Jack" and "Jill", "child" and "adult", "her" and "him".


## A. Relative pronouns that relate to antecedent things or situations

The two relative pronouns we use are "which" and "that". We begin the section with a discussion of the different uses of these relative pronouns and of the relative clauses associated with them.

**a.** Relative pronouns that relate to antecedent situations.

There is no problem here: you are bound to use "which", and you are bound to separate the antecedent clause from the relative clause with a comma.

They have been working hard, **which** has made them tired.[1]

**b.** Relative pronouns that relate to antecedent things.

Here you have a choice between "which" and "that", and you also have a choice of punctuation. The choice of relative pronoun is a difficult choice to make, because usage has changed in the past few decades. The choice of punctuation is clearer.

## Usage

Until about the middle of the twentieth century, the distinction between "that" and "which", and the distinction in punctuation, were pretty rigid.

**i.** The relative pronoun "that" was associated with defining relative clauses, and these clauses were not separated from their antecedent clauses with commas.

I am looking for a play **that** will interest me.[1]

**ii.** The relative pronoun "which" was associated with defining relative clauses if, and only if, it was preceded by a preposition — but even then you could transform the "which" relative pronoun into a "that" relative pronoun by shifting the preposition to the end of the sentence. In either case, you didn't separate the relative clauses from the antecedent clauses with commas.

I am looking for a play **in which** I can take an interest.[3]
I am looking for a play **that** I can take an interest **in**.[3]

**iii.** The relative pronoun "which" was associated with nondefining relative clauses, and these clauses were separated from their antecedent clauses with commas.

You could try reading *Hamlet*, **in which** lots of people are interested.[3]
You could try reading *Hamlet*, **which** lots of people are interested **in**.[3]

(Incidentally, if you have a problem accepting two of the example sentences above because they end with the preposition "in", please read chapter 1, section C, dealing with this matter.)

Nowadays, the punctuation distinction between defining and nondefining relative clauses still holds. But fewer people are bothering to discriminate between "that" for defining relative clauses, and "which" for nondefining relative clauses. There is a trend towards using "which" in both cases.

---

1 Standard formal: *use this, and you can't go wrong in formal contexts.*
2 Standard formal with consistent options: *choose one and stick to it.*
3 Standard formal with flexible options: *choose any one, any time.*
4 Old-fashioned: *still all right, but fading from modern usage.*
5 Standard informal: *fine in conversation or in personal letters.*
6 Nonstandard: *you jez'gotta be kidding.*

Nevertheless, the distinction is still there, and you will find it used in the pages of quality books and publications. We have chosen, therefore, to label the use of "that" at the head of a defining relative clause as the standard formal usage, and "which" in the same context as the standard informal usage — unless "which" follows a preposition, in which case it becomes standard formal again.

DEFINING

Give me a bag **that** is not made of plastic.[1]
Give me a bag **which** is not made of plastic.[5]
Give me a bag **that** I can fit these things **in**.[3]
Give me a bag **in which** I can fit these things.[3]

NONDEFINING

Here is my bag, **in which** you can fit these things.[3]
Here is my bag, **which** you can fit these things **in**.[3]

There is another distinction between defining and nondefining relative clauses.

**i.** You may choose to omit the defining relative pronoun in two circumstances.

When the relative pronoun is the object of a verb —

DEFINING

I am looking for a car **that** I can **afford**.[3]
I am looking for a car I can **afford**.[3]

When the relative pronoun is the object of a preposition —

DEFINING

I am looking for a car **that** I will be happy **with**.[3]
I am looking for a car I will be happy **with**.[3]

**ii.** In the case of nondefining relative clauses, the choice of omitting the relative pronoun does not exist.

## Usage

When the relative pronoun is the object of a verb —

NONDEFINING

Buy my car, **which** I am sure you can afford.[1]
(Buy my car, I am sure you can afford.[6])

When the relative pronoun is the object of a preposition —

NONDEFINING

Buy my car, **with which** I am sure you will be happy.[3]
Buy my car, **which** I am sure you will be happy **with**.[3]
(Buy my car, I am sure you will be happy **with**.[6])

So much for the preliminary discussion. Now for a look at all the options. As you read the example sentences, you will see that we have not used commas to separate defining relative clauses from their antecedent clauses. We have used commas to separate nondefining and situational clauses from their antecedent clauses.

**1. The relative pronoun relates to a situation.**
The whole of the antecedent clause — rather than one specific word in it — acts as the antecedent of the relative pronoun. "Which" is the only suitable relative pronoun.

They introduced me to some friends, **which** ended my loneliness.[1]
When they got home, **which** was after nine, they had a rest.[1]
They helped me to study, **for which** I am very grateful.[3]
They helped me to study, **which** I am very grateful **for**.[3]

**2. The relative pronoun relates to a thing, and it is the subject of a verb.**
a. If the relative clause is defining, "that" and "which" are the options.

---

1 Standard formal: *use this, and you can't go wrong in formal contexts.*
2 Standard formal with consistent options: *choose one and stick to it.*
3 Standard formal with flexible options: *choose any one, any time.*
4 Old-fashioned: *still all right, but fading from modern usage.*
5 Standard informal: *fine in conversation or in personal letters.*
6 Nonstandard: *you jez'gotta be kidding.*

# "Who", "whom", "which", "that"

I am looking for a computer **that** is not too expensive.[1]
I am looking for a computer **which** is not too expensive.[5]
I want to live in a house **that** faces north.[1]
I want to live in a house **which** faces north.[5]

**b.** If the relative pronoun is nondefining, use "which".

My computer, **which** is an older model, was not too expensive.[1]
I met them at their house, **which** faces north.[1]

**3. The relative pronoun relates to a thing, and it is the object of a verb.**
**a.** If the relative clause is defining, the options are "that", "which" and no relative pronoun at all.

This is the computer **that** I bought.[3]
This is the computer I bought.[3]
This is the computer **which** I bought.[5]
I received the letter **that** she sent.[3]
I received the letter she sent.[3]
I received the letter **which** she sent.[5]

**b.** If the relative clause is nondefining, use "which".

My computer, **which** I bought recently, is a laptop.[1]
Last Monday I sent you a letter, **which** you should have received by now.[1]

Note that, while it's all right to omit the relative pronoun from the defining relative clauses, this doesn't work for the nondefining relative clauses. This indicates that there is a real distinction between defining and nondefining relative clauses.

**4. The relative pronoun relates to a thing, and it is the object of a preposition.**
**a.** If the relative clause is defining, the options are "that", "which" or no relative pronoun at all. There are also options in the placement of the preposition.

## Usage

These are the essays **that** I told you **about**.[3]
These are the essays **about which** I told you.[3]
These are the essays I told you **about**.[3]
These are the essays **which** I told you **about**.[5]

**b.** If the clause is nondefining, use "which".

I have just reread Orwell's essays, **for which** I have a great liking.[3]
I have just reread Orwell's essays, **which** I have a great liking **for**.[3]

### B. Relative pronouns that relate to antecedent persons

Remember, in our discussion at the start of section A, we said that fewer people nowadays are bothering to discriminate between what relative pronoun to select for the start of defining and nondefining relative clauses relating to things? Well, the same goes for relative pronouns relating to people — only more so.

Let us see what the situation was in the past, and what it is nowadays.

Five decades or so ago, the principle held that you used "that" at the head of a defining relative clause, and "who" or "whom" at the start of a nondefining relative clause.

DEFINING

I know the child **that** drew this picture.[1]

NONDEFINING

My eldest child, **who** also likes to draw, does not draw so well.[1]

In current English, the first of these two sentences, which accords with the strict canons of midcentury grammar, sounds almost quaint. People — many quality writers included — would be more likely to use "who" than "that" at the start of the defining relative clause. We bow to this modern convention and designate "that" and "who" as equally valid in modern usage.

---

1 Standard formal: *use this, and you can't go wrong in formal contexts.*
2 Standard formal with consistent options: *choose one and stick to it.*
3 Standard formal with flexible options: *choose any one, any time.*
4 Old-fashioned: *still all right, but fading from modern usage.*
5 Standard informal: *fine in conversation or in personal letters.*
6 Nonstandard: *you jez'gotta be kidding.*

# "Who", "whom", "which", "that"

DEFINING

I know the child **that** drew this picture.[3]
I know the child **who** drew this picture.[3]

But while the distinction between "that" and "who" no longer strictly applies, two other distinctions still do.

One is a distinction in punctuation: you don't separate defining relative clauses from their antecedent clauses with commas; you do separate nondefining relative clauses from their antecedent clauses.

DEFINING

Parents **that pamper their children** may end up with brats on their hands.[3]
Parents **who pamper their children** may end up with brats on their hands.[3]

NONDEFINING

My parents, **who never pampered me,** still ended up with a brat on their hands.[1]

The other distinction is that — in a defining relative clause — you may omit the relative pronoun when it functions as the object of a verb or of a preposition. In a nondefining relative clause, the omission of the relative pronoun doesn't work.

DEFINING

Can you name an author **that** you admire?[3]
Can you name an author **whom** you admire?[3]
Can you name an author you admire?[3]
I need someone **with whom** I can talk.[3]
I need someone **that** I can talk **with**.[3]
I need someone I can talk **with**.[3]
I need someone **whom** I can talk **with**.[3]

NONDEFINING

This is my eldest sister, **whom** you have not previously met.[1]
(This is my eldest sister, you have not previously met.[6])

**Usage**

This is my youngest brother, **about whom** I have told you.[3]
This is my youngest brother, **whom** I have told you **about**.[3]
(This is my youngest brother, I have told you **about**.[6])

One more point. In the overview we said that you use "who" if the relative pronoun is a subject, and "whom" if the relative pronoun is an object. This holds good in formal contexts. In informal contexts, you can use "who" indiscriminately.

This is my mother, **whom** we have just been talking about.[1]
This is my mother, **who** we've just been talking about.[5]

After these preliminaries, we take a closer look at the variations and the options.

**5. The relative pronoun relates to a person, and it is the subject of a verb.**

**a.** If the relative clause is defining, use "that" or "who".

I have two brothers in Australia. The one **that** lives in Sydney is a singer; the one **that** lives in Melbourne is a truck driver.[3]
I have two brothers in Australia. The one **who** lives in Sydney is a singer; the one **who** lives in Melbourne is a truck driver.[3]

**b.** If the relative clause is nondefining, use "who".

My only sister, **who** lives in Perth, is a journalist.[1]

**6. The relative pronoun relates to a person, and it is the object of a verb.**

**a.** If the relative clause is defining, there are four options, including the omission of the relative pronoun.

This is the same person **that** you met last week.[3]
This is the same person **whom** you met last week.[3]

---

1 Standard formal: *use this, and you can't go wrong in formal contexts.*
2 Standard formal with consistent options: *choose one and stick to it.*
3 Standard formal with flexible options: *choose any one, any time.*
4 Old-fashioned: *still all right, but fading from modern usage.*
5 Standard informal: *fine in conversation or in personal letters.*
6 Nonstandard: *you jez'gotta be kidding.*

## "Who", "whom", "which", "that"

This is the same person you met last week.³
This is the same person **who** you met last week.⁵

**b.** If the relative clause is nondefining, neither the use of "that" nor the omission of the relative pronoun are options. There are, however, two other options.

This is my youngest child, **whom** I am coaching in mathematics.¹
This is my youngest child, **who** I am coaching in mathematics.⁵

**7. The relative pronoun is the object of a preposition.**
**a.** If the relative clause is defining, there are five choices, including the option of omitting the relative pronoun.

Direct me to someone **from whom** I can get the information.³
Direct me to someone **whom** I can get the information **from**.³
Direct me to someone **that** I can get the information **from**.³
Direct me to someone I can get the information **from**.³
Direct me to someone **who** I can get the information **from**.⁵

**b. If the relative clause is nondefining, there are three options.**

Direct me to your manager, **from whom** I can get the information.³
Direct me to your manager, **whom** I can get the information **from**.³
Direct me to your manager, **who** I can get the information **from**.⁵

# CHAPTER 9
# Parenthetic elements

## Overview

Parenthetic elements are throwaway parts of sentences, and sometimes whole sentences. They are bits that you can leave out without affecting the essential structure of the text in which they occur, but that you insert for the sake of making some point. Because they stand apart from the text of which they form a part, you normally separate them from the rest of the sentence with some form of punctuation.

Here are examples of the kinds of uses to which you can put parenthetic elements.

**a.** To define a term in the associated sentence.

They went to PNG, **Papua New Guinea**, last week.[1]

**b.** To explain or elaborate a point in the associated sentence.

We were unable — **it was a moonless night** — to find our way across the fields.[1]

**c.** To mark an aside.

As far as I'm concerned (**and I hope you're taking note of this**) I don't mind if I never see you again.[1]

**d.** To express a reservation on a point in the associated sentence.

They have never, **with possibly one exception**, broken any of their promises.[1]

---

1 Standard formal: *use this, and you can't go wrong in formal contexts.*
2 Standard formal with consistent options: *choose one and stick to it.*
3 Standard formal with flexible options: *choose any one, any time.*
4 Old-fashioned: *still all right, but fading from modern usage.*
5 Standard informal: *fine in conversation or in personal letters.*
6 Nonstandard: *you jez'gotta be kidding.*

**e.** To give an equivalence of something in the associated sentence.

Each villager owns 100 hectares (**247.1 acres**) of land.[1]

**f.** To add an explanatory sentence in a passage.

Michael Tal lost the world chess championship in 1962. (**He was ill during the contest.**) But he continued until his death in 1992 to be active in tournament play.[1]

**g.** To avoid ambiguity.

When Tom met Dick, he (**Tom**) invited him to dinner.[1]

To sum up so far, the examples we have given show that:

**i.** the parenthetic element is grammatically superfluous to the text with which it is associated;

**ii.** the parenthetic element can be of different lengths and grammatical structures;

**iii.** you can use commas, dashes or brackets to separate off the parenthetic element;

**iv.** the parenthetic element can serve various functions in a text.

We deal with parenthetic elements in this chapter under three heads.

## A. Ways of separating off parenthetic elements in texts
Here we give the different kinds of punctuation you can use to separate off parenthetic elements, and the different parts of sentences in which the parenthetic elements can occur.

## B. Punctuation of parenthetic elements and of associated texts of the same and of different moods
What if the text is a statement and the parenthetic element is a question — how do we punctuate the sentence? This is the kind of problem we deal with in this section.

## C. Multiple parenthetic elements in a text
You can have two, even more, parenthetic elements in a sentence. You can even have a parenthetic element inside a parenthetic element inside a sentence. How to handle these structures is the topic of this section.

**Usage**

## A. Ways of separating off parenthetic elements in texts

There are six different ways of separating off a parenthetic element from its associated text —

  i. a comma
  ii. a pair of commas
  iii. a dash
  iv. a pair of dashes
  v. a pair of brackets.
  vi. nothing at all (see point **2.a.** below).

Which of these options you choose will depend on a number of factors —

  i. the position of the parenthetic element in the associated text;
  ii. the tone or flavour that you want to impart to the parenthetic element and its associated text;
  iii. the other punctuation in the associated text.

We look at each of these factors below.

### 1. The position and punctuation of parenthetic elements.

**a.** At the beginning of a sentence you can choose a comma or a dash to separate off a parenthetic element.

> **Believe it or not,** they do know what they are doing.[3]
> **Believe it or not** — they do know what they are doing.[3]

A pair of brackets also works, but only in a very specialised context.

> **(Aloud)**: "So here you are at last!"[1]

**b.** In the middle of a sentence you can choose a pair of commas, a pair of dashes, or a pair of brackets to separate off a parenthetic element.

---

1 Standard formal: *use this, and you can't go wrong in formal contexts.*
2 Standard formal with consistent options: *choose one and stick to it.*
3 Standard formal with flexible options: *choose any one, any time.*
4 Old-fashioned: *still all right, but fading from modern usage.*
5 Standard informal: *fine in conversation or in personal letters.*
6 Nonstandard: *you jez'gotta be kidding.*

They did the job, **or so I believe,** on their own.[3]
They did the job — **or so I believe** — on their own.[3]
They did the job (**or so I believe**) on their own.[3]

**c.** At the end of a sentence you can choose a comma, a dash or a pair of brackets to separate off a parenthetic element.

They did the job on their own, **or so I believe.**[3]
They did the job on their own — **or so I believe.**[3]
They did the job on their own (**or so I believe**).[3]

It is worth noting, in the last of these examples, that the full stop comes outside the closing bracket.

**d.** You can put a whole sentence inside a pair of brackets.

I took my family to the zoo. (**One of the neighbours' children tagged along too.**) We had a great time there.[1]

Because the whole sentence is within brackets the full stop comes within the closing bracket.

**2. The tone or flavour imparted to a text by the punctuation used to separate off the parenthetic element.**

**a.** A comma or a pair of commas — or nothing at all — is the weakest form of separating off a parenthetic element. A parenthetic element separated off by this means is still intended to form an integral part of the sentence. However, if you read the sentence aloud, you would read the parenthetic element in a slight undertone.

I am, **in my present mood,** not ready for visitors.[3]
I am **in my present mood** not ready for visitors.[3]

**b.** A dash or a pair of dashes is an intermediate form of separating off a parenthetic element, and a very subtle one at that. Although insulating the parenthetic element from the rest of the sentence, the dash or pair of dashes also gives the whole sentence a tinge of drama. You would read it aloud with significant pauses before and after the parenthetic element.

I am really disappointed — **and not for the first time either** — with their performance.[1]

## Usage

**c.** A pair of brackets is the strongest form of separating off a parenthetic element. It suggests that the parenthetic element is there to tell the readers something just in case they don't already know it, or to add something that is of lesser importance than the surrounding text. Aloud, you would gloss over the parenthetic element by reading it in a rapid undertone.

They ran 10 kilometres (**6.214 miles**) in relays.[1]

### 3. Punctuating a sentence that contains parenthetic and other commas.

Commas are the most usual means of separating off parenthetic elements. Commas are also the most common of punctuation marks in general. If you use a number of parenthetic commas and punctuating commas within the same sentence, you run the risk of ending up with a sentence that contains a confusing mass of commas. There are several ways of avoiding the confusion, all exemplified below. (In each of the next four examples, the parenthetic element consists of the words "six in all".)

**a.** Retain the punctuation commas, and separate off the parenthetic element with brackets or dashes.

> Since our new neighbours moved into the house next door, their children often come over to spend a few hours at our place, and the whole bunch of them — **six in all** — work together on their homework.[3]

> Since our new neighbours moved into the house next door, their children often come over to spend a few hours at our place, and the whole bunch of them (**six in all**) work together on their homework.[3]

**b.** Use parenthetic commas, and upgrade the punctuation comma to a semicolon.

Since our new neighbours moved into the house next door, their children often come over to spend a few hours at our place; and the whole bunch of them, **six in all**, work together on their homework.[3]

---

1 Standard formal: *use this, and you can't go wrong in formal contexts.*
2 Standard formal with consistent options: *choose one and stick to it.*
3 Standard formal with flexible options: *choose any one, any time.*
4 Old-fashioned: *still all right, but fading from modern usage.*
5 Standard informal: *fine in conversation or in personal letters.*
6 Nonstandard: *you jez'gotta be kidding.*

**c.** Use parenthetic commas, and reduce the number of other commas.
Since our new neighbours moved into the house next door their children often come over to spend a few hours at our place, and the whole bunch of them, **six in all**, work together on their homework.[3]

## B. Punctuation of parenthetic elements and of associated texts of the same and of different moods

Mood, in grammar, is the mode of expression conveyed by the verb and, through the verb, by the sentence as a whole. The expression may be one of assertion ("It **is** late") or of denial ("It **is not** late") or of command ("**Don't be** late") and so forth. In this section we are interested in three moods, indicated by three different terminal punctuation marks.

**a.** Statements ending in full stops.

> I need more space.[1]

**b.** Exclamations or commands ending in exclamation marks.

> What a fool I was![1]
> Run for your life![1]

**c.** Questions ending in question marks.

> What is the time?[1]

Moods can affect the way in which we punctuate parenthetic elements and their associated texts. There are usually no problems if the parenthetic element and the associated text feature the same mood; but there may be problems if they feature different moods. In this section we examine both the problematic and the unproblematic cases.

### 4. The parenthetic element and the associated sentence feature the same mood.

**a.** If both the parenthetic element and the associated sentence are statements, end the sentence as a whole with a full stop.

> They were, **to the best of my knowledge,** a happy couple.[1]
> We drove all night — **it was raining heavily** — to reach home.[1]
> It was two inches (**50.8 mm**) long.[1]

## Usage

If you want to add a punctuating (as distinct from a parenthesising) comma after a parenthetic element, you can do so only if you have separated off the parenthetic element with a pair of brackets.

> Early one morning (**it was some time last month**), I thought I saw an apparition.[1]

**b.** If the parenthetic element and the associated sentence are both questions, use only one question mark and put it at the end of the whole sentence.

> Are you now, **or have you ever been**, ill with meningitis?[1]
>
> Have you — **has anybody** — ever seen such an amazing thing?[1]
>
> Can I expect (**could you, for example, guarantee**) that I will get good service there?[1]

**c.** If both the parenthetic element and the associated sentence are exclamations (or commands), use only one exclamation mark and put it at the end of the whole sentence.

> Don't you dare, **don't you ever dare**, do that again![1]
>
> What a surprise — **goodness gracious me** — to see you here![1]
>
> So there you are (**as if I hadn't known**)![1]

**5. The parenthetic element and the associated text feature different moods.**

**a.** If the parenthetic element is a question, and the associated sentence is a statement, you need some form of punctuation to separate the elements. These are the options.

> **i.** When the parenthetic element is in the middle of the sentence —
>
> They were happy — **and who wouldn't be?** — to be alive.[3]
>
> They were happy (**and who wouldn't be?**) to be alive.[3]

---

1 Standard formal: *use this, and you can't go wrong in formal contexts.*
2 Standard formal with consistent options: *choose one and stick to it.*
3 Standard formal with flexible options: *choose any one, any time.*
4 Old-fashioned: *still all right, but fading from modern usage.*
5 Standard informal: *fine in conversation or in personal letters.*
6 Nonstandard: *you jez'gotta be kidding.*

**ii.** When the parenthetic element is at the end of the sentence —

They were happy to be alive, **and who wouldn't be?**[3]
They were happy to be alive — **and who wouldn't be?**[3]
They were happy to be alive (**and who wouldn't be?**).[3]

The third of these sample sentences ends in two different punctuation marks separated by the closing bracket. This double terminal punctuation is unique to brackets. For another example, see **b.ii.** below.

**b.** If the parenthetic element is an exclamation, and the associated sentence is a statement, these are the options.

**i.** When the parenthetic element is in the middle of the sentence —

There were hundreds of people — **unbelievable!** — at the wedding.[3]
There were hundreds of people (**unbelievable!**) at the wedding.[3]

**ii.** When the parenthetic element is at the end of the sentence—

There were hundreds of people at the wedding, **unbelievable!**[3]
There were hundreds of people at the wedding — **unbelievable!**[3]
There were hundreds of people at the wedding (**unbelievable!**).[3]

Note that the last of these sample sentences ends in two different punctuation marks separated by the closing bracket.

**c.** If the parenthetic element is an exclamation in the middle of a question sentence, these are the options.

Do you realise — **stop fidgeting for once!** — that I am talking to you?[3]
Do you realise (**stop fidgeting for once!**) that I am talking to you?[3]

**d.** If the parenthetic element is a statement in the middle of a question sentence, these are the options.

Will they ever, **and I hope they will**, come back again?[3]
Will they ever — **and I hope they will** — come back again?[3]
Will they ever (**and I hope they will**) come back again?[3]

**e.** If the parenthetic element is a statement in the middle of an exclamation (or a command) sentence, the options are these:

> What a surprise — **I really never expected it** — to see you again![3]
> What a surprise (**I really never expected it**) to see you again![3]

### C. Multiple parenthetic elements in a text

You can — as in the sentence you are now reading — have more than one parenthetic element (not an indefinite number, though) in a sentence. You can even (what will they, in their wisdom, think of next?) have a parenthetic element inside a parenthetic element inside a sentence. We don't advocate overusing this device: the result may be ugly and confusing. But, used with discretion, it can be a handy tool for writers.

**6. Multiple parenthetic elements all separated off with the same kind of punctuation.**

**a.** You may use all commas or all brackets to separate off multiple parenthetic elements within the same sentence.

> There is, **it seems to me**, no good reason, **not even a bad reason**, for people to fight over religion or, **for that matter**, over any other ideological question.[3]
> There is (**it seems to me**) no good reason (**not even a bad reason**) for people to fight over religion or (**for that matter**) over any other ideological question.[3]

**b.** With dashes it doesn't work — it becomes too confusing to figure out which particular dash begins or ends which particular parenthetic element.

> There is — **it seems to me** — no good reason — **not even a bad reason** — for people to fight over religion or — **for that matter** — over any other ideological question.[6]

**7. Multiple parenthetic elements separated off with different kinds of punctuation.**

---

1 Standard formal: *use this, and you can't go wrong in formal contexts.*
2 Standard formal with consistent options: *choose one and stick to it.*
3 Standard formal with flexible options: *choose any one, any time.*
4 Old-fashioned: *still all right, but fading from modern usage.*
5 Standard informal: *fine in conversation or in personal letters.*
6 Nonstandard: *you jez'gotta be kidding.*

# Parenthetic elements

**a.** Mix and match the various kinds of punctuation.

There is **(it seems to me)** no good reason — **not even a bad reason** — for people to fight over religion or, **for that matter**, over any other ideological question.[3]

There is — **it seems to me** — no good reason, **not even a bad reason,** for people to fight over religion or **(for that matter)** over any other ideological question.[3]

**b.** If any of the parenthetic elements differs from the associated sentence in mood, use brackets or dashes to separate such elements off. In the examples below, the associated sentence is a statement; one of the parenthetic elements is a question.

There is, **it seems to me,** no good reason **(or can you see a reason?)** for people to fight over religion or, **for that matter,** over any other ideological question.[3]

There is, **it seems to me,** no good reason — **or can you see a reason?** — for people to fight over religion or, **for that matter,** over any other ideological question.[3]

**8. A parenthetic element inside a parenthetic element inside a sentence.**
**a.** There are various options for separating off such nested parenthetic elements, when all three parts (the two parenthetic elements and the associated sentence) feature the same mood:

**i.** All commas —

They say, **and I for one have no reason, none at all, to doubt their word,** that they are happy.[3]

**ii.** A mix of dashes and commas —

They say — **and I for one have no reason, none at all, to doubt their word** — that they are happy.[3]

**iii.** A mix of brackets and commas —

They say **(and I for one have no reason, none at all, to doubt their word)** that they are happy.[3]

## Usage

**iv.** A mix of brackets and dashes —

They say (**and I for one have no reason — none at all — to doubt their word**) that they are happy.³

**v.** A mix of brackets, dashes and commas —

They say (**and I, for one, have no reason — none at all — to doubt their word**) that they are happy.³

In specialised texts such as mathematics or logic, it is acceptable to separate off parenthetic elements nested within each other by using brackets within brackets or dashes within dashes. In ordinary prose this is unaesthetic and confusing.

**b.** If a parenthetic element inside a parenthetic element features a different mood from that of the associated text, separate off the inner parenthetic element with dashes or brackets (not commas). Our example shows a parenthetic question inside a parenthetic statement inside a statement sentence.

They say (**and I have no reason — do you have any reason? — to doubt their word**) that they are happy.³

They say — **and I have no reason (do you have any reason?) to doubt their word** — that they are happy.³

---

1 Standard formal: *use this, and you can't go wrong in formal contexts.*
2 Standard formal with consistent options: *choose one and stick to it.*
3 Standard formal with flexible options: *choose any one, any time.*
4 Old-fashioned: *still all right, but fading from modern usage.*
5 Standard informal: *fine in conversation or in personal letters.*
6 Nonstandard: *you jez'gotta be kidding.*

# CHAPTER 10
# Transforming direct speech into reported speech

## Overview
When you quote verbatim the words used by another person, the words so quoted are called direct speech. Normally, but not invariably, you can recognise direct speech by the quotation marks that enclose it. When you report in your own words what someone else has said or written, but stick as closely as possible to the sense and wording of the original, the words so reported are called reported speech (or "indirect speech" or "oblique speech", in the terminology of some grammarians). Here is an example of each of the two kinds of speech.

| DIRECT SPEECH | REPORTED SPEECH |
|---|---|
| They said, "Hello, we're happy to see you." | They greeted us and said that they were happy to see us. |

The above examples show that the transformation of a sentence from direct into reported speech entails a number of verbal and structural changes. And it is with these changes that the present chapter deals. The chapter comes in three sections.

## A. The introductory clause in reported speech
The introductory clause of a sentence in reported speech is that part of the sentence that starts with some such wording as these examples.

| | |
|---|---|
| They said that | They asked whether |
| They told me | They answered that |

In this section of the chapter we deal with the problem of what introductory verb (for example, "said" or "asked") we should use in the introductory clause, and what conjunction (for example, "that" or "whether") we need at the end of the introductory clause.

## Usage

### B. Changes to the quoted words transformed from direct speech into reported speech

Here we look at the changes that occur to direct speech when we transform it into reported speech.

### C. Transformation of a sustained passage of direct speech into reported speech

This section deals with the techniques for transforming a longer passage from direct into reported speech.

### A. The introductory clause in reported speech

Both the wording and the structure of the introductory clause in reported speech depend on the grammatical mood of the quoted words. What do we mean by "grammatical mood"? Well, it means the mode of expression of a verb — whether, for example, it is a statement or a question or a command. In this section of the chapter we consider three grammatical moods.

**a.** the indicative mood, which expresses —

    **i.** a positive statement ("I am ready"), or
    **ii.** a negative statement ("I am not ready");

**b.** the interrogative mood, which expresses —

    **i.** a positive question ("Are you ready?"), or
    **ii.** a negative question ("Aren't you ready?");

**c.** the imperative mood, which expresses —

    **i.** a positive command ("Get ready"), or
    **ii.** a negative command ("Don't get ready").

We will be looking at how the mood of the directly quoted words affects the introductory clause of the reported speech in two regards —

---

1 Standard formal: *use this, and you can't go wrong in formal contexts.*
2 Standard formal with consistent options: *choose one and stick to it.*
3 Standard formal with flexible options: *choose any one, any time.*
4 Old-fashioned: *still all right, but fading from modern usage.*
5 Standard informal: *fine in conversation or in personal letters.*
6 Nonstandard: *you jez'gotta be kidding.*

# Direct speech to reported speech

**a.** whether and what kind of conjunction — joining word — we need to use following the introductory clause, and

**b.** what verb we need to use in the introductory clause of the reported speech.

**1. The conjunction "that", when the direct speech is in the indicative mood.**
The use of "that" is optional.

| DIRECT SPEECH | REPORTED SPEECH |
|---|---|
| They said, "It is getting late." | They said **that** it was getting late.[3] |
| | They said it was getting late.[3] |

**2. The conjunction "whether" or "if", when the direct speech is in the interrogative mood.**
You can use either "whether" or "if", but one is standard formal while the other is standard informal.

| DIRECT SPEECH | REPORTED SPEECH |
|---|---|
| They said, "Is it green?" | They asked **whether** it was green.[1] |
| | They asked **if** it was green.[5] |

**3. Other conjunctions when the direct speech is in the interrogative mood.**
If the direct question already contains question words such as "where", "when", "how" and the like, simply use those words at the end of the introductory clause.

| DIRECT SPEECH | REPORTED SPEECH |
|---|---|
| They said, "**Where** are you going?" | They asked me **where** I was going.[1] |

**4. Introductory verbs in introductory clauses reporting indicative direct speech.**
The two most common introductory verbs are "said" and "told". But you are certainly not restricted to these two alone. Here is a small sampling of introductory verbs you may use.

**Usage**

| DIRECT SPEECH | REPORTED SPEECH |
|---|---|
| They said, "We need it." | They **said** that they needed it.[3] |
| | They **told** us they needed it.[3] |
| | They **argued** that they needed it.[3] |
| | They **claimed** they needed it.[3] |

**5. Introductory verbs in introductory clauses reporting interrogative direct speech.**

The most usual introductory verb is "asked", but there is a whole range of introductory verbs among which to choose. Here are a few of the available options.

| DIRECT SPEECH | REPORTED SPEECH |
|---|---|
| I said, "When will they come?" | I **asked** when they would come.[3] |
| | I **wondered** when they would come.[3] |
| | I **inquired** when they would come.[3] |
| | I **wanted to know** when they would come.[3] |

**6. Introductory verbs in introductory clauses reporting imperative direct speech.**

The two most common introductory verbs are "asked" (that's the polite one) and "told" (that's the sharp one). But there is a range of other introductory verbs you can use as well. Here is a sampling of the possibilities.

| DIRECT SPEECH | REPORTED SPEECH |
|---|---|
| Someone said, "Take a seat." | Someone **asked** me to take a seat.[3] |
| | Someone **told** me to take a seat.[3] |
| | Someone **ordered** me to take a seat.[3] |
| | Someone **commanded** me to take a seat.[3] |

1 Standard formal: *use this, and you can't go wrong in formal contexts.*
2 Standard formal with consistent options: *choose one and stick to it.*
3 Standard formal with flexible options: *choose any one, any time.*
4 Old-fashioned: *still all right, but fading from modern usage.*
5 Standard informal: *fine in conversation or in personal letters.*
6 Nonstandard: *you jez'gotta be kidding.*

Direct speech to reported speech

## B. Changes to the quoted words transformed from direct speech into reported speech

Let's examine one example.

| DIRECT SPEECH | REPORTED SPEECH |
|---|---|
| She said, "**This is** what **I want**." | She said that **that was** what **she wanted**.[1] |

There are five words within quotation marks in the direct speech. Four of them undergo some change or other when we transform them into reported speech. In this section, we look in a systematic way at the changes that occur in the process of transformation.

### 7. Changes to pronouns.

If you are reporting Jack's speech, the "I" in his direct speech becomes "he" in the reported speech; if you are reporting Jill's speech, "I" becomes "she". This and similar changes are a simple matter of common sense.

| DIRECT SPEECH | REPORTED SPEECH |
|---|---|
| Jack said, "**I** went up the hill." | Jack said **he** had gone up the hill, and |
| Jill said, "**I** went too." | Jill said **she** had gone too.[1] |

### 8. Terms indicating nearness change into terms indicating remoteness.

The following changes take place.

| DIRECT SPEECH | REPORTED SPEECH |
|---|---|
| here | there |
| this | that |
| these | those |
| now | then |

| DIRECT SPEECH | REPORTED SPEECH |
|---|---|
| Jack said, "I need **this** pail and **these** climbing boots, and I need them **here** and **now**." | Jack asserted that he needed **that** pail and **those** climbing boots, and that he needed them **there** and **then**.[1] |

131

### Usage

**9. Changes to time designations.**
The following changes take place.

| DIRECT SPEECH | REPORTED SPEECH |
|---|---|
| today | that day / the same day |
| tonight | that night / the same night |
| yesterday | the day before / the previous day |
| the day before yesterday | two days before / two days earlier |
| last night (week, etc) | the previous night (week, etc) / the night (week, etc) before |
| | |
| tomorrow | the next day / the following day |
| the day after tomorrow | two days later |
| next week (month, etc) | the following week (month, etc) |
| recently / lately | in the recent past |

| DIRECT SPEECH | REPORTED SPEECH |
|---|---|
| He said, "**Last week** I lent you a book that I would like back **today** rather than **next week**." | He told me that **the previous week** he had lent me a book that he would like back **that day** rather than **the following week**.[1] |

**10. Changes to verb tenses.**
Whether tense changes occur in the quoted words of the reported speech depends on the tense of the verb in the introductory clause.
**a.** If the verb in the introductory clause is in the present tense ("She says that) or in the future tense ("He will say that"), the tenses of the verbs in the quoted part of the sentence remain unchanged.

---

1 Standard formal: *use this, and you can't go wrong in formal contexts.*
2 Standard formal with consistent options: *choose one and stick to it.*
3 Standard formal with flexible options: *choose any one, any time.*
4 Old-fashioned: *still all right, but fading from modern usage.*
5 Standard informal: *fine in conversation or in personal letters.*
6 Nonstandard: *you jez'gotta be kidding.*

### Direct speech to reported speech

| DIRECT SPEECH | REPORTED SPEECH |
|---|---|
| She **says**, "Things **were** bad, they **are changing**, and they **will become** better." | She **says** that things **were** bad, they **are changing**, and they **will become** better.[1] |
| He **will say**, "I **did** it, I **am doing** it again, and I **will do** it some more." | He **will say** that he **did** it, he is **doing** it again, and he **will do** it some more.[1] |

**b.** If the verb in the introductory clause is in the past tense ("She said that") or in the future in the past tense ("He would say that"), the following changes occur to the tenses of the verbs in the quoted part of the sentence.

**i.** The present tense changes into the past tense.

| DIRECT SPEECH | REPORTED SPEECH |
|---|---|
| She **said**, "I **know** what to do." | She **said** that she **knew** what to do.[1] |
| He **said**, "I **am writing** a letter." | He **said** that he **was writing** a letter.[1] |

There is one exception to this rule. If the quoted part of the sentence in which the verb occurs expresses some universal truth or matter of common fact, you may opt between leaving the verb in the present tense and changing it into the past tense.

| DIRECT SPEECH | REPORTED SPEECH |
|---|---|
| She **said**, "Mars **is** a planet." | She **said** that Mars **is** a planet.[3] |
|  | She **said** that Mars **was** a planet.[3] |

**ii.** The past tense changes into the past perfect tense.

| DIRECT SPEECH | REPORTED SPEECH |
|---|---|
| She **said**, "I **took** my vacation in June." | She **said** she **had taken** her vacation in June.[1] |

If the quoted part of the direct speech is already in the past perfect tense, it stays that way.

## Usage

| DIRECT SPEECH | REPORTED SPEECH |
|---|---|
| He said, "I **hadn't thought** of that." | He said he **had not thought** of that.[1] |

**iii.** The future tense changes into the future in the past tense.

| DIRECT SPEECH | REPORTED SPEECH |
|---|---|
| He **said**, "I **will be going** there on Monday" | He **said** that he **would be going** there on Monday.[1] |

**iv.** The future in the past tense changes into the future in the past perfect tense.

| DIRECT SPEECH | REPORTED SPEECH |
|---|---|
| She **said**, "I **would know** him anywhere." | She **said** that she **would have known** him anywhere.[1] |

If the quoted part of the sentence is already in the future in the past perfect tense, it stays that way.

| DIRECT SPEECH | REPORTED SPEECH |
|---|---|
| He **said**, "I **would have done** it differently." | He **said** that he **would have done** it differently.[1] |

**11. Changes in the moods of the verbs.**
**a.** The positive and the negative indicative moods don't change: the positive remains positive; the negative remains negative.

| DIRECT SPEECH | REPORTED SPEECH |
|---|---|
| She said, "**I am managing** though **I am not rich**." | She said that **she was managing** though **she was not rich**.[1] |

---

1 Standard formal: *use this, and you can't go wrong in formal contexts.*
2 Standard formal with consistent options: *choose one and stick to it.*
3 Standard formal with flexible options: *choose any one, any time.*
4 Old-fashioned: *still all right, but fading from modern usage.*
5 Standard informal: *fine in conversation or in personal letters.*
6 Nonstandard: *you jez'gotta be kidding.*

# Direct speech to reported speech

**b.** The interrogative (question) mood changes into the positive mood.

DIRECT SPEECH | REPORTED SPEECH
He asked me, "**Do you understand?**" He asked whether **I understood**.[1]

When one is transforming direct speech into reported speech, leaving the interrogative mood in the interrogative is a trap for the unwary. It's all right at the colloquial level, but it's not standard formal English.

DIRECT SPEECH | REPORTED SPEECH
She said, "**Are you going** home?" | She asked me **was I going** home.[5]
She asked me whether **I was going** home.[1]

**c.** The negative-interrogative mood (a negative question) transforms into the negative mood.

DIRECT SPEECH | REPORTED SPEECH
She said, "**Aren't you coming?**" | She asked me whether **I was not coming**.[1]
She asked **was I not coming**.[5]

**d.** The imperative mood (the mood of command) transforms into the infinitive (a base-form verb with "to" in front of it).

DIRECT SPEECH | REPORTED SPEECH
He said, "**Tell** me a story." | He asked me **to tell** him a story.[1]
She said, "**Don't hurry**." | She told me **not to hurry**.[1]

You can include the "please" concept of an imperative either in the introductory clause or in the quoted part of the sentence.

DIRECT SPEECH | REPORTED SPEECH
He said, "**Please** come back." | He **pleaded** with me to come back.[3]
He **asked me please** to come back.[3]

The polite command "would you please" is really a question. You therefore treat it as an interrogative (point **11.b.** above).

## Usage

| DIRECT SPEECH | REPORTED SPEECH |
|---|---|
| She said, "**Would you please shut** the door?"[1] | She asked me whether **I would please shut** the door.[1] |
| | She asked **would I please shut** the door.[5] |

**12. Various transformations from direct into reported speech: greetings, "thanks", "yes", "no".**

**a.** Here are the options for the most common greetings

| DIRECT SPEECH | REPORTED SPEECH |
|---|---|
| They said, "**Hello.**" | They **greeted** me.[3] |
| | They **said hello**.[3] |
| They said, "**Goodbye.**" | They **took their leave**.[3] |
| | They **said goodbye**.[3] |
| | They **bade me farewell**.[4] |
| They said, "**Good morning.**" | They **wished me a good morning**.[3] |
| | They **said good morning**.[3] |
| They said, "**Good afternoon.**" | They **wished me a good afternoon**.[3] |
| | They **said good afternoon**.[3] |
| They said, "**Good night.**" | They **wished me goodnight**.[3] |
| | They **said good night**.[3] |
| They said, "**Merry Christmas.**" | They **wished me a merry Christmas**.[3] |
| | They **said merry Christmas**.[3] |
| They said "**Happy New Year.**" | They **wished me a happy New Year**.[3] |
| | They **said happy New Year**.[3] |

---

1 Standard formal: *use this, and you can't go wrong in formal contexts.*
2 Standard formal with consistent options: *choose one and stick to it.*
3 Standard formal with flexible options: *choose any one, any time.*
4 Old-fashioned: *still all right, but fading from modern usage.*
5 Standard informal: *fine in conversation or in personal letters.*
6 Nonstandard: *you jez'gotta be kidding.*

### Direct speech to reported speech

They said, "**Happy birthday**." | They **wished me a happy birthday**.[3]
| They **said happy birthday**.[3]

**b.** "Thanks" or "thank you".

| DIRECT SPEECH | REPORTED SPEECH |
|---|---|
| He said, "**Thanks** for the dinner." | He **thanked** us for the dinner.[3] |
| | He **said thanks** for the dinner.[3] |

**c.** "Yes" and "no".
Here are the major options.

| DIRECT SPEECH | REPORTED SPEECH |
|---|---|
| She asked, "Is it late?" | She asked whether it was late. |
| He answered, "**Yes**." | He **answered that it was**.[3] |
| | He **answered in the affirmative**.[3] |
| | He **affirmed that it was**.[3] |
| | He **acknowledged that it was**.[3] |
| | He **said yes**.[3] |
| He said, "Did you do it?" | He asked me whether I had done it. |
| I said, "**No**." | I **replied that I had not**.[3] |
| | I **answered in the negative**.[3] |
| | I **denied that I had**.[3] |
| | I **said no**.[3] |

## C. Transformation of a sustained passage of direct speech into reported speech

**13. Transform the direct speech into a continuous passage of reported speech.**

In sections **A** and **B** of this chapter we dealt with the transformation of individual sentences from direct into reported speech. Most of the transformed sentences began with an introductory clause: "They said", "They asked", or the like. In a sustained passage it would obviously be clumsy to start each sentence with such an introductory clause. Instead, what we do — using equal dollops of common sense and the guidelines developed in sections **A** and **B** above — is to take the separate sentences

## Usage

of the passage of direct speech and stitch them together into a continuous passage of reported speech.

There are two things worth noting about sustained passages of speech. One is that, in direct speech, each paragraph opens with quotation marks; but only the last paragraph opens and closes with quotation marks. The other is that, in reported speech, you vary the introductory verbs and scatter them throughout the passage as needed.

To show how this works, we take as an example excerpts from George F Kennan's acceptance speech on receiving the Albert Einstein Peace Prize for 1981. The title of Kennan's address: "The only way out of the nuclear nightmare."

DIRECT SPEECH

"What can we do?

"Adequate words are lacking to express the full seriousness of our present situation. It is not just that the US is for the moment on a collision course politically with the Soviet Union; it is also — and even more importantly — the fact that the ultimate sanction behind the conflicting policies of these two governments is a type and volume of weaponry which could not possibly be used without utter disaster for us all.

REPORTED SPEECH

George F Kennan began by asking his audience what the US could do.

Adequate words, he said, were lacking to express the full seriousness of America's position at that time. It was not just that the US was for the moment on a collision course politically with the Soviet Union; it was also — and even more importantly — the fact that the ultimate sanction behind the conflicting policies of those two governments was a type and volume of weaponry which could not possibly be used without utter disaster for them all.

1 Standard formal: *use this, and you can't go wrong in formal contexts.*
2 Standard formal with consistent options: *choose one and stick to it.*
3 Standard formal with flexible options: *choose any one, any time.*
4 Old-fashioned: *still all right, but fading from modern usage.*
5 Standard informal: *fine in conversation or in personal letters.*
6 Nonstandard: *you jez'gotta be kidding.*

## Direct speech to reported speech

"The danger is so obvious. So much has already been said. What is to be gained by reiteration? What good would it now do? Look at the record. Over all these years the competition in the development of nuclear weaponry has proceeded steadily, relentlessly, without the faintest regard for all these warning voices.

"We have gone on piling weapon upon weapon, missile upon missile. We have done this helplessly, almost involuntarily: like the victims of some sort of hypnotism, like lem-mings heading for the sea.

"And the result is that today the Americans and the Russians have achieved, in the creation of these devices and their means of delivery, levels of redundancy of such grotesque dimensions as to defy rational understanding.

The danger, Kennan continued, was so obvious. So much had already been said. Kennan then asked his audience what was to be gained by reiteration, and what good such reiteration would then do. He appealed to his audience to look at the record. Over all those years, he pointed out, the competition in the development of nuclear weaponry had proceeded steadily, relentlessly, without the faintest regard for all those warning voices.

The superpowers had gone on piling weapon upon weapon, missile upon missile. They had done that helplessly, almost involuntarily: like the victims of some sort of hypnotism, like lemmings heading for the sea.

And the result was that, by that day, the Americans and the Russians had achieved, in the creation of those devices and their means of delivery, levels of redundancy of such grotesque dimensions as to defy rational understanding.

## Usage

"What I would like to see the president do, after due consultation with the congress, would be to propose to the Soviet government an immediate across-the-board reduction by fifty percent of the nuclear arsenals now being maintained by the two superpowers, all this to be implemented at once and without further wrangling among the experts, and to be subject to such national means of verification as now lie at the disposal of the two powers.

"In the final week of his life, Albert Einstein signed a collective appeal against the development of nuclear weapons. He was dead before it appeared. It was an appeal drafted, I gather, by Bertrand Russell. I had my differences with Russell at the time, but I quote one sentence from the final paragraph of the statement, not only because it was the last one Einstein ever signed, but because it sums up, I think, all that I have to say on the subject.

Kennan went on to state that what he would have liked to see the president do, after due consultation with the congress, would have been to propose to the Soviet government an immediate across-the-board reduction by fifty percent of the nuclear arsenals then being maintained by the two superpowers, all that to be implemented at once and without further wrangling among the experts, and to be subject to such national means of verification as then lay at the disposal of the two powers.

In the final weeks of his life, Kennan reminded his audience, Albert Einstein had signed a collective appeal against the development of nuclear weapons. Einstein had died before the appeal had appeared. It had been an appeal, Kennan gathered, drafted by Bertrand Russell. Kennan acknowledged that he had had his differences with Russell at the time, but he went on to quote one sentence from the final paragraph of the statement, not only because it had been the last one Einstein had ever signed, but because it summed up, Kennan thought, all that Kennan himself had to say on the subject.

1 Standard formal: *use this, and you can't go wrong in formal contexts.*
2 Standard formal with consistent options: *choose one and stick to it.*
3 Standard formal with flexible options: *choose any one, any time.*
4 Old-fashioned: *still all right, but fading from modern usage.*
5 Standard informal: *fine in conversation or in personal letters.*
6 Nonstandard: *you jez'gotta be kidding.*

## Direct speech to reported speech

"It reads as follows: 'We appeal, as human beings to human beings: remember your humanity, and forget the rest.'"

In the sentence that Kennan quoted, the signatories appealed to their readers — as human beings to human beings — to remember their humanity and to forget the rest.[1]

# CHAPTER 11
# Italic print and underlined roman print or writing

## Overview
Italic print (*which consists of sloping writing that looks like this*) and underlined roman print (<u>which is underlined upright print</u>) are alternative and equally legitimate ways of distinguishing words from a surrounding text. Normally, a word-processed or a printed text will make use of italic print, while a handwritten or a typed text will make use of underlining. We divide this chapter into two sections.

### A. Names and titles of literary and other works
These appear in italic print, or in underlined roman print or handwriting.

### B. Letters, words, expressions and reverse italics
Here come the other uses.

### A. Names and titles of literary and other works
Instances that come under this section range from Beethoven's *Emperor Concerto* (or <u>Emperor Concerto</u>) to NASA's *Challenger* (or <u>Challenger</u>). Apart from the print style there is another factor to consider: in many cases the overall title of a work is in italic print, or in underlined roman print or writing, while the title of a subsidiary part is enclosed in quotation marks. This holds, for example, for the title of a book and of a component chapter, and for the title of a music album and of a component track.

---

1 Standard formal: *use this, and you can't go wrong in formal contexts.*
2 Standard formal with consistent options: *choose one and stick to it.*
3 Standard formal with flexible options: *choose any one, any time.*
4 Old-fashioned: *still all right, but fading from modern usage.*
5 Standard informal: *fine in conversation or in personal letters.*
6 Nonstandard: *you jez'gotta be kidding.*

## Italic and underlined roman print

**1. Titles of major written works and their component parts.**
Format the title of the major work in italics (or underlining); enclose the title of the component part in single or double quotation marks.
**a.** A book and a component chapter.

> There is a chapter called '**Abstract Art**' in *How to Paint and Draw*.[2]
> There is a chapter called "**Abstract Art**" in *How to Paint and Draw*.[2]
> There is a chapter called '**Abstract Art**' in <u>How to Paint and Draw</u>.[2]
> There is a chapter called "**Abstract Art**" in <u>How to Paint and Draw</u>.[2]

The titles of sacred texts are an exception: they appear in roman print without underlining.

> I have read parts of **the Bible, the Talmud** and **the Koran**.[1]

**b.** A report or booklet, and a component chapter or section.

> I got the information from the chapter '**Grains**', in the booklet *Healthy Foods*.[2]
> I got the information from the chapter "**Grains**", in the booklet *Healthy Foods*.[2]
> I got the information from the chapter '**Grains**', in the booklet <u>Healthy Foods</u>.[2]
> I got the information from the chapter "**Grains**", in the booklet <u>Healthy Foods</u>.[2]

**c.** A newspaper or periodical, and a component news story or article.

> There was an article headed '**Road funding**' in *The Economist*.[2]
> There was an article headed "**Road funding**" in *The Economist*.[2]
> There was an article headed '**Road funding**' in <u>The Economist</u>.[2]
> There was an article headed "**Road funding**" in <u>The Economist</u>.[2]

Since the definite article "The" forms part of the title of the periodical, it too is italicised or underlined.

**2. Legislation and law reports.**
Use italic print or underlining for the titles of bills, acts and legal cases.

> Parliament debated the *Dairy Industry Promotion Bill 1991*.[2]
> Parliament debated the <u>Dairy Industry Promotion Bill 1991</u>.[2]

## Usage

Since the definite article "the" is not part of the title of the bill, it is neither italicised nor underlined.

> The attorney referred to the case of *Regina v. Such-and-Such Company*.[2]
> 
> The attorney referred to the case of **Regina v. Such-and-Such Company**.[2]

**3. Poetic works.**

**a.** The titles of longer poetic works.

> Have you read Milton's *Paradise Lost* and Shakespeare's *Venus and Adonis*?[2]
> 
> Have you read Milton's **Paradise Lost** and Shakespeare's **Venus and Adonis**?[2]

The former work is book length; the latter is more than ten pages long.

**b.** The titles of shorter poetic works.

> I've read Milton's 'On His Blindness' and Shakespeare's 'Under the Greenwood Tree'.[2]
> 
> I've read Milton's "On His Blindness" and Shakespeare's "Under the Greenwood Tree".[2]

The former work is a sonnet; the latter is two verses long.

**4. Musical works.**

**a.** The name of a musical work is in roman print, without quotation marks, when it specifies the musical form and key or number of the work. If it has a descriptive name, use italics or underlining.

> Beethoven's **symphony in D minor, number 9**, is known as the *Choral Symphony*.[2]

---

1 Standard formal: *use this, and you can't go wrong in formal contexts.*
2 Standard formal with consistent options: *choose one and stick to it.*
3 Standard formal with flexible options: *choose any one, any time.*
4 Old-fashioned: *still all right, but fading from modern usage.*
5 Standard informal: *fine in conversation or in personal letters.*
6 Nonstandard: *you jez'gotta be kidding.*

Beethoven's **symphony in D minor, number 9**, is known as the **Choral Symphony**.²

**b.** The name of a musical album and of a component track.

My favourite track from *The Best of the Beatles* is '**Yesterday**'.²
My favourite track from *The Best of the Beatles* is "**Yesterday**".²
My favourite track from **The Best of the Beatles** is 'Yesterday'.²
My favourite track from **The Best of the Beatles** is "Yesterday".²

**5. Various works from the fields of the arts and entertainment.**
We include the titles of plays, films, television and radio programs, paintings and statues.

I have seen both the stage version of *Hamlet* and Olivier's film version of *Hamlet*.²
I have seen both the stage version of **Hamlet** and Olivier's film version of **Hamlet**.²
*Letter from America* is a long-running radio series; *Coronation Street*, a long running TV series.²
**Letter from America** is a long-running radio series; **Coronation Street**, a long running TV series.²
Michelangelo's *David* is as famous a sculpture as Picasso's *Guernica* is a painting.²
Michelangelo's **David** is as famous a sculpture as Picasso's **Guernica** is a painting.²

**6. Vehicles — trains, planes, boats, spacecraft and so on.**
**a.** The particular names of vehicles.

**HMAS** *Otway* is an Oberon class submarine.²
**HMAS Otway** is an Oberon class submarine.²
*HMAS Otway* is an Oberon class submarine.²
**HMAS Otway** is an Oberon class submarine.²

They crossed Australia on the *Indian-Pacific* train.²
They crossed Australia on the **Indian-Pacific** train.²

**Usage**

The president arrived in his aircraft, *Airforce One*.[2]
The president arrived in his aircraft, **Airforce One**.[2]
I saw the launching of the space shuttle *Columbia*.[2]
I saw the launching of the space shuttle **Columbia**.[2]

**b.** The names of the makes or models of vehicles need no distinction from the surrounding text.

They drove to the airport in a **Ford Laser** and flew overseas in a **Boeing 707** aircraft.[1]

**7. A plural or a genitive "s" added to an italicised or underlined name or title.**
You have four options.

I have two *Macbeths* sitting on my bookshelf.[2]
I have two **Macbeths** sitting on my bookshelf.[2]
I have two *Macbeth*s sitting on my bookshelf.[2]
I have two **Macbeth**s sitting on my bookshelf.[2]
*Hamlet's* end is tragic.[2]
**Hamlet's** end is tragic.[2]
*Hamlet*'s end is tragic.[2]
**Hamlet**'s end is tragic.[2]

**B. Letters, words, expressions and reverse italics**
Here we deal with the italicising or underlining of individual letters, words and expressions, as well as with reverse italics.

**8. Letters of the alphabet.**
If you want to refer to individual letters as letters — as distinct from using the letters to make up a word — distinguish them from the surrounding text.

---

1 Standard formal: *use this, and you can't go wrong in formal contexts.*
2 Standard formal with consistent options: *choose one and stick to it.*
3 Standard formal with flexible options: *choose any one, any time.*
4 Old-fashioned: *still all right, but fading from modern usage.*
5 Standard informal: *fine in conversation or in personal letters.*
6 Nonstandard: *you jez'gotta be kidding.*

## Italic and underlined roman print

IN THE SINGULAR

Not many words start with an *x*.[2]
Not many words start with an *X*.[2]
Not many words start with an x.[2]
Not many words start with an **X**.[2]
Not many words start with an x.[2]
Not many words start with an **X**.[2]
Not many words start with an 'x'.[2]
Not many words start with an '**X**'.[2]
Not many words start with an "x".[2]
Not many words start with an "**X**".[2]

IN THE PLURAL

Mind your *p*s and *q*s.[2]
Mind your *P*s and *Q*s.[2]
Mind your ps and qs.[2]
Mind your **P**s and **Q**s.[2]
Mind your ps and qs.[2]
Mind your **P**s and **Q**s.[2]
Mind your 'p's and 'q's.[2]
Mind your '**P**'s and '**Q**'s.[2]
Mind your "p"s and "q"s.[2]
Mind your "**P**"s and "**Q**"s.[2]
Mind your p's and q's.[4]
Mind your **P**'s and **Q**'s.[4]

### 9. Words as words.

If you want to refer to individual words as words — as distinct from using them to make up a sentence — you have these options.

The word *series* may be either singular or plural.[2]
The word series may be either singular or plural.[2]
The word 'series' may be either singular or plural.[2]
The word "series" may be either singular or plural.[2]

### 10. Foreign words, expressions and sentences.

**a.** Distinguish them from the English text if they have not yet become naturalised into English.

## Usage

Chess was probably derived from *chaturanga*, an old Indian board game.[2]

Chess was probably derived from <u>chaturanga</u>, an old Indian board game.[2]

*Et tu, Brute*? This is now a way of expressing surprise at betrayal by a friend.[2]

<u>Et tu, Brute</u>? This is now a way of expressing surprise at betrayal by a friend.[2]

**b.** Don't distinguish them from the English text if they have become naturalised into English.

**i.** Examples of words that became naturalised in the nineteenth century or earlier—

| mutton[1] | (French) | incognito[1] | (Italian) |
| algebra[1] | (Arabic) | leviathan[1] | (Hebrew) |

**ii.** Examples of words that became naturalised in the twentieth century—

| kibbutz[1] | (Hebrew) | ombudsman[1] | (Swedish) |
| glasnost[1] | (Russian) | intifada[1] | (Arabic) |

It's a feature of the English language that it is hospitable to foreign words. When such words make their first appearance, the tendency is to italicise (or underline) them. If the words prove useful, and if they stay around long enough — usually a matter of months — people (including publishers) accept them into the language and stop distinguishing them from the surrounding text.

**11. Emphasis.**
Use italics or underlining for emphasis.

This book is *mine* and you will *not* get hold of it.[2]
This book is <u>mine</u> and you will <u>not</u> get hold of it.[2]

---

1 Standard formal: *use this, and you can't go wrong in formal contexts.*
2 Standard formal with consistent options: *choose one and stick to it.*
3 Standard formal with flexible options: *choose any one, any time.*
4 Old-fashioned: *still all right, but fading from modern usage.*
5 Standard informal: *fine in conversation or in personal letters.*
6 Nonstandard: *you jez'gotta be kidding.*

## 12. Reverse italics or underlining.

**a.** This occurs, for example, if the title of a book contains the title of another work that is ordinarily italicised or underlined.

I have read Andrew Pearson's *Imagery in Shakespeare's* **Macbeth**.[2]
I have read Andrew Pearson's <u>Imagery in Shakespeare's</u> **Macbeth**.[2]

**b.** It also occurs in a text that is routinely printed in italics. Some books and periodicals, for example, write the picture captions in italics. A caption under a picture of Shakespeare might then read as follows.

*William Shakespeare, the author of* **Hamlet**.[1]

# CHAPTER 12
# Capital letters and small letters

## Overview

Capital letters (or just simply "capitals") are the big letters "A", "B", "C". Small letters are the letters "a", "b", "c". The two kinds of letters are also known as upper and lower case letters from the practice of printers of old who kept the capitals in the upper part of their letter cases, and the small letters in the lower part.

There is no uniform set of rules for upper and lower casing. Different publications and publishing houses follow different house rules. But there is a trend, and that is towards fewer capitals. So if you want to write in a modern way, use as few capitals as you think you can get away with. To illustrate the trend, we give below an excerpt from the instructions given to Captain James Cook before he set out on his first journey in 1768.

> Whereas we have, in Obedience to the Kings Commands, caused His Maj$^s$ Bark the *Endeavour*, whereof you are Commander, to be fitted out in a proper manner for receiving such Persons as the Royal Society should think fit to appoint to observe the Passage of the Planet Venus over the Disk of the Sun on the 3$^d$ of June 1769 . . . I have desir'd that the Observation may be made at Port Royal Harbour . . .

A bit weird by modern standards. But what are the modern standards?

Well, for most cases, your sense of the language will serve to tell you what they are. You know, for example, that "January" and "Canberra" start

1 Standard formal: *use this, and you can't go wrong in formal contexts.*
2 Standard formal with consistent options: *choose one and stick to it.*
3 Standard formal with flexible options: *choose any one, any time.*
4 Old-fashioned: *still all right, but fading from modern usage.*
5 Standard informal: *fine in conversation or in personal letters.*
6 Nonstandard: *you jez'gotta be kidding.*

## Capital letters and small letters

with capitals;" . . . cat sat on a mat" with small letters. But what about "the Education Department" or "the education department", "the Director General" or "the director general"? Our chapter starts with these tough cases.

### A. Capital and small letters for the names of organisations and for the titles of office bearers
At its most general, our rule of thumb is this —
   **a.** use initial capital letters for the full formal name or title;
   **b.** use initial small letters for the short informal name or title.

We also discuss the exceptions and the refinements to this rule.

### B. Capital and small letters in proper nouns and their derivatives
Proper names are names like "Victoria" and "Scotland"; their derivatives are "Victorian" and "Scottish".

### C. Capital and small letters in the titles of written and artistic works, in the names of journals and in headings
We have written the above section heading using one capital alone. But there are two other ways in which we might have written it.

   Capital and Small Letters in the Titles of Written and Artistic Works, in the Names of Journals and in Headings, or
   CAPITAL AND SMALL LETTERS IN THE TITLES OF WRITTEN AND ARTISTIC WORKS, IN THE NAMES OF JOURNALS AND IN HEADINGS.

We discuss the status of these three methods in this section.

### D. Capital and small letters in prose and poetry
You are probably pretty certain that there is always an initial capital letter for the first word after a full stop, a question mark or an exclamation mark that ends a sentence, and for the first word in every line of a poem. Well, not really; at least, not always.

### E. Various other uses of capital letters and small letters
Is it "UNESCO" or "Unesco", "Come, O Night" or "Come, oh night"? The answers are in this section.

# Usage

## A. Capital and small letters for the names of organisations and for the titles of office bearers

This is an area in which chaos reigns. Some people write "the Minister", others "the minister". Yet there is a modern trend emerging in quality books and publications, and it is this —

> **i.** if you cite the full official name or title in a text, use initial capital letters;

> **ii.** if you cite a short unofficial name or title in a text, use initial small letters.

We will show refinements and exceptions to this guideline, but it's a good one to keep in mind as you go through the rest of this section.

**1. The names of organisations and the titles of office bearers in address blocks, salutations and signature blocks.**
When these names and titles appear outside a prose text — that is, when they appear in an address block, a salutation or a signature block — start the names and titles with capital letters, whether the names and titles are full and official or short and unofficial.

> **The Director**
> **Personnel Section**
> Dear **Director**
> Thank you for the information you have sent me.
> Yours faithfully
> Sam Brown
> **Policy Branch.**[1]

---

1 Standard formal: *use this, and you can't go wrong in formal contexts.*
2 Standard formal with consistent options: *choose one and stick to it.*
3 Standard formal with flexible options: *choose any one, any time.*
4 Old-fashioned: *still all right, but fading from modern usage.*
5 Standard informal: *fine in conversation or in personal letters.*
6 Nonstandard: *you jez'gotta be kidding.*

**The Prime Minister**
Parliament House
Canberra ACT 2600
Dear **Prime Minister**
I accept your invitation to the reception.
Yours faithfully
Sam Green
**Managing Director**
**Such-and-Such Company.**[1]

**2. The names of organisations in a prose text.**
In a prose text — as distinct from an address block, a salutation or a signature block — capitalisation or lower casing depends on four variables. Three of these variables are whether the name is —

**i.** the full formal name of the organisation or the short informal name;

**ii.** the name of a major umbrella organisation or the name of a relatively minor component of that organisation;

**iii.** the name of a specific organisation or a general name for any organisation of that kind.

**iv.** The fourth variable is psychological rather than technical in nature. It is whether you are a member of the organisation or not. In the former case — say, if you are an employee of the organisation — you might be inclined to capitalise even the short informal title of the organisation. But if you are an outsider — say, a journalist writing about the organisation — you would be inclined to use initial small letters for the short informal title of the organisation.

The guidelines for using initial capital letters or small letters are as follows.

**a.** If you use the full formal name of a specific major organisation, use initial capital letters.

the **Australian Institute** of **Sport**[1]
the **World Health Organisation**[1]

**b.** If you use the short or informal name of a specific organisation, use initial small letters. Capitalising the initial letters is old-fashioned.

## Usage

the **sports institute**[1]
the **institute of sport**[1]
the **institute**[1]
the **Sports Institute**[4]
the **Institute**[4]

the **health organisation**[1]
the **organisation**[1]
the **Health Organisation**[4]
the **Organisation**[4]

**c.** For the name of a relatively minor component of a specific major organisation, you may choose between initial small letters (in the modern mode) and initial capital letters (in the old-fashioned mode):

the **finance and resources branch**[1]
the **Finance and Resources Branch**[4]

Here too your relationship to the organisation may determine your choice. As a member of the organisation you may opt for the initial capital letters; as an outsider you may opt for the initial small letters.

**d.** For the name of a nonspecific organisation, or a nonspecific component part of an organisation, use initial small letters in any case — regardless of whether you are citing a full formal name or a short informal name.

a **sports institute**[1]
an **institute**[1]

a **finance and resources branch**[1]
a **branch**[1]

The following table shows all possible variations, taking into account the first three variables and the guidelines above. For the purposes of the table, we assume that the full formal name of the major organisation is "THE DEPARTMENT OF EDUCATION", the short informal name is "THE DEPARTMENT" or "THE EDUCATION DEPARTMENT"; the full formal name of the minor component of the organisation is "THE POLICY BRANCH", the short informal name of the minor component is "THE BRANCH".

---

1 Standard formal: *use this, and you can't go wrong in formal contexts.*
2 Standard formal with consistent options: *choose one and stick to it.*
3 Standard formal with flexible options: *choose any one, any time.*
4 Old-fashioned: *still all right, but fading from modern usage.*
5 Standard informal: *fine in conversation or in personal letters.*
6 Nonstandard: *you jez'gotta be kidding.*

154

## Capital letters and small letters

USE OF INITIAL CAPITAL LETTERS AND SMALL LETTERS FOR THE NAMES OF ORGANISATIONS

| *Full formal name* | *Major organisation* | *Specific organisation* | |
|---|---|---|---|
| yes | yes | yes | I like working for this **Department of Education**.[1] |
| yes | yes | no | I would like to work in any **department of education**.[1] |
| no | yes | yes | I like working in this **department**.[3] <br> I like working in this **education department**.[3] <br> I like working in this **Department**.[4] <br> I like working in this **Education Department**.[4] |
| no | yes | no | I would like to work in any **education department**.[3] <br> I would like to work in any **department**.[3] |
| yes | no | yes | I like working in this **policy branch**.[1] <br> I like working in this **Policy Branch**.[4] |
| yes | no | no | I would like to work in any **policy branch**.[1] |
| no | no | yes | I like working in this **branch**.[1] <br> I like working in this **Branch**.[4] |
| no | no | no | I would like to work in any **branch**.[1] |

### 3. The titles of office bearers in a prose text.

Whether you should use initial capital letters or initial small letters for the titles of office bearers in a prose text depends on five variables. Four of these variables are whether the title is —

**i.** the full formal one or a short informal one;

**ii.** attached to the office bearer's name or not attached to the office bearer's name;

**iii.** related to a specific person or used in a generalised sense;

**iv.** used vocatively — that is, as a form of address — or not.

**v.** The fifth variable is psychological rather than technical in nature. If you are a colleague of the office bearer, you might wish to opt to use initial capital letters — especially when you use the full formal title. On the other hand, if you are an outsider — say, a journalist writing about the office bearer — you would be more inclined to use initial small letters.

**Usage**

The guidelines for using initial capital letters or small letters, taking account of these four variables, are as follows.

**a.** If you use the title of the office bearer vocatively, use initial capital letters regardless of the other variables.

> Good morning, **Sergeant**.[1]
> Yes, **Minister**.[1]

**b.** If the office bearer's title is attached to his or her name use capital letters regardless of the other variables.

> I have met **Secretary Brown**.[1]
> I wish to introduce **Professor Green**.[1]

**c.** If you use the title in a generalised way — that is, not as the title of any specific individual — use initial small letters, whether the title is full and formal or short and informal.

> Dr Green is a **professor**.[1]
> Most **prime ministers** work hard.[1]

**d.** If you use the full formal title to refer to a specific office bearer, but you don't use it vocatively or attached to the office bearer's name, you can opt between initial small letters and initial capital letters.

> I spoke to the **director general**.[2]
> I spoke to the **Director General**.[2]
> I saw the **prime minister**.[2]
> I saw the **Prime Minister**.[2]

**e.** If you use a short or informal title to refer to a specific office bearer, but you don't use it vocatively or attached to the office bearer's name, lower casing is modern, capitalising is old-fashioned.

---

1 Standard formal: *use this, and you can't go wrong in formal contexts.*
2 Standard formal with consistent options: *choose one and stick to it.*
3 Standard formal with flexible options: *choose any one, any time.*
4 Old-fashioned: *still all right, but fading from modern usage.*
5 Standard informal: *fine in conversation or in personal letters.*
6 Nonstandard: *you jez'gotta be kidding.*

## Capital letters and small letters

I briefed the **minister**.[1]
I briefed the **Minister**.[4]

The following table shows all the possible variations, taking into account the first four variables and the guidelines above. For the purposes of the table, we assume that the name of the office bearer is "JONES", the full formal title of the office bearer is "MINISTER FOR EDUCATION", and the short informal title is either "MINISTER" or "EDUCATION MINISTER".

## Usage

USE OF INITIAL CAPITAL LETTERS AND SMALL LETTERS FOR THE TITLES OF OFFICE BEARERS

| Full formal title | Attached to a name | Specific person | Used in the vocative | |
|---|---|---|---|---|
| yes | yes | yes | yes | There is no time, **Minister for Education Jones**, for you to lose.[1] |
| no | yes | yes | yes | There is no time, **Minister Jones**, for you to lose.[3]<br>There is no time, **Education Minister Jones**, for you to lose.[3] |
| yes | no | yes | yes | There is no time, **Minister for Education**, for you to lose.[1] |
| yes | yes | yes | no | There is no time for **Minister for Education Jones** to lose.[1] |
| no | no | yes | yes | There is no time, **Minister**, for you to lose.[3]<br>There is no time, **Education Minister**, for you to lose.[1] |
| no | yes | yes | no | There is no time for **Minister Jones** to lose.[3]<br>There is no time for **Education Minister Jones** to lose.[3] |
| yes | no | yes | no | There is no time for the **minister for education** to lose.[2]<br>There is no time for the **Minister for Education** to lose.[2] |
| no | no | yes | no | There is no time for the **minister** to lose.[3]<br>There is no time for the **education minister** to lose.[3]<br>There is no time for the **Minister** to lose.[4]<br>There is no time for the **Education Minister** to lose.[4] |
| yes | no | no | no | There is no time for any **minister for education** to lose.[1] |
| no | no | no | no | There is no time for any **minister** to lose.[3]<br>There is no time for any **education minister** to lose.[3] |

## Capital letters and small letters

**4. Select names of organisations and titles of office bearers in a text.**
There are certain stock institutional names and office titles that occur frequently in texts and that follow their own conventions. We list the major ones under three subheadings.

**a.** Words conventionally capitalised in current usage.

the **Queen**[1]  
the **Crown**[1]  
the **Treasury**[1]

the **Community**[1] (the European Community)  
**Labor**[1] (a political party)  
the **Commonwealth**[1] (referring, for example, to Australia)

**b.** Words used optionally with initial capitals or lower case letters.

the **parliament**[2]  
the **Parliament**[2]

the **congress**[2]  
the **Congress**[2]

**c.** Words conventionally lower cased in modern usage — or capitalised in old-fashioned usage.

the **government**[1]  
the **Government**[4]  
the **opposition**[1]  
the **Opposition**[4]  
the **state**[1]  
the **State**[4]  
**federal**[1]  
**Federal**[4]  
the **establishment**[1]  
the **Establishment**[4]

the **cabinet**[1]  
the **Cabinet**[4]  
the **church**[1]  
the **Church**[4]  
the **press**[1]  
the **Press**[4]  
the **bar**[1] (in the legal profession)  
the **Bar**[4]  
the **bench**[1] (in the legal profession)  
the **Bench**[4]

## B. Capital and small letters in proper nouns and their derivatives

Proper nouns — also called proper names — are the particular names of people ("Albert Einstein"), geographic place names ("Snowy River") and of other things ("the Milky Way" and "the *Orient Express*").

## Usage

In proper nouns consisting of several words, not every word needs to start with a capital letter. The names of some people may contain elements such as "de" or "van" that start with small letters. The same may be the case with geographic place names and other types of proper nouns. There are no rules for using capital or small letters in such cases. If you are not sure how to write such names, look them up in a reference work — a telephone book or a gazetteer, for example — and follow the usage given there.

**5. People's names and their derivatives.**
**a.** People's names may be all in capitals or in a mix of capitals and small letters.

> **William Morris Hughes**[1]
> 
> **Louis Charles** de la **Bourdonnais**[1]

**b.** The names of some systems derived from people's names start with capitals.

> **Darwinism**[1]
> 
> **Stalinism**[1]

**c.** Some adjectives derived from people's names start with capital letters, others start with small letters. When you are not sure which is which, consult a modern dictionary.

> a **Shakespearean** sonnet[1]    the **Elizabethan** age[1]
> 
> **platonic** love[1]    a **machiavellian** plot[1]

**6. Proprietary names.**
**a.** Start the names with capital letters.

> a **Hoover** carpet cleaner[1]
> 
> a **Xerox** photocopier[1]

---

1 Standard formal: *use this, and you can't go wrong in formal contexts.*
2 Standard formal with consistent options: *choose one and stick to it.*
3 Standard formal with flexible options: *choose any one, any time.*
4 Old-fashioned: *still all right, but fading from modern usage.*
5 Standard informal: *fine in conversation or in personal letters.*
6 Nonstandard: *you jez'gotta be kidding.*

**b.** Some proprietary names and/or their derivatives have become assimilated into the English language as ordinary words. In those cases, start the words with small letters.

    I drank a **coke**.[1]

    I **velcroed** it shut.[1]

**7. The names of vehicles.**
**a.** Makes and models start with capital letters.

    a **Honda Civic**[3]
    a **Honda**[3]
    a **Civic**[3]

**b.** If the vehicle bears a proper name, use initial capitals and italicise the whole name.

    the *Orient Express*[1]
    the *SS Titanic*[1]

**c.** When you refer to these vehicles by the common nouns alone, start the words with small letters.

    the **express**[1]
    the **steam ship**[1]

**8. The names of town features such as buildings, bridges, streets and the like.**
**a.** Start the names with capitals, or a mix of capitals and small letters, when you refer to the full name.

    the **Leaning Tower of Pisa**[1]
    the **Sydney Harbour Bridge**[1]

**b.** When you refer to the town features by the common names alone, start the words with small letters.

    the **tower**[1]
    the **bridge**[1]

## Usage

**9. The names of settlements (towns, cities, etc) and of bounded areas (shires, states, countries, continents, etc).**

**a.** Start the names with capitals — or with a mix of capitals and small letters — when you refer to the full name.

    the **State** of **Victoria**[1]          **Europe**[1]
    **New York City**[1]             **Japan**[1]

**b.** When you refer to the names by the common nouns alone, start the words with small letters.

    the **state**[1]                     the **continent**[1]
    the **city**[1]                       the **country**[1]

**c.** Adjectives derived from such names start with capital letters.

    **Victorian**[1]
    **Japanese**[1]

**d.** When you attach a prefix that is not normally capitalised to an adjective that is normally capitalised, start the prefix with a small letter and the adjective with a capital letter.

    pro-**Australian**[1]
    non-**British**[1]

**e.** Some of the names in this class have become assimilated into English as common nouns or adjectives. In those cases, start the names with small letters.

    a **china** plate[1]
    **venetian** blinds[1]

---

1 Standard formal: *use this, and you can't go wrong in formal contexts.*
2 Standard formal with consistent options: *choose one and stick to it.*
3 Standard formal with flexible options: *choose any one, any time.*
4 Old-fashioned: *still all right, but fading from modern usage.*
5 Standard informal: *fine in conversation or in personal letters.*
6 Nonstandard: *you jez'gotta be kidding.*

## Capital letters and small letters

**10. Descriptive place names.**
The modern trend is towards starting the words in such names with small letters.

the **demilitarised zone**[1]
the **Demilitarised Zone**[4]
newly **industrialised countries**[1]
**Newly Industrialised Countries**[4]

**11. The names of natural geographic features such as rivers and mountains.**
**a.** If you are in doubt over which words in the names to start with capitals, and which with small letters, look the names up in a reference work.

Mount **Fuji**[1]              the **Sea** of **Marmara**[1]
the **Hunter River**[1]        the **Valley** of the **Kings**[1]

**b.** When you refer to such natural geographic features by the common nouns alone, start the words with small letters.

the **mountain**[1]            the **sea**[1]
the **river**[1]               the **valley**[1]

**12. The points of the compass.**
**a.** The points of the compass (whether used as nouns or as adjectives) start with small letters if they stand alone or if they are used descriptively.

the **west**[1]                **southern** Africa[1]
the **east**[1]                **northern** Europe[1]

**b.** When you use these words in a political sense, you have two options.

Most of the **East** has recently abandoned communism.[2]
Most of the **east** has recently abandoned communism.[2]

**c.** When the names of the points of the compass form parts of proper geographic names or of proper regional names, start the names with capital letters.

## Usage

South America[1]
the Northern Territory[1]

the Middle East[1]
the Middle Western states (of the USA)[1]

**13. The proper names of cosmic objects.**
**a.** Start these names with capital letters.

Alpha Centauri[1]
the Milky Way[1]

Mars[1]
Venus[1]

**b.** The names of some cosmic objects — our earth, for example, or the sun — have become household words through frequent and familiar use. The modern trend is to start those names with small letters. Initial capital letters, though still all right, are becoming old-fashioned.

the earth[1]
the Earth[4]
the sun[1]
the Sun[4]
the moon[1]
the Moon[4]

the solar system[1]
the Solar System[4]
the universe[1]
the Universe[4]

**14. The names of deities.**
**a.** The proper names of deities start with capital letters.

Jehovah[1]
Zeus[1]

Jesus[1]
Allah[1]

**b.** Common nouns that are used to stand for the deities of the major religions start with capital letters.

God[1]
the Almighty[1]

the Lord[1]
the Holy Spirit[1]

**c.** Used in a generalised sense, common nouns that are used to stand for deities start with small letters.

---

1 Standard formal: *use this, and you can't go wrong in formal contexts.*
2 Standard formal with consistent options: *choose one and stick to it.*
3 Standard formal with flexible options: *choose any one, any time.*
4 Old-fashioned: *still all right, but fading from modern usage.*
5 Standard informal: *fine in conversation or in personal letters.*
6 Nonstandard: *you jez'gotta be kidding.*

## Capital letters and small letters

The Roman **gods** have affinities with the Greek **gods**.[1]

**d.** Some people, out of respect for their deity, use a capital letter at the start of pronouns that refer to the deity. But there is no ground for this in normal usage. Even the King James version of the Bible starts these pronouns with small letters.

Where is **he** that is born King of the Jews? For we have seen **his** star in the east, and are come to worship **him**.[1]

**15. The names of religions, their adherents, religious festivals and adjectives derived from these words.**

**a.** Most of the words in this class start with capital letters.

| **Judaism** | **Christianity** | **Islam** |
|---|---|---|
| **Jews** | **Christians** | **Moslems** |
| **Jewish**[1] | **Christian**[1] | **Islamic**[1] |

**b.** Some words in this class have become common English words and therefore start with small letters.

**antisemitism**[1]
**protestant** work ethic[1]
**puritan** morals[1]

**c.** For the names of religions outside the mainstream, and for words derived from these names, start the words with small letters.

**animism**[1]
**animist**[1]
**pagan**[1]
**paganism**[1]

**d.** The names of religious festivals start with capital letters.

**Yom Kippur**[1]
**Christmas Day**[1]
**Ramadan**[1]

**Usage**

**16. Names associated with time and with historical events.**

**a.** The names of the days and the months start with capital letters.

Sunday[1]
January[1]

**b.** The names of the seasons and of centuries start with small letters.

summer[1]
the **twentieth century**[1]

**c.** The names of special days in the calendar start with capital letters.

the **Fourth** of **July**[1]
**Melbourne Cup Day**[1]
**New Year**[1]

**d.** The names of most other historical events and eras now start with small letters, though some people still prefer the old-fashioned capitals.

the **second world war**[1]       the **industrial revolution**[1]
the **Second World War**[4]       the **Industrial Revolution**[4]
the **middle ages**[1]            the **cold war**[1]
the **Middle Ages**[4]            the **Cold War**[4]

## C. Capital and small letters in the titles of written works, in the names of journals and in headings

We distinguish between major works (books, for example) and their component parts (chapters, for example).

**17. Titles of major written works and of their component parts, and headings.**

Under major written works, we include such works as books, long poems, reports and legislation (bills, acts and regulations). Under their component parts we include such items as chapters and sections. Under headings

---

1 Standard formal: *use this, and you can't go wrong in formal contexts.*
2 Standard formal with consistent options: *choose one and stick to it.*
3 Standard formal with flexible options: *choose any one, any time.*
4 Old-fashioned: *still all right, but fading from modern usage.*
5 Standard informal: *fine in conversation or in personal letters.*
6 Nonstandard: *you jez'gotta be kidding.*

## Capital letters and small letters

we include both newspaper and journal headlines, essay headings, and subheadings.

There are three methods now in use for writing such titles and headings. Two of the methods are modern and equally valid; the third method — method **iii.** below — is old-fashioned and fading from use.

**i.** All the letters of the title are in capital letters.

HOW TO WRITE ABOUT SCIENCE AND TECHNOLOGY FOR THE POPULAR PRESS [2]

**ii.** The first word of the title starts with an initial capital letter, and all the other words with initial small letters.

**How** to write about science and technology for the popular press.[2]
(If you opt for this method you will, of course, still need to capitalise proper nouns and the like.)

**iii.** Every major word in the title starts with an initial capital letter, and every minor word — unless it stands at the start of the title or heading — with an initial small letter.

**How** to **Write** about **Science** and **Technology** for the **Popular Press**.[4]

In method **iii.** above, the four classes of minor words that you start with small letters are —

the articles "a", "an", "the";

the prepositions (words such as "in", "under", "between");

the adverb "to" used in front of a base-form verb, as in "to Go", "to Read", "to Write";

the conjunctions (words such as "and", "but", "or", "nor").

If you cite the title of an extant major written work or, say, the title of a component chapter in the major written work, or if you cite a newspaper headline, we suggest that the sensible thing to do is to use the capitalisation and the lower casing of the original title or headline. That will automatically solve any problem you may have about whether to use initial capital or small letters. But if you are composing the title of a major

167

## Usage

written work, or of a component chapter or section, or if you are composing a heading or headline, we offer the following guidelines.

**a.** Use the method of your choice for the full formal title of the major work.

**THE REPORT ON THE CONTROL OF COASTAL AND RIVERINE FISHERIES**[2]
**The** report on the control of coastal and riverine fisheries[2]
**The Report** on the **Control** of **Coastal** and **Riverine Fisheries**[4]

**b.** Use the method of your choice for the full formal title of a component part of the major written work.

**CHAPTER 4. FISHING IN COASTAL WATERS**[2]
**Chapter** 4. **Fishing** in coastal waters[2]
**Chapter** 4. **Fishing** in **Coastal Waters**[4]

**c.** When you are citing the short or the informal title of a major written work or any component part of a major written work, use small initial letters. The use of capitals is decidedly old-fashioned.

the **report**[1]      the **chapter**[1]
the **fisheries report**[1]      the **coastal fishing chapter**[1]
the **Report**[4]      the **Chapter**[4]
the **Fisheries Report**[4]      the **Coastal Fishing Chapter**[4]

**d.** Use the method of your choice for a heading or headline.

**SOCK-KNITTING CONTEST ENDS IN A TIE**[2]
**Sock**-knitting contest ends in a tie[2]
**Sock-Knitting Contest Ends** in a **Tie**[4]

---

1 Standard formal: *use this, and you can't go wrong in formal contexts.*
2 Standard formal with consistent options: *choose one and stick to it.*
3 Standard formal with flexible options: *choose any one, any time.*
4 Old-fashioned: *still all right, but fading from modern usage.*
5 Standard informal: *fine in conversation or in personal letters.*
6 Nonstandard: *you jez'gotta be kidding.*

**18. Titles of newspapers and journals, plays and movies, and works of art.**

The current convention is that the major words in this group all have initial capital letters, the minor words have initial small letters. Another current convention — when you cite the titles — is that all the words in the titles appear in italic print or in underlined roman print.

> I read it in *The Sydney Morning Herald*.[2]   (Title of a newspaper.)
> I read it in <u>The Sydney Morning Herald</u>.[2]
> I read it in *The Bulletin*.[2]   (Title of a magazine.)
> I read it in <u>The Bulletin</u>.[2]
> I have seen *Much Ado about Nothing*.[2]   (Title of a play.)
> I have seen <u>Much Ado</u> about <u>Nothing</u>.[2]
> I enjoyed *The Great Escape*.[2]   (Title of a movie.)
> I enjoyed <u>The Great Escape</u>.[2]
> I have seen Rembrandt's *A Girl with a Broom*.[2]   (Title of a painting.)
> I have seen Rembrandt's <u>A Girl</u> with a <u>Broom</u>.[2]

For a more detailed discussion of italics and underlining, see chapter 11.

## D. Capitals and small letters in prose and poetry

**19. Capital letters in a prose passage.**

**a.** At the beginning of a prose passage, use an initial capital letter.

> One day I awoke to a loud bang.[1]

**b.** In the middle of a prose passage, use an initial capital letter after any of the following punctuation marks — if the punctuation mark indicates the end of a sentence.

> **i.** a full stop,
> **ii.** a question mark,
> **iii.** an exclamation mark.

> One day I awoke to a loud bang.  **Where** could it have come from? **What** a mystery!  **But** the mystery was soon solved.[1]

**c.** If the question mark or the exclamation mark comes within a pair of brackets or a pair of dashes, it may form part of a sentence; and then you don't follow it with a capital letter.

**Usage**

It was (how shall I put it?) a complete surprise.[2]
It was — how shall I put it? — a complete surprise.[2]
They took my book (what impudence!) **and** walked away with it.[2]
They took my book — what impudence! — **and** walked away with it.[2]

### 20. What happens after a colon?
Nothing. You continue with a lower case letter.

We will need a few things: **maps**, compasses, hiking shoes.[1]
As Oscar Wilde once said: **the** truth is rarely pure and never simple.[1]
What I want to know is this: **where** do we go from here?[1]

### 21. Capital and small letters at the beginning of quotations set off with quotation marks.

**a.** Use an initial capital letter at the beginning of a complete quotation set off with quotation marks.

Oscar Wilde wrote: "**The** truth is rarely pure and never simple."[1]
I asked them, "**Where** do we go from here?"[1]

**b.** Use an initial small letter for a fragmentary quotation, even if it is set off with quotation marks.

They called what I had done "**a** good job" and gave me another task.[1]

For a more detailed discussion of quotations and quotation marks see chapter 23.

### 22. Capital and small letters for the first word of each line of a poem.
Poets conventionally start the first word of each line with a capital letter, even if that word is not the first word of a new sentence.

**I'll** write because I'll give
**You** critics means to live;

---

1 Standard formal: *use this, and you can't go wrong in formal contexts.*
2 Standard formal with consistent options: *choose one and stick to it.*
3 Standard formal with flexible options: *choose any one, any time.*
4 Old-fashioned: *still all right, but fading from modern usage.*
5 Standard informal: *fine in conversation or in personal letters.*
6 Nonstandard: *you jez'gotta be kidding.*

> **For** should I not supply
> **The** cause, th'effect would die.[1]
>
> Robert Herrick (1591–1674)

Some poets break this convention, and you can feel free to do so too.

## E. Various other uses of capital and small letters
### 23. The pronoun "I" and the interjection "O".
These are, by convention, written with capital letters.

> Listen to what **I** have to say, **O** you people.[1]

Note, though, that the interjection "oh" comes with an initial small letter.

> Where, **oh** where, can they have gone?[1]

### 24. Personified abstract nouns.
**a.** Use initial capital letters if you use the personified abstract noun in the vocative — that is, if you use it as a form of address.

> Come heal me, **Mother Nature**.[1]

**b.** In nonvocative uses, start the abstract personified nouns with small letters. The use of initial capital letters is old-fashioned.

> Many ills are cured by **mother nature**.[1]
> Many ills are cured by **Mother Nature**.[4]

### 25. Acronyms.
Acronyms come in three types.

**a.** All the letters in the acronym are capitals — even though, when you spell the words out, some or all of the words may start with small letters.

> **GBS**[1]   (George Bernard Shaw)
> **GDP**[1]   (gross domestic product)
> **BC**[1]    (before Christ)

**b.** All the letters in the acronym are small letters.

> **ie**[1]   (*id est*)
> **eg**[1]   (*exempli gratia*)

**Usage**

| | |
|---|---|
| **am**[1] | (*ante meridiem*) |
| **pm**[1] | (*post meridiem*) |
| **scuba**[1] | (self-contained underwater breathing apparatus) |
| **radar**[1] | (radio detecting and ranging) |

**c.** The acronyms consist of a mix of capital and small letters, or all capital or all small letters.

| | |
|---|---|
| **LlB**[1] | (bachelor of laws) |
| **PhD**[1] | (doctor of philosophy) |
| | |
| **Unesco**[2] | (United Nations Educational, Scientific and Cultural |
| **UNESCO**[2] | Organisation) |
| | |
| **Aids**[2] | (acquired immune deficiency syndrome) |
| **aids**[2] | |
| **AIDS**[2] | |

There are two modern trends worth noting about the writing of acronyms.

**i.** One is the trend towards omitting the full stops between the letters.

| | |
|---|---|
| **GPO**[1] | (General Post Office) |
| **G.P.O.**[4] | |

**ii.** The other is towards using small letters where possible.

| | |
|---|---|
| **Anzac**[1] | (Australian and New Zealand Army Corps) |
| **ANZAC**[4] | |

---

1 Standard formal: *use this, and you can't go wrong in formal contexts.*
2 Standard formal with consistent options: *choose one and stick to it.*
3 Standard formal with flexible options: *choose any one, any time.*
4 Old-fashioned: *still all right, but fading from modern usage.*
5 Standard informal: *fine in conversation or in personal letters.*
6 Nonstandard: *you jez'gotta be kidding.*

# PART II
# PUNCTUATION

|     |                             | Page |
|-----|-----------------------------|------|
| 13. | Full stops                  | 175  |
| 14. | Exclamation marks           | 183  |
| 15. | Question marks              | 189  |
| 16. | Commas                      | 197  |
| 17. | Semicolons                  | 226  |
| 18. | Colons and dashes           | 236  |
| 19. | Brackets                    | 246  |
| 20. | Apostrophes                 | 250  |
| 21. | Hyphens                     | 265  |
| 22. | Slashes                     | 281  |
| 23. | Quotation marks             | 284  |
| 24. | Ellipses                    | 301  |
| 25. | Asterisks and allied symbols| 310  |

# CHAPTER 13
# Full stops

## Overview

The full stop (you can also call it "the stop" or "the period", if you like) is a dot at line level (.). It is one of the three terminal punctuation marks, the other two being the question mark (?) and the exclamation mark (!). Its main function is to mark the end of an indicative sentence — that is, one that makes either a positive or a negative statement.

| | |
|---|---|
| POSITIVE: | It has been a good day.[1] |
| NEGATIVE: | It has not been such a good week.[1] |

To end a sentence that is an exclamation or a question you use, respectively, an exclamation mark or a question mark.

| | |
|---|---|
| EXCLAMATION: | What a great painting this is![1] |
| QUESTION: | Where are you going?[1] |

You will find the discussion of these two punctuation marks in chapters 14 and 15.

Incomplete sentences can end in either of two other punctuation marks as well: an ellipsis or a dash.

To be or not to be . . .[2]
To be or not to be —[2]

For a discussion of the ellipsis and the dash, see chapters 24 and 18.

In this chapter, though, we shall be dealing with the full stops, and the discussion comes in two sections.

175

**Punctuation**

### A. Full stops as terminal punctuation marks of indicative and other sentences

Here we classify some of the sentences that come under this category and discuss the use of full stops and of some optional terminal punctuation marks.

### B. Other uses of full stops

In this section we have acronyms ("V.C.R." or "VCR" for "video cassette recorder"); abbreviations ("ph." or "ph" for "telephone"); and contractions ("Mr." or "Mr" for "Mister"). We also discuss a fascinating question: can you ever end a sentence with two full stops?

There are other uses of full stops as well — with decimal numbers, for example, or with dates when expressed as digits. We deal with these uses in the chapter on numbers — chapter 7.

### A. Full stops as terminal punctuation marks of indicative and other sentences

1. Full stops and indicative sentences.

**a.** Use a full stop to end an indicative positive or negative sentence.

**They are coming soon.**[1]   (Indicative positive)

**They will not be coming home.**[1]   (Indicative negative)

**b.** Note that an indicative sentence can consist of as little as a single word.

"Are you hungry?"
**"Yes."**[1]

**c.** You can end what is, technically speaking, an indicative sentence with a question mark or an exclamation mark. The former then has the function of a question; the latter, of an exclamation.

---

1 Standard formal: *use this, and you can't go wrong in formal contexts.*
2 Standard formal with consistent options: *choose one and stick to it.*
3 Standard formal with flexible options: *choose any one, any time.*
4 Old-fashioned: *still all right, but fading from modern usage.*
5 Standard informal: *fine in conversation or in personal letters.*
6 Nonstandard: *you jez'gotta be kidding.*

# Full stops

**You think** I believe you?[1]
(Compare this with the question: "**Do you think** I believe you?")
**I was right!**[1]
(Compare this with the exclamation: "How right I was!")

## 2. Full stops and reported questions.

Reported questions are statements about questions. Since they are statements, they end in full stops.

I asked them **what they were doing.**[1]

I inquired **what the matter was.**[1]

Compare these reported questions with their direct question counterparts.

I asked them, "**What are you doing?**"[1]

I inquired, "**What is the matter?**"[1]

For a discussion of direct and reported questions see chapter 10.

## 3. When to omit the full stops at the end of indicative sentences.

**a.** A sentence that constitutes the title of a book, film or play, when you write it on its own — say, on the title page of a book.

**Charley Is My Darling**[1]

If you write it at the end of a sentence it does, of course, get its own terminal punctuation mark.

I've read Joyce Cary's *Charley Is My Darling*.[1]

The same goes also for the title of a chapter, a poem, a painting and other artistic works.

**b.** A sentence that constitutes a heading or headline, when you write it on its own — say, a headline in a newspaper.

**Lack of concrete holds up bridge**[1]

In a sentence it does get its own terminal punctuation mark.

I saw this funny headline: "**Lack of concrete holds up bridge.**"

**Punctuation**

c. A sentence in quotation marks, when the sentence in which the quotation occurs continues.

"I would like to borrow this," he said.[1]
"You can take it," she told him.[1]

**4. Full stops as substitutes for question marks.**
"Could you", "Would you please", and sentences beginning with similar constructions are technically question sentences. They can therefore legitimately end in question marks. But because they are really requests, rather than genuine inquiries, you can opt to end such sentences with full stops or — if the requests are peremptory — with exclamation marks.

Would honourable members please resume their seats?[3]
Would honourable members please resume their seats.[3]
Would honourable members please resume their seats![3]

Could you please stop that noise?[3]
Could you please stop that noise.[3]
Could you please stop that noise![3]

**5. Full stops as substitutes for exclamation marks.**
A sentence in the imperative mood — the mode of command — often ends in an exclamation mark. By substituting a full stop for the exclamation mark, and possibly also by adding "please", you can take the sharpness out of the command.

Hold this![3]
Hold this.[3]
Don't bother me now![3]
Don't bother me now.[3]
Please don't bother me now.[3]

---

1 Standard formal: *use this, and you can't go wrong in formal contexts.*
2 Standard formal with consistent options: *choose one and stick to it.*
3 Standard formal with flexible options: *choose any one, any time.*
4 Old-fashioned: *still all right, but fading from modern usage.*
5 Standard informal: *fine in conversation or in personal letters.*
6 Nonstandard: *you jez'gotta be kidding.*

# Full stops

If the command consists of one word — or of "Don't" and one word — the exclamation mark is standard formal.

**Help!**[1]

**Don't move!**[1]

**6. Artificial full stops for the sake of dramatic effect.**
Artificial, how? The answer is in the middle of what is normally a single sentence. This was a favourite of writers, especially American writers, of the "tough school" in the middle decades of the twentieth century. Today, advertisers still fancy this device.

**She knocked on the door. Hard.**[5]
**She knocked on the door — hard.**[1]
**Our product is tested. And tested over again.**[5]
**Our product is tested, and tested over again.**[1]

## B. Other uses of full stops

**7. Full stops and acronyms conventionally pronounced as words.**
**a.** The evolution of some of these acronyms has been from complexity to simplicity. Take, for example, the acronym for the North Atlantic Treaty Organisation.

It started off as "**N.A.T.O.**"[4]
It soon became "**NATO**".[4]
Nowadays you can often come across it as "**Nato**".[1]

The same has happened with the United Nations Educational, Scientific and Cultural Organisation, and with the Queensland and Northern Territory Aerial Service.

**U.N.E.S.C.O.**[4]   **Q.A.N.T.A.S.**[4]
**UNESCO**[4]        **QANTAS**[4]
**Unesco**[1]        **Qantas**[1]

**b.** Some acronyms have reached a further stage of evolution. Even the first letter of the acronym is a lower case letter — except, of course, if it comes at the beginning of a sentence.

**Punctuation**

    **radar**[1]        (radio detection and ranging)
    **scuba**[1]        (self-contained underwater breathing apparatus)
    **quango**[1]     (quasi-autonomous nongovernmental organisation)
    **eftpos**[1]      (electronic funds transfer at point of sale)

**8. Full stops and acronyms not pronounced as words.**
These are of three types.
**a.** Fully capitalised acronyms.

    **UK**[1]         (United Kingdom)
    **U.K.**[4]
    **ACT**[1]        (Australian Capital Territory)
    **A.C.T.**[4]
    **IMF**[1]        (International Monetary Fund)
    **I.M.F.**[4]

When you are writing the initial letters of a person's name, the same principle holds.

    **GBS**[1]        (George Bernard Shaw)
    **G.B.S.**[4]

When you spell the person's surname out, there are two equally valid modern options.

    **G.B. Shaw**[2]
    **G B Shaw**[2]

**b.** Fully lower cased acronyms.

    **am**[1]         (*ante meridiem* — Latin for "before noon")
    **a.m.**[4]
    **ie**[1]          (*id est* — Latin for "that is")
    **i.e.**[4]

---

1 Standard formal: *use this, and you can't go wrong in formal contexts.*
2 Standard formal with consistent options: *choose one and stick to it.*
3 Standard formal with flexible options: *choose any one, any time.*
4 Old-fashioned: *still all right, but fading from modern usage.*
5 Standard informal: *fine in conversation or in personal letters.*
6 Nonstandard: *you jez'gotta be kidding.*

# Full stops

c. Partly capitalised acronyms.

**PhD**[1]     (doctor of philosophy)
**Ph.D.**[4]
**MSc**[1]     (master of science)
**M.Sc.**[4]

## 9. Full stops and contractions.

A contraction is a shortened form of a word in which the first and last letters of the contraction are the same as the first and last letters of the full word. In old-fashioned usage a contraction ended with a full stop; in modern usage you omit the full stop.

Park St[1]
Park St.[4]
**Mr** Jones[1]
**Mr.** Jones[4]
St George[1]
St. George[4]

## 10. Full stops and abbreviations.

An abbreviation is a shortened form of a word in which the final letter of the shortened form is not the same as the final letter of the full word. In old-fashioned usage there was always a full stop at the end of the abbreviation; in modern usage you omit the full stop.

**cm**[1]     (centimetre)
**cm.**[4]
**Prof** Brown[1]     (Professor Brown)
**Prof.** Brown[4]

## 11. Double full stops.

**a.** If a contraction or an abbreviation comes at the end of a sentence — even if you choose to terminate all your abbreviations with full stops — the sentence terminates with only one full stop.

He is now working for the Automatic Car Co.[1]
He is now working for the Automatic Car Co..[6]

**Punctuation**

**b.** There are two, and only two, cases in which you can choose to terminate a sentence with two full stops. Both cases are old-fashioned, and in both cases there is some other punctuation mark that separates the two full stops. The cases are as follows.

**i.** When the first full stop marks an abbreviation or a contraction, and the full stop comes inside a pair of brackets at the end of a sentence.

He is now working for the A.C.C. (the Automatic Car Co.).[4]
He is now working for the ACC (the Automatic Car Co).[1]

**ii.** When the first full stop marks an abbreviation or a contraction, and the full stop forms part of a fragmentary quotation enclosed by a pair of quotation marks at the end of a sentence.

He said he was working for some outfit called "the A.C.C. — the Automatic Car Co.".[4]
He said he was working for some outfit called "the ACC — the Automatic Car Co".[1]

A full quotation — even if you opt to terminate the abbreviation with a full stop — ends with one full stop. The use of two full stops is nonstandard.

He said, "I am working for the Automatic Car Co."[1]
He said, "I am working for the Automatic Car Co.".[6]

For an extended discussion of where to place terminal punctuation marks in full and in fragmentary quotations, see chapter 23.

---

1 Standard formal: *use this, and you can't go wrong in formal contexts.*
2 Standard formal with consistent options: *choose one and stick to it.*
3 Standard formal with flexible options: *choose any one, any time.*
4 Old-fashioned: *still all right, but fading from modern usage.*
5 Standard informal: *fine in conversation or in personal letters.*
6 Nonstandard: *you jez'gotta be kidding.*

# CHAPTER 14
# Exclamation marks

## Overview
The exclamation mark is a vertical line with a dot below it (!). There are two things to bear in mind about the exclamation mark. One is that its main use is to emphasise the word or words that go before it. For that reason, it's best not to overuse it, or it loses its impact. The other thing is that in most, though not in all, cases there is a handy alternative to the exclamation mark.

We deal with exclamation marks in the following sections.

### A. Exclamation marks after interjections or exclamations
Interjections are specialised words such as "ouch" and "wow". Exclamations are nonspecialised words used in an exclamatory way. A case in point is the word "marvellous", used when you are overwhelmed by a strong emotion.

### B. Exclamation marks after various kinds of sentences
You can feel free to use an exclamation mark after virtually any kind of sentence — a command, a statement, even certain kinds of questions — for the sake of emphasis.

### C. Exclamation marks and capitalisation
What happens when you put an exclamation mark at the end of a sentence, and what happens when you put one in the middle of a sentence?

### D. Multiple exclamation marks and other curiosities
How weird can you get?!

### A. Exclamation marks after interjections or exclamations
Let's first look at the difference between interjections and exclamations.

## Punctuation

Interjections are members of the class of words that express some emotion or feeling. Most usually, they are a verbal way of letting off steam. "Alas" is an interjection that gives vent to a feeling of sorrow; "bah" is an interjection that expresses contempt or disgust. Typically, interjections are single words and, also typically, they have no other grammatical function.

By way of contrast, exclamations are words or phrases that function as ordinary nouns, verbs or the like, but that you may also use in an exclamatory way. "Nitwit" is an ordinary noun. "My foot" is an ordinary phrase. But give them exclamation marks, and they become exclamations.

We can deal with interjections and exclamations together because, for the purposes of punctuation, they function in the same way.

**1. Exclamation marks after interjections or exclamations.**
**a.** When you use an interjection on its own, follow it with an exclamation mark.

**Ouch!**[1]
**Wow!**[1]

**b.** When you use an exclamation on its own, follow it with an exclamation mark:

**i.** whether it is an exclamatory word —

**Brilliant!**[1]
**Never!**[1]

**ii.** or an exclamatory phrase —

**What a shame!**[1]
**My word!**[1]

---

1 Standard formal: *use this, and you can't go wrong in formal contexts.*
2 Standard formal with consistent options: *choose one and stick to it.*
3 Standard formal with flexible options: *choose any one, any time.*
4 Old-fashioned: *still all right, but fading from modern usage.*
5 Standard informal: *fine in conversation or in personal letters.*
6 Nonstandard: *you jez' gotta be kidding.*

# Exclamation marks

**c.** Technically, greeting words (such as "hello") are interjections. Normally, you wouldn't follow them with exclamations marks — but you may, if you want to give them particular emphasis.

    **Goodbye!**[3]
    **Goodbye.**[3]

**2. Exclamation marks after interjections or exclamations with associated sentences.**

When you use an interjection or an exclamation with an associated sentence, there are two options.

    **Hey!** That hurts.[3]
    **Hey,** that hurts![3]
    **How delightful!** They've arrived.[3]
    **How delightful** — they've arrived![3]

## B. Exclamation marks after various kinds of sentences

Sentences don't have to have interjections or exclamations to earn exclamation marks. Other sentences can take them just as well.

**3. Imperative sentences.**

These are sentences that express commands. "Go home" and "Don't come near me" are examples of imperative sentences.

**a.** If the imperative sentence consists of a single word ("Sit" or "Stand"), or if it consists of a single word preceded by "don't" ("Don't complain" or "Don't cry"), punctuate it with an exclamation mark.

    **Help!**[1]
    **Don't touch!**[1]

**b.** If the imperative forms part of a longer sentence, choose between an exclamation mark and a full stop. The exclamation mark makes the command more urgent.

    **Help** me, please!ureka[3]
    **Help** me, please.[3]
    **Don't touch** that switch![3]
    **Don't touch** that switch.[3]

# Punctuation

### 4. Subjunctive sentences.

Subjunctive sentences are sentences whose structure indicates some sort of state of unreality — wishful thinking, for instance, or hope. You can end subjunctive sentences either with exclamation marks or with full stops. The exclamation mark gives the subjunctive sentence greater emphasis than does the full stop.

**Heaven help us!**[3]
**Heaven help us.**[3]
**If only I hadn't forgotten!**[3]
**If only I hadn't forgotten.**[3]

### 5. Indicative sentences.

These are sentences whose structure suggests that they are about the realm of facts (as distinct from commands or wishful thinking). Indicative sentences come in four subtypes, any of which you may end in an exclamation mark or in some other punctuation mark noted below.

**a.** A positive indicative sentence is one that states that the action (or state) expressed by the verb exists.

**They have definitely finished the job!**[3]
**They have definitely finished the job.**[3]

**b.** A negative indicative sentence is one that denies that the action (or state) expressed by the verb exists.

**They aren't right!**[3]
**They aren't right.**[3]

**c.** An interrogative sentence is one that poses the question of whether the action (or state) expressed by the verb exists. Normally such a sentence ends with a question mark. But an interrogative sentence (especially one that starts with "would you" or "could you") may also be a veiled request or command. If that is the case, you may opt to use a full stop, a question

---

1 Standard formal: *use this, and you can't go wrong in formal contexts.*
2 Standard formal with consistent options: *choose one and stick to it.*
3 Standard formal with flexible options: *choose any one, any time.*
4 Old-fashioned: *still all right, but fading from modern usage.*
5 Standard informal: *fine in conversation or in personal letters.*
6 Nonstandard: *you jez'gotta be kidding.*

mark or an exclamation mark. Each of these terminal punctuation marks gives the sentence a different flavour.

**Would you mind** closing that window.[3]   (A somewhat grumpy request.)
**Would you mind** closing that window?[3]   (A polite request.)
**Would you mind** closing that window![3]   (A firm command.)

**d.** A negative-interrogative sentence is one that combines the forms and functions of a negative and of an interrogative sentence.

**Aren't they ready yet?**[3]
**Aren't they ready yet!**[3]

The question mark makes the sentence a genuine inquiry. The exclamation mark expresses your exasperation. It also suggests that you don't really expect an answer, because you know darn well that they aren't ready yet.

## C. Exclamation marks and capitalisation
When do you — and when don't you — follow a question mark with a capital letter?

**6. The exclamation mark with accompanying text enclosed within a pair of brackets or a pair of dashes.**
If the sentence runs on after the brackets, don't use a capital letter.

I want to see you (**if you don't mind!**) early next week.[3]
I want to see you — **if you don't mind!** — early next week.[3]

**7. The exclamation mark with accompanying text enclosed within quotation marks.**
If the sentence runs on after the quotation, don't use a capital letter.

"**What a marvellous sight!**" she cried.[1]

**8. The sentence doesn't run on after the exclamation mark.**
Use a capital letter.

**Please keep quiet!**  We are trying to read.[1]

## Punctuation

### D. Multiple exclamation marks and other curiosities
We examine one standard formal use and a few informal ones.

**9. The exclamation mark on its own enclosed within a pair of brackets.**
Use this device to draw attention to the fact that the text that precedes the exclamation mark is astounding.

> According to one estimate, the number of possible chess positions is $10^{120}$, and it would take a modern supercomputer about **a billion centuries** (!) to go through them all.[1] (*New Scientist*, 10 September 1992.)

**10. Multiple exclamation marks.**
These multiply the effect of single exclamation marks. Use them — but use them sparingly — to get an effect of special drama.

> **This is my last warning!!**[5]
> **This is my last warning!**[1]
> **Oh, how I love you!!!**[5]
> **Oh, how I love you!**[1]

**11. Exclamation marks with question marks.**
Depending on the context, such combinations can express a variety of emotions such as indignation or puzzlement.

> **What — you're not ready yet!?**[5]
> **What — you're not ready yet?**[1]
> **Who on earth could have done this!?!**[5]
> **Who on earth could have done this?**[1]

---

1 Standard formal: *use this, and you can't go wrong in formal contexts.*
2 Standard formal with consistent options: *choose one and stick to it.*
3 Standard formal with flexible options: *choose any one, any time.*
4 Old-fashioned: *still all right, but fading from modern usage.*
5 Standard informal: *fine in conversation or in personal letters.*
6 Nonstandard: *you jez'gotta be kidding.*

# CHAPTER 15
# Question marks

## Overview

The question mark looks like a hook floating above a dot (?). It's no secret that you use question marks after questions. But that's not the end of the story. As we shall see, you can also use question marks after what are (formally speaking) statements, and you can put full stops or exclamation marks after what are (formally, again) questions.

Let's start, though, by looking at what it is that makes a question a question. The answer, for most purposes, is the mood of the verb. Grammarians use the word "mood" to describe the form that a verb (and perhaps some accompanying words) can take in order to indicate its function in a sentence. The moods that come into this chapter are all indicative, which connotes a matter of fact ("You are going home") — in distinction, say, to the imperative, which connotes a command ("Go home").

    **i.** The positive indicative indicates that the state or action expressed by the verb exists ("They like cheese").
    **ii.** The negative indicative denies that the state or action expressed by the verb exists ("They don't like cheese").
    (We can also refer to **i.** and **ii.** above as "statements".)
    **iii.** The interrogative indicative questions whether the state or action expressed by the verb exists ("Do they like cheese?").
    **iv.** The negative-interrogative indicative combines the functions of **ii.** and **iii.** above ("Don't they like cheese?").
    (We can also refer to **iii.** and **iv.** above as "questions".)

Next we look at what it is that characterises questions. The sign that a sentence is in the interrogative (or in the negative-interrogative) is the presence in the sentence of a certain kind of finite verb in front of the

## Punctuation

subject (that is, in front of the doer, or agent) of the verb. We give twenty-four example sentences below, with the finite verbs printed in bold letters.

| STATEMENTS | QUESTIONS |
|---|---|
| I am well. | **Am** I well?[1] |
| She is happy. | **Is** she happy?[1] |
| They are coming. | **Are** they coming?[1] |
| He was ready. | **Was** he ready?[1] |
| They were there. | **Were** they there?[1] |
| We have done it. | **Have** we done it?[1] |
| He has eaten. | **Has** he eaten?[1] |
| She had finished. | **Had** she finished?[1] |
| I can tell. | **Can** I tell?[1] |
| They could work. | **Could** they work?[1] |
| We may go. | **May** we go?[1] |
| They might come. | **Might** they come?[1] |
| We shall overcome. | **Shall** we overcome?[1] |
| They will dine. | **Will** they dine?[1] |
| We should do it. | **Should** we do it?[1] |
| They would regret it. | **Would** they regret it?[1] |
| We must study. | **Must** we study?[1] |
| We ought to be there. | **Ought** we to be there?[1] |
| We need to hurry. | **Need** we hurry?[1] |
| They dare do it. | **Dare** they do it?[1] |
| You used to live there. | **Used** you to live there?[1] |
| They know the answer. | **Do** they know the answer?[1] |
| She leaves tomorrow. | **Does** she leave tomorrow?[1] |
| He cooked my goose. | **Did** he cook my goose?[1] |

1  Standard formal: *use this, and you can't go wrong in formal contexts.*
2  Standard formal with consistent options: *choose one and stick to it.*
3  Standard formal with flexible options: *choose any one, any time.*
4  Old-fashioned: *still all right, but fading from modern usage.*
5  Standard informal: *fine in conversation or in personal letters.*
6  Nonstandard: *you jez'gotta be kidding.*

# Question marks

Note that each question sentence in the above examples starts with a different finite verb ("Am", "Is", "Are", etc). The twenty-four finite verbs in these twenty-four examples are the only finite verbs that can stand before a subject in modern English. That makes these twenty-four finite verbs unusual, and it is for this reason that grammarians have dubbed them the "anomalous finite verbs" (or "anomalous finites"). The word "anomalous" means unusual or abnormal.

Our discussion comes in three sections.

## A. Question marks and single questions
These are cases in which you have one question to a sentence.

## B. Question marks and multiple questions
These are cases in which questions come in pairs or groups within a single sentence or in separate sentences.

## C. A statement and a question in the same sentence
How do you punctuate a sentence that contains both a statement and a question? The answers come in this section.

## A. Question marks and single questions
These are the relatively straightforward cases. You ask a question and end the sentence with a question mark: "How are you?" There are other cases, but you will find these familiar too.

### 1. Questions with interrogative verbs.
In each sentence there is an anomalous finite before the subject, and the sentence ends with a question mark.

**a.** Sentences starting with anomalous finites.

**Did** they finish the job?[1]
**Could** you not have done it?[1]
**May** I see you again?[1]

**b.** Sentences starting with question words followed by anomalous finites.

**Where have** they gone?[1]
**Why should** we not do it?[1]
**When did** they arrive?[1]

**Punctuation**

**2. Questions preceded by "who", "what" or "which".**
**a.** In some contexts there are no anomalous finites before the subjects, but you use question marks anyway.

**Who** thinks it is true?[1]

**What** wants my attention?[1]

**Which** of you volunteers to be first?[1]

**b.** In other contexts you use "who", "what" or "which" with anomalous finites before the subjects. Again you need question marks.

**Who do** you think you are?[1]

**What do** they need?[1]

**Which** book **did** she want?[1]

**3. Question marks after single words.**
This use of question marks occurs, typically, in dialogue.

    JACK:    I've heard an interesting piece of news.
    JILL:    **Yes?**[1]
    JACK:    It's about your friends.
    JILL:    **Really?**[1]
    JACK:    Somebody saw them last night.
    JILL:    **Who?**[1]

And so on with the dialogue. Notice that you use question marks after words that may or may not be question words in themselves, in order to prompt the talker or to express surprise or elicit more information.

**4. Questions that are really requests or commands.**
We often express a request or a command using an interrogative verb. Because of the mood of the verb, you may end the sentence with a question mark. But because the sentence is really intended as a request or

---

1 Standard formal: *use this, and you can't go wrong in formal contexts.*
2 Standard formal with consistent options: *choose one and stick to it.*
3 Standard formal with flexible options: *choose any one, any time.*
4 Old-fashioned: *still all right, but fading from modern usage.*
5 Standard informal: *fine in conversation or, in personal letters.*
6 Nonstandard: *you jez'gotta be kidding.*

a command, it also makes sense to end it with a full stop or an excla- mation mark. This gives you three options. The one you choose will depend on the nuance that you want your request or command to have. The question mark is the request or command at its most polite; the exclamation mark, at its most peremptory; the full stop, somewhere in between.

> **Would you mind closing that window?**[3]
> **Would you mind closing that window.**[3]
> **Would you mind closing that window!**[3]
> **Could you please stop making that noise?**[3]
> **Could you please stop making that noise.**[3]
> **Could you please stop making that noise!**[3]

### 5. Statement sentences that are really questions.

It's quite feasible to use a verb that is not interrogative — with a rising intonation in speech, or with a question mark in writing — as one way in which to ask a question. The difference between a statement and an interrogative used as a question is one of nuance. In our first set of examples, the statement sentence suggests a challenge; the question sentence suggests a genuine inquiry.

> **You really think I did this?**[3]
> **Do you really think I did this?**[3]

In our second set, the statement sentence suggests surprise; the question sentence suggests a genuine inquiry.

> **They aren't coming after all?**[3]
> **Aren't they coming after all?**[3]

### 6. Indirect questions with "whether".

You can ask indirect questions preceded by the word "whether" (or by a question word such as "when", "why", etc) with a positive or a negative verb. In such cases you don't use question marks at all.

> I asked them **whether they were busy.**[1]
> I asked them **why they were not going.**[1]

For a fuller treatment of indirect questions, see chapter 10.

**Punctuation**

## B. Question marks and multiple questions

Suppose you have two, three or more questions to ask in a burst of curiosity. Here is how you handle the sentence structures and the punctuation.

### 7. Multiple questions with an introductory clause.
Roll all the questions up into a single sentence and start it with an introductory clause.

> **I ask the honourable minister**: has the government investigated the matter; what has it found as a result of the investigation; what is it planning to do about the matter?[3]

Separate the clauses into discrete sentences, each with its own terminal punctuation mark.

> **I ask the honourable minister the following**. Has the government investigated the matter? What has it found as a result of the investigation? What is it planning to do about the matter?[3]

Combine the above two methods.

> **I ask the honourable minister**: has the government investigated the matter? What has it found as a result of the investigation, and what is it planning to do about the matter?[3]

### 8. Multiple questions without an introductory clause.
Apply the same three methods used in point **7** above.

> **Where are you going; how are you going to get there; what will you do when you get there?**[3]
> **Where are you going? How are you going to get there? What will you do when you get there?**[3]
> **Where are you going? How are you going to get there, and what will you do when you get there?**[3]

---

1 Standard formal: *use this, and you can't go wrong in formal contexts.*
2 Standard formal with consistent options: *choose one and stick to it.*
3 Standard formal with flexible options: *choose any one, any time.*
4 Old-fashioned: *still all right, but fading from modern usage.*
5 Standard informal: *fine in conversation or in personal letters.*
6 Nonstandard: *you jez'gotta be kidding.*

## C. A statement and a question in the same sentence

This is a tricky one, because the question part of the sentence begs for a question mark; the statement part, for a full stop.

### 9. Questions with question tags.

These are questions that call for agreement from the respondent. They are also called anticipatory questions. They consist of a statement clause followed by a comma, and then the question tag followed by a question mark.

**a.** A statement with a question tag alone ends with a question mark.

> You can do it, **can't you?**[1]
>
> They don't like it, **do they?**[1]

**b.** If the statement sentence runs on, you have three choices.

> You can do it, **can't you,** if I lend you a hand?[3]
> You can do it — **can't you?** — if I lend you a hand.[3]
> You can do it (**can't you?**) if I lend you a hand.[3]

### 10. The question is first, the statement is last.

**a.** Put a question mark after the question if it is quoted; a comma, if it is not.

> "What will they do?" **I wonder.**[3]
> What will they do, **I wonder.**[3]

**b.** If the question is separated from the statement, each part gets its own sentence.

> **What will they do?** I don't really know.[1]

### 11. The statement is first, the question is last.

The sentence ends with a question mark.

> I wonder: "**What will they do?**"[3]
> I wonder — **what will they do?**[3]
> I wonder: **what will they do?**[3]

**Punctuation**

**12. The question is in the middle of a statement sentence.**
Give the question its own question mark, and separate it from the rest of the sentence with a pair of dashes or a pair of brackets.

> I'm not sure — **are you?** — whether we ought to do this.[3]
> I'm not sure (**are you?**) whether we ought to do this.[3]

---

1 Standard formal: *use this, and you can't go wrong in formal contexts.*
2 Standard formal with consistent options: *choose one and stick to it.*
3 Standard formal with flexible options: *choose any one, any time.*
4 Old-fashioned: *still all right, but fading from modern usage.*
5 Standard informal: *fine in conversation or in personal letters.*
6 Nonstandard: *you jez'gotta be kidding.*

# CHAPTER 16
# Commas

## Overview

Commas are the most prevalent and among the most useful of all the punctuation marks. They give the sentence its pace and cadence. They also give it its breath; for commas mark the places where the reader takes a short pause. Without commas we would be left either with insufferably longwinded sentences or — if we were to replace them with full stops — with intolerably staccato ones. Commas can give a sentence a special nuance. Take, for example, these two sentences.

>**Then** they swarmed across the land.[3]
>**Then,** they swarmed across the land.[3]

One sentence is as well punctuated as the other. But the first is in a more dramatic and breathless mode; the second in a more casual, story teller's mode.

Commas can also serve to determine the meaning of a sentence.

>Churchill**, said Hitler,** was a beast.[2]
>Churchill **said Hitler** was a beast.[2]

The sentences are identical in their wording: the punctuation makes them different in meaning.

The chapter comes in five sections.

### A. Commas between pairs or series of words and phrases

When you're writing about "Jane, Jean(,) and Janice" — or "Tom, Dick(,) and Harry" — do you need that second comma?

# Punctuation

## B. Sentence ancillaries and commas
Sentence ancillaries are single words or phrases that you can stick onto (even into) a sentence without affecting its basic structure or meaning. Some examples are: "Once upon a time . . .", "So . . .", "Feeling lazy . . ." and the like.

## C. Clauses and commas
Here we get into big sentence chunks — called clauses — connected with conjunctions such as "and" — "They took one look at my face(,) and they let out a howl of laughter." Question: is the bracketed comma necessary? Answer: read section C to find out.

## D. Commas in addresses and correspondence
Do you need a comma at the end of every line of an address? Do you need one after the salutation "Dear Friend"?

## E. Miscellaneous uses of commas
Everything else you ever wanted to know about commas goes into this section — from the comma after the designation of the person you are addressing ("You there, what's your name?") to the comma that you need, or maybe don't need, before or after "namely".


## A. Commas between pairs or series of words and phrases
In this section we deal with pairs ("poor . . . honest") and with series ("tall . . . dark . . . handsome") that do and that don't have "and" before the last member of the series. Everything we say below about "and" applies also to "but" or "or".

### 1. Repeated words without "and".
Put a comma between the repeated words.

> They were **very, very** happy.[1]
>
> Our motto is **service, service, service**.[1]

---

1 Standard formal: *use this, and you can't go wrong in formal contexts.*
2 Standard formal with consistent options: *choose one and stick to it.*
3 Standard formal with flexible options: *choose any one, any time.*
4 Old-fashioned: *still all right, but fading from modern usage.*
5 Standard informal: *fine in conversation or in personal letters.*
6 Nonstandard: *you jez'gotta be kidding.*

# Commas

**2. A pair of adjectives without "and".**
**a.** If the adjectives qualify the noun separately use a comma.

> They were a **happy, devoted** couple.[1]

You can tell that the adjectives "happy" and "devoted" qualify "couple" separately from the fact that you could insert the word "and" between them without incongruity.

> They were a happy **and** devoted couple.[1]

**b.** If the adjectives qualify the noun jointly don't use a comma.

> I had a **big black** labrador.[1]

You can tell that the adjectives "big" and "black" qualify "labrador" jointly from the fact that it would be incongruous to insert the word "and" between them.

> I had a big **and** black labrador.[6]

**3. A series of words without "and".**
**a.** In all normal circumstances (other than that in paragraph **c.** below), separate the members of the series with commas.

> I took along some **knives, forks, spoons**.[1]

**b.** If "etc" (or "et cetera") occurs at the end of the series, treat it as just another member of the series and separate if off with a comma.

> I took along some **knives, forks, etc**.[3]
> I took along some **knives, forks, et cetera**.[3]

If the sentence runs on after "etc" (or "et cetera"), you don't need an extra comma after "etc".

> I took along some **knives, forks, etc** in a bag.[1]

**4. A series of words with "and" before the last member of the series.**
**a.** This is the one that sparks innumerable arguments. Well, you can have it either way — just as long as you are consistent about it.

> I have visited Thailand, Indonesia **and** Singapore.[2]

## Punctuation

I have visited Thailand, Indonesia, **and** Singapore.[2]

**b.** If the last member of the series is a member that itself contains an "and" put a comma before the last member.

We toured Jamaica, Barbados, **and** Trinidad **and** Tobago.[1]

I like carrots, peas, **and** fish **and** chips.[1]

**c.** If the last member of the series is preceded by a parenthetic element enclosed by a pair of commas, omit the comma before "and".

They acted well, promptly and, **to my surprise**, effectively.[1]

Please let me introduce Kitty, John, Clare and, **last but not least**, Joe.[1]

**5. A series of phrases that doesn't have "and" before the last member of the series.**

**a.** In normal circumstances a comma is sufficient between the phrases. If you want to give the individual phrases more emphasis, though, you may choose semicolons.

They were **willing to work, eager to help, ready for anything.**[3]

They were **willing to work; eager to help; ready for anything.**[3]

**b.** If any of the phrases have internal commas, use semicolons between the phrases.

They were willing to work; eager, **or so I gather,** to help; ready for anything.[1]

**6. A series of phrases that has "and" before the last member of the series.**

**a.** If you choose to put commas (as distinct from semicolons) between the phrases, you have two options.

---

1 Standard formal: *use this, and you can't go wrong in formal contexts.*
2 Standard formal with consistent options: *choose one and stick to it.*
3 Standard formal with flexible options: *choose any one, any time.*
4 Old-fashioned: *still all right, but fading from modern usage.*
5 Standard informal: *fine in conversation or in personal letters.*
6 Nonstandard: *you jez'gotta be kidding.*

> They were willing to work, eager to help **and** ready for anything.[2]
> They were willing to work, eager to help**,** **and** ready for anything.[2]

**b.** But if the omission of the comma could result in ambiguity or a false reading-on of the sentence, keep the comma before "and".

> They were aware of the latest discoveries, the newest methods**, and** systems recently developed.[1]

We need the comma in the above example because, without it, you might read " ... the newest methods and systems ... " before doing a double-take.

**c.** If you choose to put commas (as distinct from semicolons) between the phrases, and if one or more of the phrases contain internal conjunctions (such as "and"), keep the comma before the final "and".

> They arrived at the party happy **and** excited, ready for fun **and** frolic**, and** bearing gifts.[1]

**d.** If you choose to put semicolons (as distinct from commas) between the phrases, you will need a semicolon before "and" as well.

> They were willing to work; eager to help; **and** ready for anything.[1]

**7. A mixed series of words and phrases with "and" before the last member of the series.**

As long as there is no ambiguity, or risk of a false reading-on, the use of the comma before "and" is optional.

> I went for a hike with Adam, my sister-in-law **and** the family living next door.[2]
> I went for a hike with Adam, my sister-in-law**, and** the family living next door.[2]

## B. Sentence ancillaries and commas

Under the heading of "sentence ancillaries" we include a wide range of words and phrases that you can tack onto a sentence but that you could, as far as the structure of the sentence goes, just as well leave out. Here is a sampling of typical sentence ancillaries that we can tack onto " ... they continued on their way".

## Punctuation

| SENTENCE ANCILLARIES | MAIN PART OF SENTENCE |
|---|---|
| Last week | ... they continued on their way. |
| Elated | |
| Approaching their goal | |
| To cut a long story short | |
| Laughing | |

There are two features to note about sentence ancillaries. One is that they can be of various kinds, as the above limited selection shows. The other is that they often have optional positions in a sentence — at the beginning, in the middle or at the end.

**Elated,** they continued on their way.[3]
They continued, **elated,** on their way.[3]
They continued on their way, **elated**.[3]

In this section we look at the various types of sentence ancillaries, and at various positions they can occupy in a sentence.

**8. Attached and detached adverbs.**
There are two kinds of adverbs.
**a.** An attached adverb modifies a particular word (a verb, for example) in a sentence. You don't normally separate it with a comma from the word it modifies.

We walked **quickly**.[1]

**b.** A detached adverb modifies the sentence as a whole. You can use or omit the comma at will at the beginning of a sentence, but commas are usual when the detached adverb comes in the middle or at the end of the sentence.

**Luckily,** there was little damage.[3]
**Luckily** there was little damage.[3]

---

1 Standard formal: *use this, and you can't go wrong in formal contexts.*
2 Standard formal with consistent options: *choose one and stick to it.*
3 Standard formal with flexible options: *choose any one, any time.*
4 Old-fashioned: *still all right, but fading from modern usage.*
5 Standard informal: *fine in conversation or in personal letters.*
6 Nonstandard: *you jez'gotta be kidding.*

There was, **unfortunately,** nothing I could do about it.[3]
There was **unfortunately** nothing I could do about it.[3]
**Incidentally,** you too are invited.[3]
You too, **incidentally,** are invited.[3]
You too are invited, **incidentally**.[3]
**Yes,** we saw it.[3]
We saw it, **yes.**[3]
**No,** they didn't see it.[3]
They didn't see it, **no.**[3]

Some authorities get purple in the face over sentences that start with "hopefully".

**Hopefully** the hike can continue.[3]
**Hopefully,** the hike can continue.[3]

This sentence, the authorities claim, means that the hike can continue in a hopeful mood. But, as common sense and the above discussion show, it means nothing of the sort. "Hopefully" is just another detached adverb that modifies the rest of the sentence as a whole — not just the verb phrase "can continue". The moral of this aside is this: don't let anyone brow-beat you out of using what your common sense, and grammar properly understood, tell you is all right.

### 9. Attached and detached adverb phrases.
These are phrases that do the work of adverbs: that is, they either modify the main part of the sentence as a whole or they modify a word in the main part of the sentence.
**a.** When the adverb phrase modifies a particular word in the sentence — an attached adverb phrase — you don't usually separate it with a comma.

They worked **day and night**.[1]

**b.** When the adverb phrase modifies the sentence as a whole — a detached adverb phrase — the options are as follows.

**Once upon a time** there was a magic fountain.[3]
**Once upon a time,** there was a magic fountain.[3]
There was **once upon a time** a magic fountain.[3]

**Punctuation**

There was, **once upon a time,** a magic fountain.[3]
There was a magic fountain **once upon a time**.[3]
There was a magic fountain, **once upon a time**.[3]

The positioning and the punctuation of the detached adverb phrase depends on the rhythm and the nuance that you want to give to your sentence.

Here are other examples of detached adverb phrases.

| | |
|---|---|
| early in the morning | at the age of fifteen |
| round the corner | one more time |
| to some extent | in some cases |
| on the whole | without a doubt |
| on no account | in the last resort |

Wherever they occur, you can opt between using and omitting the commas.

**Of course,** there is no reason to doubt their word.[3]
**Of course** there is no reason to doubt their word.[3]
There were, **in all,** fifty people present.[3]
There were **in all** fifty people present.[3]
They might come second last **at best**.[3]
They might come second last, **at best**.[3]

**10. Attached and detached adjectives or adjective phrases.**
**a.** Ordinarily, adjectives and adjective phrases attach to a noun without commas.

He had a **numb** feeling and reeled back.[1]
She was **happy again** and rejoined the party.[1]

---

1 Standard formal: *use this, and you can't go wrong in formal contexts.*
2 Standard formal with consistent options: *choose one and stick to it.*
3 Standard formal with flexible options: *choose any one, any time.*
4 Old-fashioned: *still all right, but fading from modern usage.*
5 Standard informal: *fine in conversation or in personal letters.*
6 Nonstandard: *you jez' gotta be kidding.*

**Commas**

b. Detached adjectives and adjective phrases work like this.

   **Numb,** he reeled back.[3]

   He reeled back, **numb**.[3]

   **Happy again,** she rejoined the party.[3]

   She rejoined the party, **happy again**.[3]

11. **"First", "second", etc; "firstly", "secondly", etc.**
Normally you separate them off with commas.

   There are two things we must do. **First,** we must complete the job. **Second,** we must report its completion.[1]

   We have finished two tasks. **Firstly,** we completed the job. **Secondly,** we reported its completion.[1]

12. **An infinitive or an infinitive phrase.**
An infinitive is the word "to" plus the base form of a verb — "be", "have", "go" and the like. An infinitive phrase is one that incorporates an infinitive. Wherever either occurs as a sentence ancillary, you separate it from the main part of the sentence with a comma or commas.

   **To summarise,** there is nothing we can do about it.[1]

   We are**, to say the least,** astonished to hear that.[1]

   They were less than truthful**, sad to say**.[1]

13. **A present participle.**
This is the form of the verb that ends in "-ing" and that can, among other things, act as a verbal adjective. There are two distinct ways in which a present participle can function as an adjective.

a. Used adjectivally, it functions much as does a descriptive adjective (such as "good", "red", "big"), and you don't separate it with a comma from the noun that it modifies.

   I read an **exciting** poem.[1]

   I saw a **roosting** bird.[1]

In these two instances, and in similarly structured ones, we could substitute descriptive adjectives — "beautiful" or "fine", for example — for the present participles.

205

## Punctuation

**b.** Used verbally, it retains something of its function as a verb as well as its function as an adjective. In this case, the separation of the present participle from the sentence with which it is associated is optional.

**Panting** they lifted the rock.[3]
**Panting,** they lifted the rock.[3]
They emerged**, blinking,** into the sunshine.[3]
They emerged **blinking** into the sunshine.[3]
They shook hands **smiling**.[3]
They shook hands**, smiling**.[3]

**14. A present participle phrase.**
This is a phrase that contains a present participle. The use of a comma or commas with such a phrase is optional.

**Realising the time** the group hurried along.[3]
**Realising the time,** the group hurried along.[3]
The group**, realising the time,** hurried along.[3]
The group **realising the time** hurried along.[3]
The group hurried along **realising the time**.[3]
The group hurried along**, realising the time**.[3]

A note on dangling participles. You will have seen, in the above set of example sentences, that the participle phrase implicitly shares the subject of the main part of the sentence. It was "the group" that realised the time as well as "hurried along". When the participle phrase doesn't have the same implicit subject as the main part of the sentence, grammarians call it a dangling participle — and they get very irate over it.

**Walking home one day,** there was a lovely sunset.[6]
**Walking home one day,** I saw a lovely sunset.[1]

---

1 Standard formal: *use this, and you can't go wrong in formal contexts.*
2 Standard formal with consistent options: *choose one and stick to it.*
3 Standard formal with flexible options: *choose any one, any time.*
4 Old-fashioned: *still all right, but fading from modern usage.*
5 Standard informal: *fine in conversation or in personal letters.*
6 Nonstandard: *you jez'gotta be kidding.*

## Commas

**15. An absolute construction.**
An absolute construction is a participle phrase (see number **14** above) that has its own subject. You need to separate it with a comma or commas from the main body of the sentence.

> **The armies having assembled,** the battle began.[1]
>
> We made camp, **night having fallen,** to rest the horses.[1]
>
> The battle came to an end, **the trumpet having sounded.**[1]

**16. A past participle.**
The past participle is the form of the verb exemplified by "seen", "known", "taken" and so forth. Like the present participle (see number **14** above), it can function as an adjective. And, like the present participle, it can carry out that function in two distinct ways.

**a.** Used adjectivally, it functions much as does a descriptive adjective (such as "good", "red", "big"), and you don't separate it from its noun with a comma.

> I heard a **recorded** message.[1]
>
> I saw a **broken** fence.[1]

Notice that, in these two instances and in many like them, we could substitute a descriptive adjective — "long", for example — for the past participles.

**b.** Used verbally, it retains something of its function as a verb as well as something of its function as an adjective. In this use, the separation of the past participle from the sentence with which it is associated is optional.

> **Undaunted** they continued on their journey.[3]
>
> **Undaunted,** they continued on their journey.[3]
>
> They proceeded, **unseen,** towards the bridge.[3]
>
> They proceeded **unseen** towards the bridge.[3]
>
> They reached the bridge **unobserved.**[3]
>
> They reached the bridge, **unobserved.**[3]

**17. A past participle phrase.**
This is a phrase that contains a past participle. The use of commas with this type of sentence ancillary is optional.

## Punctuation

**Saved by the bell,** the boxer staggered to his feet.[3]
**Saved by the bell** the boxer staggered to his feet.[3]

The fumes **released into the air** spread quickly.[3]
The fumes**, released into the air,** spread quickly.[3]

They made fast progress **helped by the wind.**[3]
They made fast progress**, helped by the wind.**[3]

To sum up: for most sentence ancillaries, you have the option of using or of omitting commas. You also have the option of positioning the ancillaries at the start, in the middle or at the end of their associated sentences. In a few cases, the choice does not exist: you have to use commas.

### C. Clauses and commas

As a preliminary to dealing with the topic of this section, we need to discuss the following concepts.

   **a.** Finite verbs.

   **b.** Clauses.

   **c.** Types of clauses —
      independent clause
      adverb clause
      relative clause
      noun clause
      coordinate clause

**a.** Finite verbs.
Verbs come in two kinds of forms: finite (or inflecting) forms, and nonfinite (or noninflecting) forms.
In their finite forms, verbs inflect — that is, they may change their forms — with a change of number (singular or plural) or of tense (present or past). Consider the verb "to be" in four of its finite forms: "is", "are", "was", "were".

1 Standard formal: *use this, and you can't go wrong in formal contexts.*
2 Standard formal with consistent options: *choose one and stick to it.*
3 Standard formal with flexible options: *choose any one, any time.*
4 Old-fashioned: *still all right, but fading from modern usage.*
5 Standard informal: *fine in conversation or in personal letters.*
6 Nonstandard: *you jez'gotta be kidding.*

My cousin **is** here.[1]
My cousins **are** here.[1]
My cousin **was** there.[1]
My cousins **were** there.[1]

You can see that "be", when it is finite, takes four different forms depending on whether we use it in the singular (with "cousin") or the plural (with "cousins"); and whether we use it in the present tense or in the past tense. We exemplified these forms with "is", "are", "was", "were". (There is a fifth finite form — "am", used in the present with "I" — which we have not exemplified.)

By way of contrast, the nonfinite forms of "to be" ("be", "being", "been") do not inflect with a change of number or tense.

My cousin is to **be** rewarded.[1]
My cousins are to **be** rewarded.[1]
My cousin was to **be** rewarded.[1]
My cousins were to **be** rewarded.[1]
My cousin is **being** watched.[1]
My cousins are **being** watched.[1]
My cousin was **being** watched.[1]
My cousins were **being** watched.[1]
My cousin has **been** in Amsterdam.[1]
My cousins have **been** in Amsterdam.[1]
My cousin had **been** in Amsterdam.[1]
My cousins had **been** in Amsterdam.[1]

Of course, the finite–nonfinite distinction obtains not only with "to be", but with all (except about half a dozen) of the tens of thousands of verbs in the English language.

**b. Clauses.**
A clause is a coherent group of words that contains a finite verb. In any given sentence, the number of clauses is, therefore, equal to the number of finite verbs.

## Punctuation

She **is** going home.[1]
(One finite verb, one clause.)

She **was** aware of / what they **were** going to be doing.[1]
(Two finite verbs, two clauses.)

I **hope** that / he **will** come / if I **ask** him to.[1]
(Three finite verbs, three clauses.)

**c. Types of clauses.**
In this preliminary survey, we confine our attention to sentences that consist of one or two clauses.

**i.** An independent clause is one that either:

constitutes the whole sentence in a single-clause sentence —

**They are here**[1], or

constitutes the clause in a multi-clause sentence to which the other clauses relate in various ways —

**They are here** / because we invited them.[1]
**I know the secret** / but I can't let it out.[1]

**ii.** An adverb clause is one that relates adverbially to the verb in the independent clause.

They came / **when nobody was looking.**[1]

"When nobody was looking" relates adverbially to "came". We can see this relationship from the fact that we could replace the adverb clause with an adverb — for example, "then".

They came **then.**[1]

There are two ways in which you can identify adverb clauses. Firstly, they always have variable positions relative to the independent clause: they can stand either before or after the independent clause —

---

1 Standard formal: *use this, and you can't go wrong in formal contexts.*
2 Standard formal with consistent options: *choose one and stick to it.*
3 Standard formal with flexible options: *choose any one, any time.*
4 Old-fashioned: *still all right, but fading from modern usage.*
5 Standard informal: *fine in conversation or in personal letters.*
6 Nonstandard: *you jez'gotta be kidding.*

They came / **when nobody was looking**.[3]
**When nobody was looking** / they came.[3]

Secondly, typically, they start with conjunctions such as —

| | | |
|---|---|---|
| when | if | because |
| after | unless | as |
| before | until | while |
| in case | lest | although |

**iii.** A relative clause (also known as an adjective clause) is one that relates adjectivally to a noun or a pronoun in the independent clause —

This is my cousin, / **who is a clever person**.[1]

You can see that "who is a clever person" relates adjectivally to "cousin", because you could replace the clause with an adjective — for example "clever".

This is my **clever** cousin.[1]

Relative clauses come in two kinds: "defining relative clauses" and "nondefining relative clauses". It's important to distinguish between them for the purposes of punctuation.

DEFINING

A defining relative clause serves to define or identify which particular noun, or what kind of noun, the clause relates to.

I admire the kind of parents / **who care for their children**.[1]

You can tell that the relative clause is defining from the fact that we need it to tell us what kind of parents we are talking about. Without the relative clause, the sentence is somehow incomplete.

I admire the kind of parents.[6]

NONDEFINING

A nondefining relative clause serves to give some additional information about an already identified noun.

211

**Punctuation**

I admire my parents, / **who cared for their children**.[1]

You can tell that the relative clause is nondefining — and hence nonessential to the sentence — from the fact that, if you left it out, the sentence would still make good sense.

I admire my parents.[1]

For a fuller discussion of relative clauses see the overview of chapter 8.

**iv.** A noun clause is one that relates as a noun to an element in the independent clause. A noun clause can do this in any one of three ways.

As the subject (or "doer") of the verb in the independent clause.

**What they wanted** / was what they got.[1]

As the object (or "target") of the verb in the independent clause.

They got / **what they wanted**.[1]

As the object of a preposition in the independent clause.

I asked them about / **what they wanted**.[1]

**v.** A coordinate clause is one that relates coordinately — that is, in parallel — to the independent clause.

They came home / **and I was there to greet them**.[1]

There are two ways to identify coordinate clauses, and to distinguish them from adverb clauses.

Firstly, unlike adverb clauses (see **b.i.** above), coordinate clauses cannot change their position relative to the independent clause.

They were ready / **but I was not**.[1]
(**But I was not** / they were ready.[6])

---

1 Standard formal: *use this, and you can't go wrong in formal contexts.*
2 Standard formal with consistent options: *choose one and stick to it.*
3 Standard formal with flexible options: *choose any one, any time.*
4 Old-fashioned: *still all right, but fading from modern usage.*
5 Standard informal: *fine in conversation or in personal letters.*
6 Nonstandard: *you jez'gotta be kidding.*

Secondly, typically, they start with conjunctions such as —

| and | but | or |
| otherwise | however | nor |
| therefore | nevertheless | for |
| yet | also | only |

Armed with these concepts and the attendant terminology, we are now ready to discuss the punctuation of clauses.

## 18. Sentences of the pattern: independent clause + conjunction + coordinate clause.

**a.** If each clause has a stated subject and a finite verb, the comma between them is optional. How you punctuate the sentence will depend on such factors as the length of the clauses or whether you want the reader to dwell on each clause separately.

> They did their work, **but we didn't.**[3]
> They did their work **but we didn't.**[3]
>
> I went for a long walk from my home to the neighbouring village, **but I didn't feel the least bit tired.**[3]
> I went for a long walk from my home to the neighbouring village **but I didn't feel the least bit tired.**[3]

As a further option, and if you really want the reader to dwell on each clause, you can put a semicolon between the clauses.

> I went for a long walk from my home to the neighbouring village; **but I didn't feel the least bit tired.**[3]

For a fuller discussion of semicolons see chapter 17.

**b.** If the coordinate clause has an implicit (but unstated) subject, there is no comma between the clauses.

> They came into the room **and searched it thoroughly.**[1]
> They did their best **but failed to reach their goal.**[1]

**c.** If the coordinate clause has an implicit (but unstated) finite verb, you have two punctuation options.

## Punctuation

> She flew to Honolulu; **and he, to Tokyo.**[3]
> She flew to Honolulu, **and he to Tokyo.**[3]

**d.** If either or both of the clauses could have internal commas, you have three punctuation options.

> They have, **to the best of my knowledge,** not arrived; but, **God willing,** they will arrive shortly.[3]
> They have **to the best of my knowledge** not arrived, but **God willing** they will arrive shortly.[3]
> They have **to the best of my knowledge** not arrived but, **God willing,** they will arrive shortly.[3]

**19.** Sentences of the pattern: independent clause (no conjunction) + coordinate clause.

**a.** If each clause has a stated subject and a stated finite verb, you have two punctuation options.

> They came into the room; **they searched it thoroughly.**[3]
> They came into the room. **They searched it thoroughly.**[3]

**b.** If the coordinate clause has an implicit (but unstated) finite verb, you have two punctuation options.

> She flew to Honolulu; **he, to Tokyo.**[3]
> She flew to Honolulu, **he to Tokyo.**[3]

**c.** If either or both of the clauses contain elements that you could punctuate with commas, you have the following options.

> They have, **to the best of my knowledge,** not arrived; **God willing,** they will arrive shortly.[3]
> They have, **to the best of my knowledge,** not arrived; **God willing** they will arrive shortly.[3]

---

1 Standard formal: *use this, and you can't go wrong in formal contexts.*
2 Standard formal with consistent options: *choose one and stick to it.*
3 Standard formal with flexible options: *choose any one, any time.*
4 Old-fashioned: *still all right, but fading from modern usage.*
5 Standard informal: *fine in conversation or in personal letters.*
6 Nonstandard: *you jez'gotta be kidding.*

They have **to the best of my knowledge** not arrived; God willing, they will arrive shortly.[3]
They have **to the best of my knowledge** not arrived; God willing they will arrive shortly.[3]
They have**, to the best of my knowledge,** not arrived. God willing, they will arrive shortly.[3]
They have**, to the best of my knowledge,** not arrived. God willing they will arrive shortly.[3]
They have **to the best of my knowledge** not arrived. God willing, they will arrive shortly.[3]
They have **to the best of my knowledge** not arrived. God willing they will arrive shortly.[3]

There are two ways in which you can react to this feast of options: with shock at its complexity, or with joy at its flexibility. We hope you take the latter view — and enjoy the freedom it gives you in your writing!

**d.** If both clauses contain comparatives ("stronger", "faster", "higher") you have several options.

**i.** Write both clauses in full, and use a comma or omit it.

The **more** people I see at the party, the **better** I like it.[3]
The **more** people I see at the party the **better** I like it.[3]

**ii.** Assuming that your reader understands the context, you can make both clauses elliptical and omit the comma.

The **more** the **better**.[1]

## 20. Sentences consisting of an independent clause and one or more adverb clauses.

**a.** If the clauses are fairly short and simple you have two options: to separate them from each other with commas or not to separate them. The options hold good wherever you position the adverb clause — before or after the independent clause.

**Whenever I get angry,** I blush.[3]
I blush, **whenever I get angry**.[3]
**Whenever I get angry** I blush.[3]
I blush **whenever I get angry**.[3]

# Punctuation

**b.** If any of the clauses are fairly long and convoluted, it makes more sense to separate them with a comma, though it is still technically feasible not to use a comma.

> **Since there is no way of getting to the root of the problem with this machine other than to take it into the workshop and completely dismantle it,** you had better take it in straight away.[3]
>
> You had better take this machine into the workshop straight away, **since there is no way of getting to the root of the problem with it other than to take it there and completely dismantle it.**[3]
>
> **Since there is no way of getting to the root of the problem with this machine other than to take it into the workshop and completely dismantle it** you had better take it in straight away.[3]
>
> You had better take this machine into the workshop straight away **since there is no way of getting to the root of the problem with it other than to take it there and completely dismantle it.**[3]

**c.** If any of the clauses have internal commas then the comma between the clauses is indispensable. This is because the dividing comma is stronger than the internal comma, and if you retain the weaker you certainly need to retain the stronger.

> Since there is no way of getting at the root of the problem with this machine**, given the intractability of the problem,** other than to take it into the workshop and completely dismantle it, you had better take it in straight away.[1]

**d.** If the independent clause is associated with two parallel adverb clauses, and the two parallel clauses are joined with a coordinating conjunction, don't separate the two parallel clauses with a comma.

> They got home **before I did but after she did.**[1]

**e.** If the independent clause is associated with more than two parallel adverb clauses, and if there is a coordinating conjunction only between the

---

1 Standard formal: *use this, and you can't go wrong in formal contexts.*
2 Standard formal with consistent options: *choose one and stick to it.*
3 Standard formal with flexible options: *choose any one, any time.*
4 Old-fashioned: *still all right, but fading from modern usage.*
5 Standard informal: *fine in conversation or in personal letters.*
6 Nonstandard: *you jez'gotta be kidding.*

last two parallel clauses, for the sake of clarity it may be preferable to put commas between each of the parallel clauses.  However, it is still legitimate to omit the comma before the coordinating conjunction.

> I am pleased **because you have passed all the examinations, because you have received a scholarship, and because you will be going to university next year.**[3]
>
> I am pleased **because you have passed all the examinations, because you have received a scholarship and because you will be going to university next year.**[3]
>
> **Because you have passed all the examinations, because you have received a scholarship, and because you will be going to university next year** I am pleased.[3]
>
> **Because you have passed all the examinations, because you have received a scholarship and because you will be going to university next year** I am pleased.[3]

**21. Sentences consisting of an independent clause and one or more defining relative clauses.**

**a.** If you have an independent clause and one defining relative clause, don't separate them with a comma.

> I like movies **that entertain me.**[1]
>
> I have a friend **who tells jokes well.**[1]

**b.** If you have an independent clause and two parallel defining relative clauses joined with a conjunction, don't separate any of the clauses with commas.

> I would like to hear a joke **that you have not told before and that I have not heard before.**[1]
>
> I know an actress **who played Ophelia and who went on to play Hamlet's mother.**[1]

**c.** With a longer series of parallel defining relative clauses — the last two linked by a conjunction — you have two options.

> I'm looking for a book **that is interesting, that is well written, and that I haven't read before.**[2]
>
> I'm looking for a book **that is interesting, that is well written and that I haven't read before.**[2]

## Punctuation

**22. Sentences consisting of an independent clause and one or more nondefining relative clauses.**

However many relative clauses there are, separate them from the independent clause with commas and — if there are two or more nondefining relative clauses — separate them from each other with commas as well.

> I have an early edition of *Animal Farm*, **which George Orwell completed in 1944.**[1]
>
> Last night I talked to my parents, **who had just returned from overseas, and who were happy to be back home.**[1]

**23. Sentences consisting of an independent clause and one or more noun clauses.**

**a.** If the independent clause has a single noun clause, don't separate it from the independent clause with a comma.

> **Who steals my purse** steals trash.[1]  (Shakespeare)
>
> I feel **that it is getting late.**[1]
>
> I will help you with **whatever you need.**[1]

**b.** If the independent clause has two parallel noun clauses not connected with a conjunction, separate the noun clauses from each other with a comma.

> Do **what I say, not what I do.**[1]

**c.** If the independent clause has two parallel noun clauses connected with a conjunction, don't use any commas.

> I want to know **where you are going and what you will be doing.**[1]
>
> **Neither where I go nor what I do** is any of your concern.[1]

**d.** If the independent clause has more than two parallel noun clauses — the last two connected with a conjunction — you have two options.

---

1 Standard formal: *use this, and you can't go wrong in formal contexts.*
2 Standard formal with consistent options: *choose one and stick to it.*
3 Standard formal with flexible options: *choose any one, any time.*
4 Old-fashioned: *still all right, but fading from modern usage.*
5 Standard informal: *fine in conversation or in personal letters.*
6 Nonstandard: *you jez'gotta be kidding.*

# Commas

I understand **that you have been playing chess, that you won second prize, and that you hope to get first prize next time.**[2]

I understand **that you have been playing chess, that you won second prize and that you hope to get first prize next time.**[2]

## D. Commas in addresses and correspondence
There are old-fashioned ways and there are modern ways.

### 24. Commas in an address.
**a.** If you write the elements of the address on separate lines, the commas are superfluous and old-fashioned.

Dr Pat Brown
14 Park Street
Woolloomooloo NSW 2010
Australia[1]

Dr Pat Brown,
14 Park Street,
Woolloomooloo, N.S.W., 2010,
Australia.[4]

**b.** If you write the address in linear form, use commas.

Dr Pat Brown, 14 Park Street, Woolloomooloo, NSW 2011, Australia.[1]

### 25. Commas after a salutation line ("Dear So-and-so") and after a complimentary closing line ("Yours such-and-such").
The commas after these lines are slowly dying out in modern usage, but of course you are still at liberty to use them if you wish.

**Dear Tia**
I have received your letter. I will reply to it soon.
**Yours sincerely**
Daphne[1]

**Dear Tia,**
I have received your letter. I will reply to it soon.
**Yours sincerely,**
Daphne[4]

**Punctuation**

### E. Miscellaneous uses of commas

In this section we deal with assorted uses (or omissions) of the comma.

**26. Nouns or noun phrases in apposition.**
We introduce the concept of apposition with a couple of examples.

> **My neighbour, Pat Jones,** is very helpful.[1]
>
> **William Shakespeare, the great dramatist,** has thrilled audiences for centuries.[1]

In the first example, the phrases "my neighbour" and "Pat Jones" both refer to the same person. In the second example, so do "William Shakespeare" and "the great dramatist". The relationship between the two members of each set is appositional. Whether you need a comma or commas to separate nouns or noun phrases in apposition depends on whether they are defining or nondefining.

**a.** We look, first, at nondefining appositional phrases. If I use the name "Winston Churchill" or "George Frideric Handel" in a sentence, people know who it is that I am referring to. An accompanying appositional phrase would not serve to define which Churchill or which Handel was under discussion — it would merely add some incidental detail. In such instances, enclose the second member of the pair in commas or dashes or in brackets.

> **Winston Churchill, Britain's wartime leader,** received a Nobel prize in literature.[3]
>
> **Winston Churchill (Britain's wartime leader)** received a Nobel prize in literature.[3]
>
> **Winston Churchill — Britain's wartime leader —** received a Nobel prize in literature.[3]
>
> **George Frideric Handel, the German composer,** spent part of his life in England.[3]

---

1 Standard formal: *use this, and you can't go wrong in formal contexts.*
2 Standard formal with consistent options: *choose one and stick to it.*
3 Standard formal with flexible options: *choose any one, any time.*
4 Old-fashioned: *still all right, but fading from modern usage.*
5 Standard informal: *fine in conversation or in personal letters.*
6 Nonstandard: *you jez'gotta be kidding.*

George Frideric Handel (the German composer) spent part of his life in England.³

George Frideric Handel — the German composer — spent part of his life in England.³

**b.** Now, let us take defining appositional phrases. If the second appositional element does define the first, then don't use commas to separate them.

**William the Conqueror** was the first Norman king of England.¹

**Tom Jones the baker** is not to be confused with **Tom Jones the singer**.¹

There are lots of Williams and lots of Tom Joneses in the world. The appositional phrases are essential to the sense of the sentences.

## 27. The vocative.

The vocative is the form of address, a concept best understood through these examples.

**Sylvie,** you're right as usual.³
**Sylvie:** you're right as usual.³
**Sylvie** — you're right as usual.³

As these examples show, you do separate vocatives from the rest of their sentences with punctuation. The punctuation depends on the position of the vocative in the sentence.

I would like it, **Pat,** if you hurried a little.³
I would like it — **Pat** — if you hurried a little.³
Where are you going, **Pat?**¹

## 28. Honorifics.

These are titles attached to people's names. "Dr", "PhD" and the like are examples of honorifics; so are "Mr" and "Esq". If the honorific stands before a person's name, you don't separate it from the name with a comma; if it stands after a person's name, you can pick between the old-fashioned comma and the modern omission of the comma.

# Punctuation

**Dr** Scott dealt with the patient.[1]
**Mr** Guthrie Featherstone **MP QC** entered his chambers.[1]
**Mr** Guthrie Featherstone, **MP, QC,** entered his chambers.[4]

## 29. Inverted names.

These are names with the surnames before the personal names as, for example, in an encyclopaedia entry. The convention still holds that you separate the names with a comma.

**Chaplin,** Charles[1]
**Curie,** Marie[1]

## 30. City and state, or city and country.

Separation with commas is the standing convention.

She lives in **Paris, Texas,** but often visits **Paris, France.**[1]

## 31. Two phrases or clauses that share the same preposition.

Separate these phrases or clauses with commas.
**a.** First we give an example with two phrases.

She steered the car **in the direction,** and **to the vicinity,** of the intersection.[1]

The two phrases share the preposition "of".

**b.** Next, an example with two clauses.

**He not only looked,** but **he also acted,** like a person in a trance.[1]

Here the two clauses share the preposition "like".

## 32. Two prepositions sharing the same prepositional object.

Separate the two segments containing the prepositions from each other and from their object.

She flew **over,** and he sailed **under,** the Sydney Harbour Bridge.[1]
My comment was directed **at,** and intended **for,** my colleagues.[1]

---

1 Standard formal: *use this, and you can't go wrong in formal contexts.*
2 Standard formal with consistent options: *choose one and stick to it.*
3 Standard formal with flexible options: *choose any one, any time.*
4 Old-fashioned: *still all right, but fading from modern usage.*
5 Standard informal: *fine in conversation or in personal letters.*
6 Nonstandard: *you jez'gotta be kidding.*

In the first example, "over" and "under" share the same object ("the Sydney Harbour Bridge"). In the second example, "at" and "for" share the same object ("my colleagues").

## 33. Question tags.

Question tags are the question segments that you add to a sentence when you are expecting, or hoping for, a specific yes or no answer. You separate these tags off with commas.

You love me, **don't you?**[1]

They aren't coming, **are they?**[1]

## 34. Parenthetic elements.

These are asides in a sentence, put there for the purpose of comment or explanation. You can separate such elements off with commas, dashes or brackets. The choice of punctuation depends on the degree of separation that you want to achieve for the parenthetic elements. Commas give you the weakest separation; brackets, the strongest; and dashes give you an intermediate degree of separation.

They are, **to the best of my knowledge,** perfectly reliable.[3]

They are — **to the best of my knowledge** — perfectly reliable.[3]

They are **(to the best of my knowledge)** perfectly reliable.[3]

Sometimes you can even get away without any punctuation at all.

They are **to the best of my knowledge** perfectly reliable.[3]

We deal with parenthetic elements in greater detail in chapter 9.

## 35. "For example", "eg"; "that is", "ie"; "namely", "viz".

After any of these expressions you can use a comma or nothing at all. Before any of these expressions there is a variety of punctuation options — colons, commas, dashes, semicolons.

I would like to visit some exotic places: **for example,** Fiji and Bali.[3]

I would like to visit some exotic places, **for example** Fiji and Bali.[3]

I would like to visit some exotic places: **eg,** Fiji and Bali.[3]

I would like to visit some exotic places, **eg** Fiji and Bali.[3]

# Punctuation

I bought a rare book — **namely,** the folio edition of Shakespeare's works.[3]
I bought a rare book — **namely** the folio edition of Shakespeare's works.[3]
I bought a rare book: **viz,** the folio edition of Shakespeare's works.[3]
I bought a rare book — **viz** the folio edition of Shakespeare's works.[3]
I wonder whether we need extra places; **that is,** whether more people will come.[3]
I wonder whether we need extra places; **that is** whether more people will come.[3]
I wonder whether we need extra places; **ie,** whether more people will come.[3]
I wonder whether we need extra places, **ie** whether more people will come.[3]

**36. Mobile conjunctions.**
These conjunctions — joining words — constitute a small class of words in English. The main members of the class are:

| | |
|---|---|
| however | nevertheless |
| moreover | consequently |
| therefore | furthermore |
| otherwise | accordingly |

They are called "mobile" because they can stand at the beginning, in the middle or at the end of a clause or a sentence. Here are the punctuation options for one of them: the others follow the same punctuation patterns.

They are late; **however,** they are still welcome.[3]
They are late; they are, **however,** still welcome.[3]
They are late; they are still welcome, **however**.[3]
They are late. **However,** they are still welcome.[3]
They are late. They are, **however,** still welcome.[3]
They are late. They are still welcome, **however**.[3]

---

1 Standard formal: *use this, and you can't go wrong in formal contexts.*
2 Standard formal with consistent options: *choose one and stick to it.*
3 Standard formal with flexible options: *choose any one, any time.*
4 Old-fashioned: *still all right, but fading from modern usage.*
5 Standard informal: *fine in conversation or in personal letters.*
6 Nonstandard: *you jez'gotta be kidding.*

## Commas

**37. To avoid ambiguity.**
The placement or the omission of a comma often determines the meaning of a sentence. In such cases the punctuation of the sentence becomes particularly important.

> Joe**, said Iris,** was very helpful.[1]
> (Iris said it of Joe.)
> Joe **said Iris** was very helpful.[1]
> (Joe said it of Iris.)
> As **she was walking past,** her friend Bernard stopped her.[1]
> (Bernard was her friend.)
> As **she was walking past her friend,** Bernard stopped her.[1]
> (Bernard wasn't necessarily her friend.)

**38. To avoid a false reading-on of the text.**
Take the following example:

> As they were standing and looking, around came their friend.[1]

Without the comma, we might start reading the sentence: "As they were standing and looking around . . ." before doing a double take and reading it as intended.

# CHAPTER 17
# Semicolons

## Overview

The semicolon looks like a comma topped by a dot (;). As a punctuation mark it is about halfway in strength between a comma and a full stop.

There are two noteworthy features of the semicolon. One is that, while it is a useful punctuation mark, it is a relatively rare one. The other is that in nearly all cases you can substitute some other punctuation mark for the semicolon — a comma, a full stop, a question mark, an exclamation mark, or even nothing at all. This means that the semicolon is virtually — though not entirely — dispensable. Nevertheless, if you choose to use it, even when alternatives are available, it will help to give your prose elegance and variety.

There are some technical terms that we use in this chapter — finite verb, phrase, clause, coordinating conjunction. We go on, now, to explore the meaning of these terms and of some associated terminology.

**a.** Finite verb.

This is a verb that inflects — that is, changes its form — if there is a change, for example, in the grammatical number or person of the subject that goes with the verb. Practically all English finite verbs inflect in the present tense, the inflection most often being marked by the addition of the letter "s" to the verb.

work / works
play / plays
go / goes

---

1 Standard formal: *use this, and you can't go wrong in formal contexts.*
2 Standard formal with consistent options: *choose one and stick to it.*
3 Standard formal with flexible options: *choose any one, any time.*
4 Old-fashioned: *still all right, but fading from modern usage.*
5 Standard informal: *fine in conversation or in personal letters.*
6 Nonstandard: *you jez'gotta be kidding.*

# Semicolons

You can see the inflection at work in the following pairs.

I **work**.[1]
She **works**.[1]
The children **play**.[1]
The child **plays**.[1]
They **go**.[1]
He **goes**.[1]

By way of contrast, the "-ing" form of the verb is not finite. It retains the same form ("-ing") regardless of other variations in the subject.

I am **working**.[1]
She is **working**.[1]
The children are **playing**.[1]
The child is **playing**.[1]
They are **going**.[1]
He is **going**.[1]

**b.** Phrases and clauses.
Both of these are coherent groups of words. The difference between them is that phrases don't contain finite verbs; clauses do.

| PHRASES | CLAUSES |
|---|---|
| **going** home one day | I **was** going home |
| **torn** to bits | I **tear** it to bits |
| **to run** a marathon | I **run** a marathon |

Phrases don't have to contain any verbs at all. The following are all examples of phrases.

not one jot
early one morning
with your permission

Among clauses, we distinguish three kinds: independent clauses, subordinate clauses, coordinate clauses.

**i.** An independent clause can stand alone as a sentence in its own right, or it may be accompanied by another clause or clauses in the same sentence.

227

## Punctuation

**I was hungry**.[1]
**They were happy** but they didn't show it.[1]
**This is my cousin**, whom you haven't met before.[1]

**ii.** A subordinate clause relates to an independent clause as a noun, as an adverb, or as an adjective. To illustrate, we take three sentences.

They told me **what they had seen**.[1]
("What they had seen" acts as a noun clause — the object of "told".)

They celebrated **when they reached home**.[1]
("When they reached home" acts as an adverb clause modifying the verb "celebrated".)

Here is the book **that you ordered**.[1]
("That you ordered" acts as an adjective clause modifying the noun "book".)

**iii.** A coordinate clause relates to an independent clause in a coordinate (co-equal) way.

I want the answer **and I want the answer now**.[1]
("And I want the answer now" is the co-equal of the independent clause. It could stand alone, making complete sense — if it weren't for the presence of the conjunction "and" at its head.)

**c.** Coordinating conjunctions.
These are the conjunctions that, typically, stand at the beginning of coordinate clauses — "and", "but", "or", "nor", "so" and some dozens more. There is one particularly interesting group of coordinating conjunctions: the mobile conjunctions. They are so called, because (unlike other coordinating conjunctions) they can shift their position within the coordinate clause. Let's look at an example with the mobile conjunction "furthermore".

---

1 Standard formal: *use this, and you can't go wrong in formal contexts.*
2 Standard formal with consistent options: *choose one and stick to it.*
3 Standard formal with flexible options: *choose any one, any time.*
4 Old-fashioned: *still all right, but fading from modern usage.*
5 Standard informal: *fine in conversation or in personal letters.*
6 Nonstandard: *you jez'gotta be kidding.*

# Semicolons

... **furthermore,** I'll lodge a complaint.[1]
... I will, **furthermore,** lodge a complaint.[1]
... I will lodge a complaint, **furthermore.**[1]

You couldn't shift the coordinating conjunction "and" around like that!

The main members of the group of mobile conjunctions are —

| | |
|---|---|
| however | therefore |
| otherwise | nevertheless |
| moreover | consequently |
| accordingly | furthermore |

The chapter comes in three sections.

## A. Semicolons or other punctuation marks between series of phrases

We need semicolons between phrases that have internal commas: "My friend, the chocolate maker; my neighbour, the gardener; my grandson, the genius."

## B. Semicolons or other punctuation marks between independent and coordinate clauses

You don't always need semicolons in such cases; however, they can be handy.

## C. Semicolons or other punctuation marks between parallel clauses that follow an introductory clause

This introductory clause is followed by four parallel clauses: now this is one parallel clause; this is another; this is one more; this is the fourth and last.

## A. Semicolons or other punctuation marks between series of phrases

In this section we deal with two specific types of phrases — phrases that constitute the titles of books or movies or the like, and appositional phrases. We define the second of these under number **2** below. For a definition of phrases see the overview to this chapter.

**Punctuation**

**1. To separate the members of a series of titles that contain internal commas.**
For our illustrative example we take three movie titles —

> *Paris, Texas*
> *Hello, Dolly*
> *The Good, the Bad and the Ugly*

If you string the titles together into a sentence, you need semicolons between the titles.

> Some movies that I have seen recently are ***Paris, Texas***; ***Hello, Dolly***; and ***The Good, the Bad and the Ugly***.[1]

**2. To separate the members of a series of appositional pairs, when the members of the pairs are separated by commas.**
An appositional pair is one in which each member of the pair refers to the same person or thing. When you separate the members of such a pair, you can do it in either of two ways. For our example we take three people.

> Ms Goodfence, my neighbour
> Ms Goodfence (my neighbour)
>
> Professor Braines, my lecturer
> Professor Braines (my lecturer)
>
> Dr Spotts, my physician
> Dr Spotts (my physician)

When you string such pairs together, the punctuation between the pairs will depend on the punctuation of the pairs themselves.

> The people I invited to dinner were **Ms Goodfence, my neighbour; Professor Braines, my lecturer;** and **Dr Spotts, my physician**.[3]
>
> The people I invited to dinner were **Ms Goodfence (my neighbour), Professor Braines (my lecturer),** and **Dr Spotts (my physician)**.[3]

---

1 Standard formal: *use this, and you can't go wrong in formal contexts.*
2 Standard formal with consistent options: *choose one and stick to it.*
3 Standard formal with flexible options: *choose any one, any time.*
4 Old-fashioned: *still all right, but fading from modern usage.*
5 Standard informal: *fine in conversation or in personal letters.*
6 Nonstandard: *you jez'gotta be kidding.*

# Semicolons

## B. Semicolons or other punctuation marks between independent and coordinate clauses

In the overview to this chapter, we explained what clauses are. To tackle the topic of this section, we have to start by distinguishing between "full clauses" and "elliptical clauses". For the purpose of this section, a "full clause" is one that has both a stated subject (that is, the "doer" of the state or action denoted by the verb) and a stated finite verb. An "elliptical clause" is one in which the finite verb (together, perhaps, with some other words) is implicit but not stated.

To illustrate both concepts, let us take a pair of clauses.

> **i.** they entered through the door
> **ii.** we entered through the window

Both clauses are full: "they" and "we" are the subjects; "entered" and "entered" are the finite verbs. Now, you can combine the two clauses into one sentence and keep both clauses full.

> They entered through the door; we entered through the window.[1]

You can also combine the two clauses into one sentence and make the second clause elliptical.

> **They entered** through the door; **we,** through the window.[3]
> **They entered** through the door — **we,** through the window.[3]

In this section we elaborate on the punctuation options for both kinds of sentences.

### 3. To separate an independent clause from a coordinate clause, when there is a coordinating conjunction between them.

**a.** If both clauses are full, you normally need either a comma or nothing at all between them. But you may wish to use a semicolon if you want the reader to linger over each clause.

> She dropped in to see whether he was ready to go on the trip; **but** he had not even got out of bed.[3]
> She dropped in to see whether he was ready to go on the trip, **but** he had not even got out of bed.[3]
> She dropped in to see whether he was ready to go on the trip **but** he had not even got out of bed.[3]

**Punctuation**

**b.** If both clauses are full, but either or both of the clauses contain parenthetic elements — that is, asides separated off from the rest of the clauses — you have the following options.

**i.** Separate the parenthetic elements off with commas, and use a semicolon between the clauses.

They have shown up, **I'm sorry to say,** late again; **and** their reason, **or so they say,** was the traffic conditions.[3]

**ii.** Separate the parenthetic elements off with dashes or brackets, and use a comma between the clauses.

They have shown up — **I'm sorry to say** — late again, **and** their reason (**or so they say**) was the traffic conditions.[3]

For a full discussion of parenthetic elements see chapter 9.

**c.** If both clauses are full, and the second clause contains a mobile conjunction, you can choose to separate the clauses with a semicolon or with a full stop.

They had a beautiful home; **however,** it was encumbered by a big mortgage.[3]

They had a beautiful home. **However,** it was encumbered by a big mortgage.[3]

They had a beautiful home; it was, **however,** encumbered by a big mortgage.[3]

They had a beautiful home. It was encumbered by a big mortgage, **however.**[3]

**d.** If the independent clause is full, and the coordinate clause is elliptical, you have the following choices.

They are on their way to Spain; **and we, on our way to Portugal.**[3]
They are on their way to Spain, **and we on our way to Portugal.**[3]

---

1 Standard formal: *use this, and you can't go wrong in formal contexts.*
2 Standard formal with consistent options: *choose one and stick to it.*
3 Standard formal with flexible options: *choose any one, any time.*
4 Old-fashioned: *still all right, but fading from modern usage.*
5 Standard informal: *fine in conversation or in personal letters.*
6 Nonstandard: *you jez'gotta be kidding.*

They are on their way to Spain; **and we, to Portugal.**[3]
They are on their way to Spain**, and we to Portugal.**[3]

**4. To separate an independent clause from a coordinate clause of similar mood, when there is no conjunction between them.**
The moods — or clause structures — that we consider below are statements, questions, exclamations.
**a.** If each of the clauses is a statement clause, combine them into the same sentence, separated by a semicolon or a dash, with a full stop at the end; or separate them into distinct sentences, each ending with a full stop.

We waited until it was dark; **still nobody showed up.**[3]
We waited until it was dark — **still nobody showed up.**[3]
We waited until it was dark. **Still nobody showed up.**[3]

**b.** If each of the clauses is a question clause, combine them into the same sentence with a semicolon between the clauses and a question mark at the end; or separate them into distinct sentences, each ending with a question mark.

Will the minister table the document; **will she undertake to implement the policy contained in it?**[3]
Will the minister table the document? **Will she undertake to implement the policy contained in it?**[3]

**c.** If each of the clauses is an exclamation clause, combine them into one sentence with a semicolon between the clauses and an exclamation mark at the end; or separate them into distinct sentences, each ending with an exclamation mark.

What daring they display; **what panache they have!**[3]
What daring they display! **What panache they have!**[3]

## C. Semicolons or other punctuation marks between parallel clauses that follow an introductory clause

Here is an example of an introductory clause.
She said . . .
Here is an example of a series of parallel clauses.

## Punctuation

Here is an example of a series of parallel clauses.

> ... that it was getting late
> ... that they had better get started
> ... that she might start without them

String them together, and you have an introductory clause followed by parallel clauses.

> She said that it was getting late, that they had better get started, that she might start without them.

Now for the punctuation options.

**5. To separate a pair of parallel clauses from each other, when the second of the parallel clauses does not start with a coordinating conjunction.**

**a.** If the introductory clause is not separated from the parallel clauses with any punctuation, use a semicolon or a comma to separate the parallel clauses from each other.

> I expect **that it is too late to make amends; that we must bear the consequences.**[3]
>
> I expect **that it is too late to make amends, that we must bear the consequences.**[3]

**b.** If the introductory clause is separated from the parallel clauses with a colon or a dash, use a semicolon to separate the parallel clauses from each other.

> There are two ways you can help me: **you can lend me your book; you can leave me in peace to read it.**[3]

---

1 Standard formal: *use this, and you can't go wrong in formal contexts.*
2 Standard formal with consistent options: *choose one and stick to it.*
3 Standard formal with flexible options: *choose any one, any time.*
4 Old-fashioned: *still all right, but fading from modern usage.*
5 Standard informal: *fine in conversation or in personal letters.*
6 Nonstandard: *you jez'gotta be kidding.*

**6. To separate a series of parallel clauses from each other, when the last of the series starts with a coordinating conjunction.**

Do you want your reader to linger over each of the parallel clauses? If so, use semicolons. Otherwise use commas — with or without a comma between the last pair of parallel clauses.

> We are here **because we want to make our voices heard; because more people should be aware of the situation; and because we hope to effect some changes.**[3]
>
> We are here **because we want to make our voices heard, because more people should be aware of the situation, and because we hope to effect some changes.**[3]
>
> We are here **because we want to make our voices heard, because more people should be aware of the situation and because we hope to effect some changes.**[3]

**7. To separate a series of parallel clauses from each other, when the last of the series does not start with a coordinating conjunction.**

**a.** If you don't separate the introductory clause from the parallel clauses with any punctuation, use semicolons or commas to separate the parallel clauses from each other.

> I think **that they are doing a good job; that they will finish on time; that the work will be up to expectation.**[3]
>
> I think **that they are doing a good job, that they will finish on time, that the work will be up to expectation.**[3]

**b.** If you do separate the introductory clause from the parallel clauses with a colon or a dash, use semicolons to separate the parallel clauses from each other.

> The builder has done a good job: **the foundations are solid; the walls are well built; the doors and windows fit.**[3]
>
> The builder has done a good job — **the foundations are solid; the walls are well built; the doors and windows fit.**[3]

# CHAPTER 18
# Colons and dashes

## Overview

The colon is written as two dots one above the other (:). The dash is a horizontal line (–). Printers recognise varying lengths of the dash, calling these —

    **i.** the en-dash (when it is as long as the width of the letter "n")
    **ii.** the em-dash (when it is as long as the width of the letter "m")
    **iii.** the double em-dash (when it is twice as long as the width of the letter "m").

For practical purposes you can ignore these distinctions, since all dashes serve the same purpose in punctuation. We suggest that, when you write a dash by hand, or by typewriter or word processor, you simply use the hyphen symbol — that is, the short horizontal bar (-) — with a space on either side of it.

In this chapter we deal with the colon and the dash under the same head, because for every function that the colon has you can also opt to use the dash. But — and this is an important point — the dash has additional uses that the colon does not have; and we deal with these additional uses of the dash as well.

You might wonder why, if we can always use a dash for a colon, the latter is necessary at all. Well, the answer is that the colon is a sober citizen in the world of punctuation; while the dash is a more flamboyant, more

---

1  Standard formal: *use this, and you can't go wrong in formal contexts.*
2  Standard formal with consistent options: *choose one and stick to it.*
3  Standard formal with flexible options: *choose any one, any time.*
4  Old-fashioned: *still all right, but fading from modern usage.*
5  Standard informal: *fine in conversation or in personal letters.*
6  Nonstandard: *you jez'gotta be kidding.*

## Colons and dashes

dramatic substitute for the colon. For that reason, we recommend that you use the dash sparingly. If you overuse it, it simply loses its impact.

One question that frequently arises in the use of the colon (or the dash) is this: do you continue the sentence with a capital letter? The answer in most cases is no. Keep an eye out for the examples in this chapter, and you will see when we do and when we don't need capitals after colons and dashes.

We deal with the colon and the dash under the following headings.

### A. Colons or dashes between introductory clauses and lists of items
This has to do with constructions such as —

> There were three courses for dinner: soup, fish and dessert.[3]
> There were three courses for dinner — soup, fish and dessert.[3]

### B. Colons, dashes or commas between introductory clauses and quotations

> Shakespeare wrote: "Few love to hear the sins they love to act."[3]
> Shakespeare wrote — "Few love to hear the sins they love to act."[3]
> Shakespeare wrote, "Few love to hear the sins they love to act."[3]

### C. Colons or dashes between certain kinds of sentence parts
Here is one example punctuated both ways.

> Thanks, I won't have a drink: I'm not thirsty.[3]
> Thanks, I won't have a drink — I'm not thirsty.[3]

### D. Dashes as alternatives to round brackets, commas, semicolons and ellipses
Yes, the versatile dash can do the work not only of a colon but also, in some functions, of other punctuation marks.

### E. Unique uses of the dash
Here we give two functions unique to the dash.

### A. Colons or dashes between introductory clauses and lists of items
You can interpose either a colon or a dash between an introductory clause ("There are several things necessary for the journey) and the list of items that follows ("backpacks, walking boots, a map"). In some cases there are

**Punctuation**

options other than colons and dashes: it all depends on how you structure the sentences.

**1. After an independent introductory clause, with a list that follows on unindented.**
An independent clause is one that can stand alone as a complete and independent sentence ("There are several things to take on the journey"). If such a clause introduces a list, and if the list follows on from the independent introductory clause in the same sentence — and without being offset from the introductory clause by indentation — you separate the clause from the list with a colon or a dash.

> **There are several things necessary for the journey:** backpacks, walking boots, a map.[3]
> 
> **There are several things necessary for the journey** — backpacks, walking boots, a map.[3]

**2. After an incomplete introductory clause, with a list that follows on unindented.**
An incomplete introductory clause is one that cannot stand alone as an independent sentence ("The things to take on the journey are"). To separate such a clause from the list that follows, you have three options.

> **The things necessary for the journey are:** backpacks, walking boots, a map.[3]
> 
> **The things necessary for the journey are** — backpacks, walking boots, a map.[3]
> 
> **The things necessary for the journey are** backpacks, walking boots, a map.[3]

**3. After an independent introductory clause, with a list that is set off by indentation.**
There are four options here, one of them old-fashioned.

---

1 Standard formal: *use this, and you can't go wrong in formal contexts.*
2 Standard formal with consistent options: *choose one and stick to it.*
3 Standard formal with flexible options: *choose any one, any time.*
4 Old-fashioned: *still all right, but fading from modern usage.*
5 Standard informal: *fine in conversation or in personal letters.*
6 Nonstandard: *you jez'gotta be kidding.*

## Colons and dashes

> There are several things necessary for the journey:
> backpacks
> walking boots
> a map.[2]

> There are several things necessary for the journey —
> backpacks
> walking boots
> a map.[2]

> There are several things necessary for the journey
> backpacks
> walking boots
> a map.[2]

> There are several things necessary for the journey:—
> backpacks
> walking boots
> a map.[4]

Apart from the full stop at the end of the list, there is no need for punctuation at the end of each indented line. The separated indented lines do the job just as well. Some people prefer commas or semicolons at the end of each indented line, and you may use these if you wish.

**4. After an incomplete introductory clause with a list that is set off by indentation.**
There are four options in this case, the last one old-fashioned.

> The things necessary for the journey are:
> backpacks
> walking boots
> a map.[2]

> The things necessary for the journey are —
> backpacks
> walking boots
> a map.[2]

**Punctuation**

The things necessary for the journey are

backpacks
walking boots
a map.[2]

The things necessary for the journey are:—

backpacks
walking boots
a map.[4]

Here, too, as in number 3 above, there is no need for punctuation at the end of each indented line — except for the full stop at the end of the last line.

## B. Colons, dashes or commas between introductory clauses and quotations

**5. Between an introductory clause and a one-sentence quotation.**
Separate the introductory clause from the quotation with a comma, a colon or a dash. The comma is the most usual and prosaic; the colon gives the quotation a more significant or dramatic tone; the dash is flamboyant. All three, though, are equally valid.

**Disraeli said:** "Almost everything that is great has been done by youth."[3]

**Disraeli said** — "Almost everything that is great has been done by youth."[3]

**Disraeli said,** "Almost everything that is great has been done by youth."[3]

**6. Between an introductory clause and a multi-sentence quotation, where the quotation runs on from the introductory clause without indentation.**
Use either a colon or a dash. The colon is the more usual punctuation; the dash is a little exotic but still perfectly legitimate.

---

1 Standard formal: *use this, and you can't go wrong in formal contexts.*
2 Standard formal with consistent options: *choose one and stick to it.*
3 Standard formal with flexible options: *choose any one, any time.*
4 Old-fashioned: *still all right, but fading from modern usage.*
5 Standard informal: *fine in conversation or in personal letters.*
6 Nonstandard: *you jez'gotta be kidding.*

**The Bible begins with the words:** "In the beginning God created the heaven and the earth. And the earth was without form and void; and darkness was upon the face of the deep."³

**The Bible begins with the words** — "In the beginning God created the heaven and the earth. And the earth was without form and void; and darkness was upon the face of the deep."³

**7. Between an introductory clause and a quotation, where the quotation is set off from the introductory clause by indentation.**

**a.** If the introductory clause is an incomplete one — that is, if it cannot stand alone as a complete sentence ("The ambassador said") — there are four punctuation options. The last still has some currency, but it is old-fashioned.

**The ambassador said:**

It is distressing when our citizens get into difficulty with authorities in other countries.²

**The ambassador said** —

It is distressing when our citizens get into difficulty with authorities in other countries.²

**The ambassador said**

It is distressing when our citizens get into difficulty with authorities in other countries.²

**The ambassador said:**—

It is distressing when our citizens get into difficulty with authorities in other countries.⁴

**b.** If the introductory clause is an independent one — that is, if it can stand alone as a complete sentence ("The ambassador made the following statement") — all four options shown above still stand. But there is also a fifth option: a full stop at the end of the introductory clause.

**The ambassador made the following statement.**

It is distressing when our citizens get into difficulty with authorities in other countries.³

## Punctuation

**8. Between speaker identification and speech in dramatic dialogue, in a transcript, or in question-and-answer format.**
In none of these cases do you enclose the speech in quotation marks.

> **Smith:** What are you doing here?
> **Brown:** Waiting for a friend.[2]
>
> **Smith** — What are you doing here?
> **Brown** — Waiting for a friend.[2]
>
> **Question:** What are you doing here?
> **Answer:** Waiting for a friend.[2]
>
> **Question** — What are you doing here?
> **Answer** — Waiting for a friend.[2]

**9. Between an introductory clause and a statement or question.**
In such cases, there is no need either for quotation marks or for a capital letter at the start of the statement or question.

> **I ask the honourable members:** what is the government going to do about it?[3]
>
> **I ask the honourable members** — what is the government going to do about it?[3]
>
> **Malcolm Fraser was right:** life is not meant to be easy.[3]
>
> **Malcolm Fraser was right** — life is not meant to be easy.[3]

### C. Colons or dashes between certain kinds of sentence parts

**10. Between two independent clauses where the second clause illustrates, explains or contrasts with the first.**
Use a colon or a dash if you want to keep the independent clauses together in one sentence.
a. Illustration.

> Many great composers were born in the seventeenth century: two of them were Bach and Handel.[3]

---

1 Standard formal: *use this, and you can't go wrong in formal contexts.*
2 Standard formal with consistent options: *choose one and stick to it.*
3 Standard formal with flexible options: *choose any one, any time.*
4 Old-fashioned: *still all right, but fading from modern usage.*
5 Standard informal: *fine in conversation or in personal letters.*
6 Nonstandard: *you jez'gotta be kidding.*

Many great composers were born in the seventeenth century — two of them were Bach and Handel.[3]

**b. Explanation.**

There is only one way to finish the job: **we must all cooperate.**[3]
There is only one way to finish the job — **we must all cooperate.**[3]

**c. Contrast.**

Man proposes: **God disposes.**[3]
Man proposes — **God disposes.**[3]

In the last example, because the two sentence parts are short, you could also use a comma.

Man proposes, **God disposes.**[3]

**d.** You can use a colon or a dash even if the first clause is a statement and the second one a question.

**I don't like it: who would?**[3]
**I don't like it — who would?**[3]

**11. Between two sentence parts, where the first part is a word or a phrase, and the second is an independent clause.**

Warning: **do not go beyond this point.**[3]
Warning — **do not go beyond this point.**[3]
On a point of order: **we cannot hear the honourable member.**[3]
On a point of order — **we cannot hear the honourable member.**[3]

**12. Between a title and a subtitle.**
Unless you need a capital letter for the start of the subtitle anyway (say, if the subtitle starts with a person's name), it's old-fashioned to use a capital letter after the colon or dash.

Education and development: **a report for the twenty-first century.**[2]
Education and development — **a report for the twenty-first century.**[2]
Education and development: **A report for the twenty-first century.**[4]
Education and development — **A report for the twenty-first century.**[4]

**Punctuation**

## D. Dashes as alternatives to round brackets, commas, semicolons and ellipses

**13. A pair of dashes as an alternative to a pair of round brackets.**
Use a pair of dashes or a pair of round brackets to separate a parenthetic element in the middle of a sentence, if the parenthetic element is a question and the rest of the sentence is a statement, or vice versa.

They were afraid — **and who wouldn't be?** — to do it.[3]
They were afraid (**and who wouldn't be?**) to do it.[3]
Aren't you afraid — **I would be** — to go there?[3]
Aren't you afraid (**I would be**) to go there?[3]

For a fuller discussion of parenthetic elements see chapter 9.

**14. Dashes as alternatives to commas, semicolons and ellipses.**
For some, but by no means all, of the uses of these other punctuation marks you may substitute dashes.

**a.** Commas or dashes for a mid-sentence vocative. (The vocative is the form of address.)

Come here**, children,** and have some milk.[3]
Come here — **children** — and have some milk.[3]

At the beginning of a sentence, a colon is another option.

**Ladies and gentlemen:** let's begin.[3]
**Ladies and gentlemen** — let's begin.[3]
**Ladies and gentlemen,** let's begin.[3]

**b.** A semicolon, a dash or a comma between an independent and an elliptical clause. (An elliptical clause is one in which the finite verb is understood but not expressed.)

---

1 Standard formal: *use this, and you can't go wrong in formal contexts.*
2 Standard formal with consistent options: *choose one and stick to it.*
3 Standard formal with flexible options: *choose any one, any time.*
4 Old-fashioned: *still all right, but fading from modern usage.*
5 Standard informal: *fine in conversation or in personal letters.*
6 Nonstandard: *you jez'gotta be kidding.*

## Colons and dashes

They went to France; **we, to Spain.**[3]
They went to France — **we, to Spain.**[3]
They went to France, **we to Spain.**[3]

(In non-elliptical form, the second clause would read: " . . . we **went** to Spain.")

**c.** A dash or an ellipsis for a censored word.

"You **b—** fool," he swore.[3]
"You **b . . .** fool," he swore.[3]

For a fuller discussion of the options in this section see

chapter 16 on commas
chapter 17 on semicolons
chapter 24 on ellipses.

### E. Unique uses of the dash

In this section we look at two cases in which the dash is the only punctuation mark for the job.

**15. To mark a sudden turn in a sentence.**
There's this story about a dog that had two tails — **but you've probably heard that story before.**[1]

**16. To gather up a scattered subject.**
Sitting here groaning, wringing your hands, wishing you were somewhere else — **all these will do you no good.**

# CHAPTER 19
# Brackets

## Overview
Brackets come in two shapes in English texts: round ( ) and square [ ]. There are other shapes as well, but these are used in mathematical or other specialised texts and don't come within the scope of this book.

The single most important use of round brackets is to enclose asides — parenthetic elements or parentheses — in a text. But for this use there are two other options: dashes or commas. Because the use of round brackets to enclose parenthetic elements is a big topic in itself, we have devoted a whole chapter to it, chapter 9. In this chapter, therefore, we deal with all the non-parenthetic uses of round brackets, and with all the uses of square brackets.

### A. Round brackets
To separate off letters, words, dates or numbers, and other material incidental or peripheral to a text.

### B. Square brackets
To separate off material that is editorially inserted into a quoted text.

### A. Round brackets
The following are the uses of round brackets in English texts, other than for parenthetic elements — which we deal with in chapter 9.

---

1 Standard formal: *use this, and you can't go wrong in formal contexts.*
2 Standard formal with consistent options: *choose one and stick to it.*
3 Standard formal with flexible options: *choose any one, any time.*
4 Old-fashioned: *still all right, but fading from modern usage.*
5 Standard informal: *fine in conversation or in personal letters.*
6 Nonstandard: *you jez'gotta be kidding.*

# Brackets

1. **To indicate a time, a date, a place or some other element incidental to, or explanatory of, a text.**

   In the Barcelona olympics (1992), Kieren Perkins (Australia) set a world record in the 1500m swimming event.[1]

2. **To indicate the optional addition of a letter or letters to a word.**
   In this use of round brackets, the slash is an equally legitimate option.

   You may borrow my book(s) if you wish.[2]
   You may borrow my book/s if you wish.[2]

3. **To indicate a number restated in a different form.**

   I owe you the sum of fifty dollars (**$50**).[3]
   I owe you the sum of $50 (**fifty dollars**).[3]
   The distance was one mile (**1.609 kilometres**).[3]
   The distance was 1.609 kilometres (**one mile**).[3]

4. **To enclose an acronym, or the words for which an acronym stands, when both occur together.**

   Papua New Guinea (**PNG**) became independent in 1975.[3]
   PNG (**Papua New Guinea**) became independent in 1975.[3]

5. **To enclose publication details of a cited work, when these details appear in a footnote.**

   S. and J. Berenstain, *The Bears' Picnic* (**Glasgow: Collins, 1966**).[1]

6. **To enclose source details, when these details are integrated in a text.**
   An article I have read (*New Scientist*, **No. 1750, p. 20**) suggests that aspirin may have beneficial effects on plants.[1]

7. **To indicate that letters or numbers are used as list markers.**
   In this use, there are several options including the use of pairs of brackets, single brackets and full stops.

   We will visit:
   - (a) Perth
   - (b) Adelaide
   - (c) Hobart.[2]

We will visit:
- a) Perth
- b) Adelaide
- c) Hobart.[2]

We will visit:
- a. Perth
- b. Adelaide
- c. Hobart.[2]

**8. To enclose either a nickname or a real name, when both are used together.**

For the nickname you have the additional option of using either single or double quotation marks.

> Edward (**Ned**) Kelly is an Australian folk hero.[2]
> Ned (**Edward**) Kelly is an Australian folk hero.[2]
> Edward '**Ned**' Kelly is an Australian folk hero.[2]
> Ned "**Edward**" Kelly is an Australian folk hero.[2]

**9. To enclose an apposition.**

An apposition is a noun or a noun phrase that refers to the same person or thing just mentioned. It does so in the special way illustrated below.

> Patrick White (**the Australian Nobel prize winner**) is the author of *Voss*.[3]
>
> Patrick White, **the Australian Nobel prize winner**, is the author of *Voss*.[3]
>
> Patrick White — **the Australian Nobel prize winner** — is the author of *Voss*.[3]

## B. Square brackets

All the uses of square brackets have this in common: they indicate some sort of editorial intervention in a quoted text.

---

1 Standard formal: *use this, and you can't go wrong in formal contexts.*
2 Standard formal with consistent options: *choose one and stick to it.*
3 Standard formal with flexible options: *choose any one, any time.*
4 Old-fashioned: *still all right, but fading from modern usage.*
5 Standard informal: *fine in conversation or in personal letters.*
6 Nonstandard: *you jez'gotta be kidding.*

# Brackets

**10. To enclose an editorial explanation or amplification.**
If you are quoting from someone else's work and you feel the need to add some word or words of your own by way of explanation or amplification, you put your contribution within square brackets. This serves to tell the reader that the word or words so enclosed do not appear in the original text.

An article I read in a journal ends with the words: "These [**migratory birds**] will return with warmer weather."[1]

In the original article, the words enclosed in square brackets did not appear in the quoted sentence. They were understood from previous sentences.

Sir John Falstaff complains: "Men of all sorts take pride to gird [**scoff**] at me."[1]

The word "scoff" in square brackets is for the benefit of readers unfamiliar with the archaic word "gird".

**11. To enclose an editorial comment.**
G.K. Chesterton wrote: "The subtle man [**was Chesterton being sexist?**] is immeasurably easier to understand than the natural man." [1]

**12. To enclose an editorial correction.**
A listener wrote to the radio station requesting, "Please let's have less music by Johann Amadeus [**correctly, Johann Sebastian**] Bach."[1]

**13. To enclose an editorial "*sic*".**
"*Sic*" is a Latin word meaning "thus". Writers use it when they are quoting a passage that contains something unusual or erroneous, to highlight the fact that what they are quoting appeared as it was in the original passage. The word "*sic*" acts in lieu of a correction.

A listener wrote to the radio station requesting, "Please let's have less music by Johann Amadeus [*sic*] Bach".[1]

# CHAPTER 20
# Apostrophes

## Overview

The apostrophe looks like a comma floating above the line ( ' ). It has two groups of uses. The first of these is to show that one or more letters are missing in:

   **i.** two words fused into one ("is not", "isn't");
   **ii.** a single contracted word in which the first and last letters of the contraction are the same as those in the whole word ("Commonwealth", "C'wealth");
   **iii.** a single abbreviated word in which the first and last letters of the abbreviation are not the same as those in the whole word ("telephone", "phone").

You normally use words in this group in informal contexts. You would, for example, use "I'm" in conversation or in personal letters; but in a contract you would use "I am". Nevertheless, throughout this book we have given examples that incorporate fusions, contractions and abbreviations — all designated with the number 1 (standard formal), rather than 5 (standard informal). The point that we were making — and we make it again in this chapter — is that if the word needs an apostrophe at all then the proper place for the apostrophe is where we have shown it to be.

Nowadays, some contracted or abbreviated words no longer come with apostrophes. "Phone" for "telephone" is an example. We will designate such words without the apostrophe as standard formal (1), and with the

1 Standard formal: *use this, and you can't go wrong in formal contexts.*
2 Standard formal with consistent options: *choose one and stick to it.*
3 Standard formal with flexible options: *choose any one, any time.*
4 Old-fashioned: *still all right, but fading from modern usage.*
5 Standard informal: *fine in conversation or in personal letters.*
6 Nonstandard: *you jez'gotta be kidding.*

# Apostrophes

apostrophe as old-fashioned (4). These designations will reflect the punctuation status of the words rather than their usage status.

The second group of uses is to show a genitive relationship in:
  I. a common noun ("the horse's coat");
  II. a proper noun ("Leslie's coat").

Apart from exemplifying the apostrophe, these two bracketed phrases also exemplify what we mean by "common noun" and "proper noun". The former is a noun that we don't normally start with a capital letter; the latter is one (such as the name of a person or of a geographic place) that we do.

This chapter has five sections.

## A. Apostrophes in fused words
An example: "I" and "will" fused into "I'll".

## B. Apostrophes in contracted and abbreviated words
"O'er" for "over" is an example of a contracted word; "deli'" for "delicatessen", an example of an abbreviated word. Nowadays, for many such words the apostrophe is old-fashioned.

## C. Apostrophes with genitive common nouns
"A baker's dozen" and "the dogs' tails" are examples. It can be hard in some cases to decide whether you need an "s" after the apostrophe.

## D. Apostrophes with genitive proper nouns
Is it "Watts' invention" or "Watts's invention", "Kansas' population" or "Kansas's population"? It can be even harder to decide the matter with such proper nouns.

## E. Pointers on when to use and when not to use apostrophes
Here we bring together such puzzlers as the differences between

  "its" and "it's"
  "ones" and "one's"
  "a teachers' college" and "a teachers college"
  "the 1990's" and "the 1990s".

# Punctuation

## A. Apostrophes in fused words

The principle to follow is to put the apostrophe at that point in the fused word where the letter or letters are omitted. The resultant fusion with an apostrophe is standard English. That's why we designate it with the superscript 1, even though you generally use such fusion in informal contexts.

**1. Words fused with verbs.**

a. Fusions with forms of the verb "be".

**I'm** on time.[1]
(I am on time.)
**Where's** the concert?[1]
(Where is the concert?)

b. Fusions with forms of the verb "have".

**I've** done it.[1]
(I have done it.)
**Who'd** eaten it?[1]
(Who had eaten it?)

c. Fusions with the verbs "shall" or "will".

**I'll** do it.[1]
(I shall do it. I will do it.)
**What'll** we do?[1]
(What shall we do? What will we do?)

d. Fusions with the verbs "should" or "would".

**I'd** do it if I were you.[1]
(I should do it if I were you. I would do it if I were you.)

---

1 Standard formal: *use this, and you can't go wrong in formal contexts.*
2 Standard formal with consistent options: *choose one and stick to it.*
3 Standard formal with flexible options: *choose any one, any time.*
4 Old-fashioned: *still all right, but fading from modern usage.*
5 Standard informal: *fine in conversation or in personal letters.*
6 Nonstandard: *you jez'gotta be kidding.*

**They'd** never have done it.[1]
(They would never have done it.)

2. **Verbs fused with "not".**

   **isn't**[1]
   (is not)
   **shouldn't**[1]
   (should not)

3. **Words fused with "and".**

A prime example of this is "rock and roll", which you may write in any of at least five ways, all equally valid.

   **rock-n-roll**[2]
   **rock'n'roll**[2]
   **rock-'n'-roll**[2]
   **rock 'n' roll**[2]
   **rock 'n roll**[2]

4. **Words fused with "of".**

This occurs in a few cases, of which we present two.

   **o'clock**[1]
   **will-o'-the-wisp**[1]

(The unfused forms have gone right out of existence.)

5. **"Let" fused with "us".**

   **Let's** go.[1]
   (Let us go.)

## B. Apostrophes in contracted and abbreviated words

In days of old, all contracted and abbreviated words had apostrophes where the letter or letters were missing. A "bus" used to be a "'bus", because the full word is "omnibus"; and an "ad" used to be an "ad'", because the full word is "advertisement". Nowadays, usage varies, and we show the variable status of some contracted and abbreviated words below.

**Punctuation**

**6. Abbreviation by omission at the beginning of words.**
The modern practice is either to contract the words without apostrophes or to write the words out in full. Using apostrophes before the contracted words is still legitimate but old-fashioned.

**bus**[1]
**'bus**[4]
(omnibus)
**phone**[1]
**'phone**[4]
(telephone)
**plane**[1]
**'plane**[4]
(aeroplane)

In all these cases the bracketed unabbreviated forms are standard formal.

**7. Contraction by omission in the middle of words.**
a. Words in which the apostrophes are old-fashioned.

**Cwealth**[1]
**C'wealth**[4]
(Commonwealth)
**dept**[1]
**dep't**[4]
(department)
**assn**[1]
**ass'n**[4]
(association)

In all these cases the bracketed full words are standard formal.

b. Archaic poetic words in which the apostrophes are standard formal.

---

1 Standard formal: *use this, and you can't go wrong in formal contexts.*
2 Standard formal with consistent options: *choose one and stick to it.*
3 Standard formal with flexible options: *choose any one, any time.*
4 Old-fashioned: *still all right, but fading from modern usage.*
5 Standard informal: *fine in conversation or in personal letters.*
6 Nonstandard: *you jez'gotta be kidding.*

**e're**[1]
(ever)
**e'en**[1]
(even or evening)
**o'er**[1]
(over)

The words with the apsotrophes are archaic. What we have shown is the standard formal way of contracting them, if contract them you must.

c. Contractions of courtesy or professional titles never have apostrophes.

**Mr**[1]
(mister)
**Dr**[1]
(doctor)

8. **Abbreviation by omission at the end of words.**
a. The abbreviated words have no apostrophes in modern English.

**pub**[1]
**pub'**[4]
(public house)
**ad**[1]
**ad'**[4]
(advertisement)
**disco**[1]
**disco'**[4]
(discotheque)

The unabbreviated words are also standard formal.

b. Abbreviated forms of words ending in "ing" take apostrophes.

**comin'** and **goin'**[1]
(coming and going)

The unabbreviated forms are standard formal.

## Punctuation

**9. Abbreviations that have omissions in more than one place.**
The practice varies for different words.

**pram**[1]
**pram'**[4]
(perambulator)
**flu**[1]
**'flu**[4]
(influenza)
**focsle**[2]
**fo'c'sle**[2]
**fo'c's'le**[2]
(forecastle)

The unabbreviated forms are also standard formal.

### C. Genitive apostrophes with common nouns

The genitive — an alternative name is "the possessive" — shows any of a variety of relationships of a noun (or a noun substitute) to some other word. "My friend's house", for example, indicates a possessing relationship between "my friend" and "house". Again: "I went on two weeks' vacation" indicates another kind of relationship between "weeks" and "vacation".

You mark the genitive relationship with an apostrophe placed immediately after the base noun in the context of the sentence. For example, we write "I saw the pony's tail", with the apostrophe immediately after "pony" because the sentence deals with the singular base word "pony". By the same token, we write "I saw the ponies' tails" with the apostrophe after "ponies", because the sentence deals with the plural base word "ponies".

---

1 Standard formal: *use this, and you can't go wrong in formal contexts.*
2 Standard formal with consistent options: *choose one and stick to it.*
3 Standard formal with flexible options: *choose any one, any time.*
4 Old-fashioned: *still all right, but fading from modern usage.*
5 Standard informal: *fine in conversation or in personal letters.*
6 Nonstandard: *you jez'gotta be kidding.*

## Apostrophes

The main problem that arises with the genitive use of the apostrophe is whether or not you add an "s" after the apostrophe. In essence, the explanation given in the paragraph above fully solves that problem. However, because the problem is a complex one and, because it stumps many people, we explain it more fully below.

**10. Apostrophes with genitive common nouns.**
A genitive common noun always ends in an apostrophe. That part is easy. The hard bit is to decide whether or not to add a genitive "s" after the apostrophe. Well, you sometimes do, and you sometimes don't.
**a.** If the genitive common noun is singular, you always add the genitive "s" after the apostrophe.

| | |
|---|---|
| my **friend's** head[1] | the **deer's** head[1] |
| (the head of my **friend**) | (the head of the **deer**) |
| the **baby's** head[1] | the **goose's** head[1] |
| (the head of the **baby**) | (the head of the **goose**) |

**b.** If the genitive common noun is plural:

**i.** you don't add the genitive "s" after the apostrophe, if the plural noun ends in a plural "s" —

my **friends'** heads[1]
(the heads of my **friends**)
the **babies'** heads[1]
(the heads of the **babies**)

**ii.** you add the genitive "s" after the apostrophe, if the plural noun doesn't end in a plural "s" —

the **deer's** heads[1]
(the heads of the **deer**)
the **geese's** heads[1]
(the heads of the **geese**)

We can show these variations in tabular form as follows.

## Punctuation

TABLE OF GENITIVE COMMON NOUNS

|  | Singular | Plural |
|---|---|---|
| GENITIVE NOUN WHOSE PLURAL FORM ENDS IN A PLURAL "S" | the baker's head<br>the poet's head<br>(See 10.a.) | the bakers' heads<br>the poets' heads<br>(See 10.b.i.) |
| GENITIVE NOUN WHOSE PLURAL FORM DOESN'T END IN A PLURAL "S" | the child's head<br>the sheep's head<br>(See 10.a.) | the children's heads<br>the sheep's heads<br>(See 10.b.ii.) |

### D. Genitive apostrophes with proper nouns

In this section we deal with genitive proper nouns — people's names and geographic names. Examples of these are "Margaret's parents" and "London's streets". The guidelines governing the use of apostrophes with these words are quite baffling. To understand them, we first have to consider four variables.

**i.** The first variable is whether or not the proper noun ends in a sibilant sound. A sibilant sound is one that sounds like a hiss or a buzz. Names like "Loftus", "Rose", "Boaz" — though they end in different letters — all end in sibilant sounds. Names like "Scott", "Megan", "Narelle" don't end in sibilant sounds.

**ii.** The second variable is whether the sibilant is voiced or voiceless. If you try to utter and to hold the sound "s-s-s", all you will hear is a hissing sound coming from your mouth, but not the sound of your voice coming from your throat. This kind of sibilant is called a voiceless sibilant. "Loftus" and "Knox" end in voiceless sibilants.

Now try to utter and to hold the sound "z-z-z". Here you will hear both the buzzing sound coming from your mouth and the sound of your voice — in a kind of humming tone — coming from your throat. This

---

1 Standard formal: *use this, and you can't go wrong in formal contexts.*
2 Standard formal with consistent options: *choose one and stick to it.*
3 Standard formal with flexible options: *choose any one, any time.*
4 Old-fashioned: *still all right, but fading from modern usage.*
5 Standard informal: *fine in conversation or in personal letters.*
6 Nonstandard: *you jez'gotta be kidding.*

is called a voiced sibilant. The names "Rose" and "Boaz" end in voiced sibilants.

**iii.** The third variable is how long the proper noun is: whether it is monosyllabic (consisting of only one syllable) or multisyllabic (consisting of more than one syllable). The names "Locke" and "Kant" are monosyllabic; the names "Plato" and "Socrates" are multisyllabic.

**iv.** Finally, among the multisyllabic names ending in sibilant sounds — whether voiced or voiceless — we have to distinguish between those names that end in consecutive sibilant sounds and those that don't. "Lysis" is a name that ends in consecutive sibilant sounds; "Empedocles" is a name that doesn't.

Now that we have dealt with the variables, we can present the guidelines.

**11. Use of apostrophes with genitive proper nouns.**
Every proper noun takes an apostrophe in the genitive. The following guidelines tell you whether or not to follow the apostrophe with an "s".
**a.** Add an "s" after the apostrophe if the proper noun is monosyllabic, regardless of whether the proper noun ends in a sibilant sound or not.

**Shaw's** play[1]
**Greece's** flag[1]

**b.** Add an "s" after the apostrophe if the proper noun is multisyllabic and either doesn't end in a sibilant sound or ends in a single voiceless sibilant sound.

**Herrick's** verse[1]
**Venice's** canals[1]

**c.** Don't add an "s" after the apostrophe if the proper noun is multisyllabic and if it ends in a single voiced sibilant sound.

Peter **Sellers'** joke[1]
**Algiers'** bazaar[1]

**d.** Don't add an "s" after the apostrophe if the proper noun is multisyllabic and if it ends in consecutive sibilant sounds.

**Menzies'** legislation[1]
**Knossos'** harbour[1]

## Punctuation

The upshot of these guidelines is as follows. You deal with a genitive proper noun in the same way as you deal with a genitive singular common noun (that is, you add an "s" after the apostrophe) except if the proper noun is multisyllabic and if it —

    i. ends in a single voiced sibilant, or
    ii. ends in consecutive sibilants (whether voiced or voiceless).

The following table sums up and exemplifies the foregoing guidelines.

TABLE OF GENITIVE PROPER NOUNS

|  | *Not ending in a sibilant* | *Ending in a voiceless sibilant* | *Ending in a voiced sibilant* |
|---|---|---|---|
| MONOSYLLABIC NAME | Hume's history<br>Perm's centre<br>(See 11.a.) | Joyce's novel<br>France's capital<br>(See 11.a) | Mills's essay<br>Cairn's hat<br>(See 11.a.) |
| MULTISYLLABIC NAME | Shelly's poem<br>Brazil's flag<br>(See 11.b.) | Harris's book<br>Tunis's people<br>(See 11.c.) | Bridges' verse<br>Athens' temple<br>(See 11.b.) |
| MULTISYLLABIC NAME ENDING IN CONSECUTIVE SIBILANTS |  | Francis' realm<br>Knossos' palace<br>(See 11.d.) | Perses' son<br>Araxes' shore<br>(See 11.d.) |

### E. Pointers on when to use and when not to use apostrophes
**12. Particular proper nouns.**
The names of some people and some geographic place names feature apostrophes. Other similar names do not feature apostrophes. Since there is no system or consistency in the choice of apostrophes in these cases, all you can do is consult a reliable source (a telephone book or a gazetteer, for instance) and use the version the source gives you.

---

1 Standard formal: *use this, and you can't go wrong in formal contexts.*
2 Standard formal with consistent options: *choose one and stick to it.*
3 Standard formal with flexible options: *choose any one, any time.*
4 Old-fashioned: *still all right, but fading from modern usage.*
5 Standard informal: *fine in conversation or in personal letters.*
6 Nonstandard: *you jez'gotta be kidding.*

## Apostrophes

MacCarthy[2]
McCarthy[2]
M'Carthy[2]
Maccarthy[2]
St John's[2]  (the capital of Newfoundland)
St Johns[2]  (a river in Florida, USA)

**13. Organisational or institutional names ending in a plural "s".**
If you are citing the name of an actual organisation or institution, check a reliable source to see the preferred usage. Otherwise, you can treat the word as a genitive plural (with an apostrophe) or as a nongenitive plural (without an apostrophe).

Australian **Writers** Services[1]
Australian **Workers'** Union[1]
a **teachers'** college[2]
a **teachers** college[2]

**14. Names of premises.**
You can opt to use either a genitive noun followed by a nongenitive noun or a genitive noun on its own.

I am going to the **grocer's shop**.[3]
I am going to the **grocer's**.[3]
I am going to my **doctor's surgery**.[3]
I am going to my **doctor's**.[3]

**15. The double genitive and its variants.**
In an expression such as "a friend of my neighbour's", both the word "of" and the form "neighbour's" indicate a genitive relationship. This gives us a double genitive, which is perfectly legitimate. But you may choose either of two other options as well, each with only one genitive element.

I spoke to a friend **of** my **neighbour's**.[3]
I spoke to a friend **of** my neighbour.[3]
I spoke to my **neighbour's** friend.[3]
I spoke to a subordinate **of** the **captain's**.[3]
I spoke to a subordinate **of** the captain.[3]
I spoke to the **captain's** subordinate.[3]

## Punctuation

**16. "Its" and "it's".**
a. "Its" is the genitive of "it".

> The dog wagged **its** tail.[1]
> The earth spins on **its** axis.[1]

b. "It's" is the fusion of "it is" or "it has".

> **It's** no use complaining.[1]
> (It is no use complaining.)
> **It's** done it again.[1]
> (It has done it again.)

Remember: you no more need the apostrophe in the genitive "its" than you do in the genitive "ours" and "yours". You need the apostrophe only in the fused "it's".

**17. "Ones" and "one's".**
a. "Ones" is the nongenitive plural of "one".

> You took a green apple; I took two red **ones**.[1]

b. "One's" is the fused form of "one is" or "one has".

> **One's** tired when **one's** done a lot of work.[1]
> (One is tired when one has done a lot of work.)

c. "One's" is the genitive singular of "one".

> One should do **one's** duty.[1]
> One has **one's** ups and downs.[1]

**18. "Others", "other's" and "others'".**
a. "Others" is the nongenitive plural of "other".

> He chose some magazines and she chose **others**.[1]

---

1 Standard formal: *use this, and you can't go wrong in formal contexts.*
2 Standard formal with consistent options: *choose one and stick to it.*
3 Standard formal with flexible options: *choose any one, any time.*
4 Old-fashioned: *still all right, but fading from modern usage.*
5 Standard informal: *fine in conversation or in personal letters.*
6 Nonstandard: *you jez'gotta be kidding.*

**b.** "Other's" is the genitive singular of "other".

They liked each **other's** friends.[1]
(They liked the friends of each other.)

**c.** "Others'" is the genitive plural of "other".

I care about **others'** troubles.[1]
(I care about the troubles of others.)

**19. The nongenitive plurals of acronyms, numbers, symbols, words and letters.**
Since these are plurals (not fusions, contractions, abbreviations or genitives) you don't use apostrophes.

**a.** Acronyms.

**MPs** are treated as **VIPs**.[1]
**MP's** are treated as **VIPs'**.[6]

**b.** Numbers.

There are two **9s** in "the **1990s**".[1]
There are two **9's** in "the **1990s'**".[6]

**c.** Symbols.

Buy here and save **$s**.[1]
Buy here and save **$'s**.[6]
Buy here and save **$s'**.[6]

**d.** Words.

They imposed a lot of **dos** and **don'ts** on us.[1]
They imposed a lot of **do's** and **don't's** on us.[6]

**e.** Letters.
This is a tricky one because, at first sight, these plurals may not seem to make sense. Nevertheless, since the letters are not actually genitive, you should avoid using the genitive apostrophe and rely on your reader's general knowledge of the language to get the right meaning. There are twelve ways of writing such plurals.

**Punctuation**

Mind your *p*s and *q*s.[2]
Mind your *P*s and *Q*s.[2]
Mind your ps and qs.[2]
Mind your Ps and Qs.[2]
Mind your ps and qs.[2]
Mind your Ps and Qs.[2]
Mind your 'p's and 'q's.[2]
Mind your 'P's and 'Q's.[2]
Mind your "p"s and "q"s.[2]
Mind your "P"s and "Q"s.[2]
Mind your p's and q's.[4]
Mind your P's and Q's.[4]

The vowels "a", "i" and "u" are special cases because the addition of the plural "s" to these vowels forms the words "as", "is", "us". When you are pluralising any of these vowels, you have four methods available.

In the word "unusual" there are three *us*.[2]
In the word "unusual" there are three Us.[2]
In the word "unusual" there are three "u"s.[2]
In the word "unusual" there are three 'u's.[2]

**f.** Verbs with the prefix "a" are not contractions — they are whimsies. They therefore appear without apostrophes.

The times they are **achanging**.[1]
The times they are **a'changing**.[6]

---

1 Standard formal: *use this, and you can't go wrong in formal contexts.*
2 Standard formal with consistent options: *choose one and stick to it.*
3 Standard formal with flexible options: *choose any one, any time.*
4 Old-fashioned: *still all right, but fading from modern usage.*
5 Standard informal: *fine in conversation or in personal letters.*
6 Nonstandard: *you jez'gotta be kidding.*

# CHAPTER 21
# Hyphens

## Overview

The hyphen is a short horizontal stroke ( - ). Its function is to join two or more words ("twenty-one", "down-at-heel") or parts of words ("pro-American", "U-turn").

There are two points worth noting about hyphens. The first is that many words that used to be hyphenated in the past are now amalgamated as a matter of course. For example, the 1901 edition of one popular dictionary (*Chambers'*) hyphenated "to-day", "to-morrow", "radio-active" and many other words that we now write as single words. The 1924 edition of another popular dictionary (*Oxford*) hyphenated such words as "co-operate", "pre-arrange", "man-handle" and many other words that, again, we now write as single words.

The second point is that, because of the continuing evolution of usage in the world of hyphenation, utter chaos reigns. One reputable writer's "lieutenant-colonel" is another reputable writer's "lieutenant colonel", and one dictionary's "out-of-doors" is another dictionary's "out of doors".

What then are we to make of these two points?

Simply this: that it is often possible nowadays to get away without using hyphens. That gives you the opportunity, in many cases, to dispense with hyphens. In other cases, though, hyphens are still either helpful (in avoiding ambiguity) or indispensable (because of convention).

Our discussion of the hyphen comes in five sections.

### A. Dangling hyphens and word division hyphens

In the class of the dangling hyphen we include the hyphen in expressions such as "pre- and postnatal care". In the class of the word division hyphen

## Punctuation

we include the hyphens you use when you show how a word like "division" splits into its component syllables: "di-vi-sion".

### B. Hyphens and compound adjectives

We start by telling you what adjectives are ("good" is an example of an adjective) and what compound adjectives are ("good-looking" is an example), and then we reveal that there are three ways of writing compound adjectives —

    i. amalgamate them ("a **heartrending** tale")
    ii. hyphenate them ("a **do-or-die** attempt")
    iii. separate them ("they were **down at heel**").

### C. Hyphens in compound nouns, prepositioned-prefixed verbs and foreign expressions

Perhaps you've been wondering whether to write "attorney-general" or "attorney general", "undergraduate" or "under-graduate", "to underpay" or "to under-pay". Well, this is the section that tells you what's what under which circumstances.

### D. Hyphens and numbers

"Twenty-one" — no problem, right? But how about "two-thirds" or "two thirds", and "twentieth-century" or "twentieth century"? This section comes up with the answers.

### E. Prefixes and capital letters joined to words

Here we take a coordinated (or "co-ordinated"?) look at these matters to preempt (or "pre-empt"?) any difficulties you may have in negotiating the hazardous S-bends (or "S bends"?) on the road to writing such compounds with confidence.

### A. Dangling hyphens and word division hyphens

In most cases, hyphens connect the end of one word with the beginning of another. In "thirty-two", for example, or in "pro-American", the hyphens immediately connect with the next word. But in "pro- and anti-

---

1 Standard formal: *use this, and you can't go wrong in formal contexts.*
2 Standard formal with consistent options: *choose one and stick to it.*
3 Standard formal with flexible options: *choose any one, any time.*
4 Old-fashioned: *still all right, but fading from modern usage.*
5 Standard informal: *fine in conversation or in personal letters.*
6 Nonstandard: *you jez'gotta be kidding.*

# Hyphens

American", the first hyphen dangles. Whether it is all right to leave it dangling is one subject of investigation in this section. Another is the word division hyphen. This is a hyphen that you use if you want to show the syllabic division of a word (for example, "di-vi-sion") or if you need it for wrapping a word around the end of a line.

**1. What is the status of the dangling hyphen?**
The short answer is that the dangling hyphen is standard formal English. But it enjoys that status if and only if you almost immediately follow it either with a related nondangling hyphen or with a related amalgamated compound. In either case, you may always, if you are so inclined, opt out of using the dangling hyphen altogether.

> I visited my **father- and my mother-in-law**.[3]
>
> I visited my **father-in-law and my mother-in-law**.[3]
>
> We studied the **pre- and the postindustrial** periods.[3]
>
> We studied the **preindustrial** and the **postindustrial** periods.[3]

In the first of our four sample sentences above, the meaning of the sentence would be different without the dangling hyphen in "father-".

**2. The word division hyphen.**
**a.** Some dictionaries show the division of words into syllables by putting hyphens between the syllables. Others use dots between the syllables.

> un-think-ing-ly[2]
> un.think.ing.ly[2]

**b.** Use a word division hyphen if you have come to the end of a line and if the line is not long enough to accommodate the whole word you are writing.

> They did it **un-
> thinkingly**.[3]
> They did it **unthink-
> ingly**.[3]
> They did it **unthinking-
> ly**.[3]

## Punctuation

### B. Hyphens and compound adjectives

We begin with a couple of definitions.

An adjective is a word that modifies a noun. Take, for example, the noun "book". Any word that modifies that noun is an adjective.

**English** book[1]
**good** book[1]
**one** book[1]
**this** book[1]
**each** book[1]
**my** book[1]
**any** book[1]
**boring** book[1]

A compound adjective is an adjective that consists of two or more words that act together to modify a noun.

**brand new** book[1]
**thought-provoking** book[1]
**half-kilogram** book[1]
**paperback** book[1]

As the above examples show, there are three ways of dealing with compound adjectives:

    i. separate the elements of the compound ("brand new"),

    ii. hyphenate the elements of the compound ("half-kilogram"),

    iii. amalgamate the elements of the compound ("paperback").

Which of these methods you follow depends on two factors.

The first of these factors is general practice. "Paperback", for example, we now generally write as a single word; "brand new" we write as two words. You may have to check a modern dictionary to find out whether the

---

1 Standard formal: *use this, and you can't go wrong in formal contexts.*
2 Standard formal with consistent options: *choose one and stick to it.*
3 Standard formal with flexible options: *choose any one, any time.*
4 Old-fashioned: *still all right, but fading from modern usage.*
5 Standard informal: *fine in conversation or in personal letters.*
6 Nonstandard: *you jez'gotta be kidding.*

compound you want to use has reached the stage of amalgamation. Better yet, keep an eye out for whether reputable modern writers, journals and publishers allow such amalgamations to appear in their works. If they do, you can allow yourself to use them as well.

The second factor is trickier. How you write a compound adjective depends on how you use the compound in the sentence: specifically on how it relates to the noun that it modifies. There are two ways in which an adjective — whether simple or compound — can modify a noun.

One of these is "attributive", which means that the adjective stands immediately before the noun that it modifies. The other is "predicative", which means that the adjective comes after the noun it modifies and that it is separated from the noun by a verb or by some other word. Below we show both ways of using adjectives.

| ATTRIBUTIVE | PREDICATIVE |
|---|---|
| I have a **good book**.[1] | The **book** I have is **good**.[1] |
| This is a **sunny day**.[1] | The **day** is **sunny**.[1] |
| I want a **one-hour rest**.[1] | I want a **rest** of **one hour**.[1] |

The distinction between the attributive use and the predicative use of compound adjectives is important for this section — indeed for this whole chapter. It often determines whether you insert or omit the hyphen between the elements of the compound.

**3. Compound adjectives containing present participles.**
The present participle is a form of the verb that you may use adjectivally. It is characterised by the ending "ing": "a **fascinating** story", a "**harrowing** tale". In the above two examples, the present participle appears alone but, as we shall see below, it may also occur in compound adjectives.
**a.** Hyphenate the compound when you use it attributively.

They bought **interest-bearing bonds**.[1]

Jogging may be a **health-giving activity**.[1]

**b.** When you use the same words predicatively, the hyphenation is optional.

These **bonds** are **interest bearing**.[2]
These **bonds** are **interest-bearing**.[2]

269

## Punctuation

As an **activity**, jogging may be **health giving**.[2]
As an **activity**, jogging may be **health-giving**.[2]

c. Some compound adjectives with present participles now commonly appear in an amalgamated form.

an **outstanding** success[1]
a **thoroughgoing** inspection[1]
a **peacekeeping** force[1]
an **underlying** reason[1]

### 4. Compound adjectives containing past participles.

The past participle is another form of the verb that you may use adjectivally. There is no particular ending that characterises past participles. Often, though, they end in the letter "n", "t" or "d".

| known | meant  | noted     |
|-------|--------|-----------|
| seen  | dreamt | delegated |
| taken | left   | lapsed    |

More importantly, you can recognise a past participle from the fact that you use it after a form of the verb "to be" (in the passive), or after a form of the verb "to have" (in the perfect aspect).

They **are known**.[1]
We **have noted** it.[1]

You can see the past participle at work in its adjectival function in expressions such as "a **broken** vase" and a "**rumpled** suit". Like the present participle, the past participle may also appear with another word to form a compound adjective.

a. Hyphenate the compound when you use it attributively.

Earth is a **medium-sized planet**.[1]
I bought some **hand-made goods**.[1]

---

1 Standard formal: *use this, and you can't go wrong in formal contexts.*
2 Standard formal with consistent options: *choose one and stick to it.*
3 Standard formal with flexible options: *choose any one, any time.*
4 Old-fashioned: *still all right, but fading from modern usage.*
5 Standard informal: *fine in conversation or in personal letters.*
6 Nonstandard: *you jez'gotta be kidding.*

# Hyphens

**b.** When you use the same words predicatively, the hyphen is optional.

> Our **planet** is **medium sized**.[2]
> Our **planet** is **medium-sized**.[2]
> I bought some **goods** that are **hand made**.[2]
> I bought some **goods** that are **hand-made**.[2]

**c.** Some compound adjectives with past participles now commonly appear in amalgamated form.

> a **simpleminded** view[1]
> the **abovementioned** item[1]
> an **outmoded** idea[1]
> my **heartfelt** thanks[1]

**5. Other two-word adjectives (that is, those not containing present or past participles).**

**a.** With these compound adjectives, you may opt either to hyphenate or to separate the elements of the compounds when you use the adjectives attributively.

> It is a **high risk** business.[2]
> It is a **high-risk** business.[2]
> The government imposed a **capital gains** tax.[2]
> The government imposed a **capital-gains** tax.[2]

**b.** When you use the same words predicatively, don't use hyphens. (Here they no longer function as adjectives.)

> The business involves a **high risk**.[1]
> They taxed my **capital gains**.[1]

**c.** Some of these compounds now commonly appear in amalgamated form.

> It was a **downright** shame![1]
> They stopped the **runaway** car.[1]

**Punctuation**

**6. Double-barrelled adjectives.**
Use hyphenation.

> We crossed the **German-French** border on an **east-west** flight.[1]

**7. Longer expressions used adjectivally.**
**a.** Hyphenate the expression when you use it attributively.

> They had an **out-of-doors** job.[1]
> It was a **once-in-a-lifetime** opportunity.[1]

**b.** When you use the same expression predicatively, omit the hyphens. (Here it no longer functions as an adjective.)

> They worked **out of doors**.[1]
> Such an opportunity comes **once in a lifetime**.[1]

**c.** When you use extra-long stock expressions attributively, your options are hyph- enation and quotation marks.

> I take a **curse-on-both-their-houses** attitude.[2]
> I take a "**curse on both their houses**" attitude.[2]

**C. Hyphens in compound nouns, preposition-prefixed verbs and foreign expressions**

Nouns come singly ("board", "light") and in compounds ("blackboard", "daylight"). Verbs too come singly ("work", "pay") and in compounds ("overwork", "underpay"). Some of these nouns and verbs are written separately, some in a hyphenated form, some in an amalgamated form. It all depends . . .

**8. Compound nouns.**
**a.** When a compound noun contains a prepositional element (that is, an element such as "in", "on", "with", "by" and the like), write it in an amalgamated form. Hyphenation is old-fashioned:

---

1 Standard formal: *use this, and you can't go wrong in formal contexts.*
2 Standard formal with consistent options: *choose one and stick to it.*
3 Standard formal with flexible options: *choose any one, any time.*
4 Old-fashioned: *still all right, but fading from modern usage.*
5 Standard informal: *fine in conversation or in personal letters.*
6 Nonstandard: *you jez'gotta be kidding.*

**i.** when the noun stands after the preposition —

a **bypass**[1]
a **by-pass**[4]
an **offshoot**[1]
an **off-shoot**[4]
an **inpatient**[1]
an **in-patient**[4]

**ii.** when the noun stands before the preposition —

a **standoff**[1]
a **stand-off**[4]
a **breakdown**[1]
a **break-down**[4]
a **takeover**[1]
a **take-over**[4]

**b.** Hyphenate double-barrelled nouns.

My friend is the **publisher-owner** of a magazine.[1]
My neighbour is an **interpreter-translator** at the UN.[1]

**c.** For compound nouns that are the titles of office bearers or military personnel, choose between hyphenation and separation.

a **governor general**[2]
a **governor-general**[2]
a **justice of the peace**[2]
a **justice-of-the-peace**[2]
an **attorney general**[2]
an **attorney-general**[2]
a **lieutenant colonel**[2]
a **lieutenant-colonel**[2]

(We deal with the capitalisation or lower casing of such titles in chapter 12, section **B**.)

**Punctuation**

At the time of writing, the chief legal officer of the Commonwealth Government of Australia goes under the title of "Attorney-General", while that person's counterpart in New South Wales goes under the title of "Attorney General". Such is the state of chaos in the realm of hyphenation.

**d.** Other compound nouns, as a matter of convention rather than of logic, divide into two classes:

   **i.** those that appear in a hyphenated form —

a **daughter-in-law**[1]
a **cross-section**[1]

   **ii.** those that appear in an amalgamated form —

a **classroom**[1]
a **necktie**[1]

**9. Preposition-prefixed verbs and phrasal verbs.**
**a.** Preposition-prefixed verbs are verbs that have a prepositional element such as "in", "on", "under", "over" before the verb. Modern usage calls for amal- gamation rather than hyphenation.

We **outdistanced** them.[1]
We **out-distanced** them.[4]
They are **overworking**.[1]
They are **over-working**.[4]

**b.** Phrasal verbs are verbs with a prepositional element such as "in", "on", "under", "over" after the verb. The modern convention is to write the two elements separately.

They **took over** the job.[1]
We **took in** a guest.[1]

---

1 Standard formal: *use this, and you can't go wrong in formal contexts.*
2 Standard formal with consistent options: *choose one and stick to it.*
3 Standard formal with flexible options: *choose any one, any time.*
4 Old-fashioned: *still all right, but fading from modern usage.*
5 Standard informal: *fine in conversation or in personal letters.*
6 Nonstandard: *you jez'gotta be kidding.*

**10. Foreign expressions.**
Many foreign expressions have become incorporated into English, though some of them still have a foreign aura about them. "Prima facie" and "joie de vivre" are two examples of such expressions. You may write these expressions in roman print (as they appear in the previous sentence), or you may write them in italic print ("*prima facie*" and "*joie de vivre*"). Roman print shows that you consider these expressions to have become naturalised into English; italic print, that you don't.

Some of these expressions also carry, with their foreign origins, a baggage of hyphens and accents. If they do, the number of valid options is mind boggling.

tete a tete$^2$  vis-a-vis$^2$
*tete a tete*$^2$  *vis-a-vis*$^2$
tête à tête$^2$  vis-à-vis$^2$
*tête à tête*$^2$  *vis-à-vis*$^2$
tete-a-tete$^2$  vis a vis$^2$
*tete-a-tete*$^2$  *vis a vis*$^2$
tête-à-tête$^2$  vis à vis$^2$
*tête-à-tête*$^2$  *vis à vis*$^2$
  viz-a-viz$^2$
  *viz-a-viz*$^2$
  viz-à-viz$^2$
  *viz-à-viz*$^2$
  viz a viz$^2$
  *viz a viz*$^2$
  viz à viz$^2$
  *viz à viz*$^2$

## D. Hyphens and numbers

In this section we consider three kinds of numbers —

    **i.** cardinal numbers ("one", "two", "three");
    **ii.** ordinal numbers ("the first", "the second", "the third");
    **iii.** fractional numbers ("a half", "a third", "a quarter").

**Punctuation**

**11. Cardinal and ordinal numbers.**
The standard convention is to put a hyphen between the tens and the units of cardinal and ordinal numbers.
**a.** Cardinal numbers.

> **twenty-two**[1]
> **thirty-four** thousand[1]
> two hundred and **sixty-seven** million[1]

**b.** Ordinal numbers.

> the **twenty-second**[1]
> the **thirty-four** thousandth[1]
> the two hundred and **sixty-seven** millionth[1]

**12. Fractional numbers.**
There is a strong — but not universal — convention in favour of putting hyphens between the elements of fractional numbers such as "three-quarters" (or "three quarters").
**a.** The convention is strongest when the fractional number stands immediately before the term it modifies.

> They are **three-quarters finished**.[1]
> The jug is **two-thirds full**.[1]

**b.** The hyphenation is optional when the fractional number stands on its own.

> I'll take **one-third** and you can have **two-thirds**.[2]
> I'll take **one third** and you can have **two thirds**.[2]

**c.** When a fractional number involves tens and units, there is always a hyphen between the tens and the units.

> A **twenty-fifth** is more than a **thirty-fifth**.[1]

---

1 Standard formal: *use this, and you can't go wrong in formal contexts.*
2 Standard formal with consistent options: *choose one and stick to it.*
3 Standard formal with flexible options: *choose any one, any time.*
4 Old-fashioned: *still all right, but fading from modern usage.*
5 Standard informal: *fine in conversation or in personal letters.*
6 Nonstandard: *you jez'gotta be kidding.*

**13. Other numeric expressions.**
**a.** Use a hyphen or a word between numbers that express a score.

> They beat us **three-one**.[2]
> They beat us **3-1**.[2]
> They beat us **three to one**.[2]
> They beat us **3 to 1**.[2]

**b.** Use a hyphen, a slash or a word between numbers that express a range.

> This is the budget for the **1993-94** financial year.[1]
> This is the budget for the **1993/94** financial year.[4]
>
> The pipe should be **4-5** metres long.[3]
> The pipe should be **4 to 5** metres long.[3]

**14. Numeric expressions joined to nonnumeric expressions.**
**a.** When you use such expressions attributively, you may choose between hyphenating or separating the elements.

> I played a **three-set** match.[2]
> I played a **three set** match.[2]
>
> Tintoretto was a **sixteenth-century** artist.[2]
> Tintoretto was a **sixteenth century** artist.[2]

**b.** When you use such expressions predicatively, separate the elements.

> I played a match of **three sets**.[1]
> Tintoretto lived in the **sixteenth century**.[1]

**c.** Sometimes you may need a hyphen to avoid ambiguity.

> These are **three-year-old** children.[1]
> These are three **year-old** children.[1]
> Here are **two-metre** lengths of wood.[1]
> Here are two **metre-lengths** of wood.[1]

Each member of each pair of sentences has a different meaning and, in each case, the difference is brought out by the hyphen.

# Punctuation

## E. Prefixes and capital letters joined to words

We may join a letter or letters to a word for either of two reasons. One reason is that the letter or letters so joined have a meaning. Examples of this kind of junction are "a-" joined to "moral" to make "amoral", "un-" joined to "friendly" to form "unfriendly". Elements such as "a-" and "un-" in our examples go under the name of prefixes. The other reason for joining a letter to a word is that the shape of the letter suggests the shape of the thing we are writing about. Examples of this type of junction are "A-frame" (or "A frame"), "L-shape" (or "L shape").

### 15. Prefixes joined to words.

**a.** Most prefixes we now as a matter of course amalgamate with their companion words.

| | |
|---|---|
| unjustified[1] | juxtaposition[1] |
| twilight[1] | triangle[1] |

**b.** With some others there is a lingering tendency to use hyphens — but this tendency is fading from modern usage.

| | |
|---|---|
| subzero[1] | minibudget[1] |
| sub-zero[4] | mini-budget[4] |
| semifinal[1] | microeconomics[1] |
| semi-final[4] | micro-economics[4] |
| postgraduate[1] | |
| post-graduate[4] | |

**c.** If the last letter of the prefix is the same as the first of the main word, the modern tendency is to amalgamate.

dissimilar[1]
dis-similar[4]
cooperate[1]
co-operate[4]

---

1 Standard formal: *use this, and you can't go wrong in formal contexts.*
2 Standard formal with consistent options: *choose one and stick to it.*
3 Standard formal with flexible options: *choose any one, any time.*
4 Old-fashioned: *still all right, but fading from modern usage.*
5 Standard informal: *fine in conversation or in personal letters.*
6 Nonstandard: *you jez'gotta be kidding.*

**preemptive**[1]
**pre-emptive**[4]

**d.** You may need a hyphen to avoid ambiguity.

The star **re-signed**.[1]
The star **resigned**.[1]

The two sentences have different meanings.

**16. Capital letters suggestive of a shape.**
**a.** Hyphenate or separate such combinations.

a **U-turn**[2]
a **U turn**[2]
a **V-sign**[2]
a **V sign**[2]
a **T-square**[2]
a **T square**[2]

**b.** Although, strictly speaking, it does not belong in this category we also include the name of the phenomenon discovered by W.K. Roentgen in 1895.

an **X-ray**[2]
an **X ray**[2]
an **x-ray**[2]

**17. Prefixes joined to words that normally begin with capital letters.**
**a.** If the capital is indispensable, put a hyphen between the prefix and the main word.

**anti-British**[1]
**pro-British**[1]
**non-British**[1]

**b.** Where feasible, dispense with the capital and amalgamate the prefix with the main word.

## Punctuation

**philosemitic**[1]
**philo-Semitic**[4]
**nonanglican**[1]
**non-Anglican**[4]
**prechristian**[1]
**pre-Christian**[4]
**antidarwinist**[1]
**anti-Darwinist**[4]

1 Standard formal: *use this, and you can't go wrong in formal contexts.*
2 Standard formal with consistent options: *choose one and stick to it.*
3 Standard formal with flexible options: *choose any one, any time.*
4 Old-fashioned: *still all right, but fading from modern usage.*
5 Standard informal: *fine in conversation or in personal letters.*
6 Nonstandard: *you jez'gotta be kidding.*

# CHAPTER 22
# Slashes

## Overview
A slash looks like a sloping bar ( / ). It has few uses but many names — among them "oblique stroke", "diagonal", "solidus", "virgule" and "slope bar". In this chapter we cover nine uses of the slash under four section headings.

### A. Slashes as indicators of alternatives
A writer may opt to use the slash in her/his work for this purpose.

### B. Slashes as separating devices
If you don't like this use of the slash, you can write to the authors c/o the publisher.

### C. Slashes with numbers
We've been working on this book during the years 1991/92.

### D. Slashes with verse written in linear sequence
The slash is handy for this use too,/ Even if it's not for you.

## A. Slashes as indicators of alternatives
In this function the slash operates to show that the words on either side of it are alternatives ("his/her"), and — when you use the slash to separate a letter from a word — to show that the additional letter is an alternative addition ("book/s").

1. **To indicate alternative words.**

   You will need a hammer **and/or** a drill.[1]

   Everyone is entitled to **her/his** opinion.[3]

   Everyone is entitled to **his/her** opinion.[3]

281

# Punctuation

**2. To indicate the optional addition of a letter.**
As an alternative to the slash you may use a pair of brackets.

> You may borrow any **book/s** you like.[2]
> You may borrow any **book(s)** you like.[2]
> Anyone can say what **s/he** thinks.[5]
> Any one can say what **(s)he** thinks.[5]

## B. Slashes as separating devices
You can use the slash to separate words (or elements of words) or the letters of some acronyms. As an alternative to using the slash, you can write the word/s out in full.

**3. To separate two units of measurement.**

> 80 **km/h**[3]
> 80 **kilometres an hour**[3]

**4. To separate the letters of some acronyms.**

> **c/o**[3]
> **care of**[3]
> **carried over**[3]
> **a/c**[3]
> **account**[3]

## C. Slashes with numbers
Here the slash has a range of functions described and exemplified below.

**5. To separate the numerator from the denominator in a fraction.**
Here the slash is an alternative to the horizontal bar.

> **1/2**[2]
> $\frac{1}{2}$[2]

---

1 Standard formal: *use this, and you can't go wrong in formal contexts.*
2 Standard formal with consistent options: *choose one and stick to it.*
3 Standard formal with flexible options: *choose any one, any time.*
4 Old-fashioned: *still all right, but fading from modern usage.*
5 Standard informal: *fine in conversation or in personal letters.*
6 Nonstandard: *you jez'gotta be kidding.*

**6. To separate the elements of a date expressed in digits.**
Full stops are the modern alternative.

    25/12/1993[4]
    25.12.1993[1]

**7. To separate the beginning and the end of a time range.**
A hyphen is the modern alternative.

    I have lodged my tax return for **1992/93**.[4]
    I have lodged my tax return for **1992-93**.[1]

    These are the figures for the **January/March** quarter.[4]
    These are the figures for the **January-March** quarter.[1]

**8. To separate the unit (or flat) number from the street number in an address.**

    They live at **4/20** Kookaburra Street, Edith Creek.[1]

## D. Slashes with verse written in linear sequence
**9. To separate lines of verse written in linear sequence.**
Gather ye rosebuds while ye may, / Old Time is still aflying; / And this same flower that smiles today, / Tomorrow will be dying.[3]

    Gather ye rosebuds while ye may,
    Old Time is still aflying;
    And this same flower that smiles today,
    Tomorrow will be dying.[3]
    Robert Herrick (1591-1674)

# CHAPTER 23
# Quotation marks

## Overview

Quotation marks (also known as inverted commas) come in two kinds: double quotation marks ( " " ) and single quotation marks ( ' ' ). Which of these you use is a matter of individual choice. The only point you have to remember is that, once you have made your choice, you have to stick to it throughout your text. There is really nothing to choose between the one and the other, and both are in use. For all the examples in the present chapter — except for the examples in this overview — we will be using double quotation marks as our primary form. But remember that single quotation marks are an equally valid option.

Two major uses of quotation marks are to enclose direct speech and to enclose quotations from texts.

> She said, "Let's go for a stroll."[2]
> She said, 'Let's go for a stroll.'[2]

> Immanuel Kant wrote, "That all our knowledge begins with experience there can be no doubt."[2]
> Immanuel Kant wrote, 'That all our knowledge begins with experience there can be no doubt.'[2]

Whether we are quoting a passing remark or Kant's *Critique of Pure Reason*, the options, methods and guidelines for using quotation marks are the same. In this chapter, therefore, we will confine ourselves to examples from speech.

---

1 Standard formal: *use this, and you can't go wrong in formal contexts.*
2 Standard formal with consistent options: *choose one and stick to it.*
3 Standard formal with flexible options: *choose any one, any time.*
4 Old-fashioned: *still all right, but fading from modern usage.*
5 Standard informal: *fine in conversation or in personal letters.*
6 Nonstandard: *you jez'gotta be kidding.*

# Quotation marks

Before we go on to preview the sections of this chapter, let us clear up two questions that often puzzle people.

**i.** Can there be two punctuation marks at the end of a sentence that contains a quotation?

The answer to this — with one minor exception — is no. The rationale for wondering whether there can in fact be two punctuation marks is that we might need one for the quotation and another for the sentence of which it forms a part — something along these lines:

He asked, "What's up?".[6]
Did she answer, "Nothing."?[6]

The two parts of each example sentence (the part within quotation marks and the part outside quotation marks) constitute a single sentence. Any single sentence can end in only one terminal punctuation mark; therefore neither of the two example sentences above can have both a full stop and a question mark. The two sentences should read as follows.

He asked, "What's up?"[1]
Did she answer, "Nothing"?[1]

The minor exception to what we have just said occurs in an example such as the following.

He said that he was working for some outfit called "the Automatic Car Co.".[4]

Here there is a full stop to mark the abbreviated word "Co.", and another full stop to mark the end of the sentence. But the full stop after Co." is old-fashioned anyway, and the more usual way of writing such a sentence is as follows.

He said that he was working for some outfit called "the Automatic Car Co".[1]

**ii.** What is the usual position of the terminal punctuation mark of a sentence that ends in a quotation mark: is it inside or outside the closing quotation mark?

# Punctuation

The answer to this question is that, in the overwhelming majority of cases, the terminal punctuation mark is inside the closing quotation mark.

He said, "I might be late."[1]
She asked, "Do you expect me to wait?"[1]

There are exceptions to this. We have shown one in the example about the Automatic Car Co, where the terminal full stop falls outside the closing quotation mark. The reason for this is that the quotation is a fragmentary — as distinct from a full — one. We deal with this and other exceptions in the body of the chapter. But it is worth keeping in mind that, in most cases, the terminal punctuation mark falls inside the closing quotation mark.

This chapter comes in four sections.

## A. Quotation marks and simple quotations
All the examples we have given so far are simple quotations: sentences cited from speech or from written works. Such quotations are called "simple" in contrast to the type that we consider in section B.

## B. Quotation marks and complex quotations
These are quotations within quotations — say, when you are quoting somebody as quoting somebody else.

## C. Quotation marks and fragmentary quotations
What she called me was "a darling", is an example. The full quotation was, "You are a darling."

## D. Other uses of quotation marks
There is a small number of specialised uses of quotation marks — for slang expressions, for example — and we consider these in this section.

---

1 Standard formal: *use this, and you can't go wrong in formal contexts.*
2 Standard formal with consistent options: *choose one and stick to it.*
3 Standard formal with flexible options: *choose any one, any time.*
4 Old-fashioned: *still all right, but fading from modern usage.*
5 Standard informal: *fine in conversation or in personal letters.*
6 Nonstandard: *you jez'gotta be kidding.*

## A. Quotation marks and simple quotations

Simple quotations are those that consist of one or more complete sentences, and that do not have quotations within quotations. For simple quotations, the matters we will be looking at in this section are these:

**i.** where to put the quotation marks;

**ii.** where to put other punctuation marks relative to the quotation marks;

**iii.** what words start with capital letters;

**iv.** where to put such introductory clauses as "she said" or "he asked" relative to the quotation.

(We call "she said" an introductory clause, not because it introduces the quotation — the clause can, in fact, come in the middle or at the end of the quotation — but because it introduces the speaker.)

Often the usage relating to these questions depends on the grammatical mood of the elements of the sentence. There is a detailed discussion of grammatical moods in chapter 5. For the purposes of this chapter, though, such a detailed discussion is not necessary. We will be dealing with only two moods:

**i.** statements —

both positive ("I am enjoying this"),

and negative ("I am not enjoying this");

**ii.** questions —

both positive ("Are you enjoying this?"),

and negative ("Aren't you enjoying this?").

## 1. Simple quotations without introductory clauses.

These are quotations without such introductory clauses as "he said" or "she answered".

"It's a fine day."[1]

"Is it a fine day?"[1]

## Punctuation

The things to note about these examples are that the whole of the quotations fall within the quotation marks; that the quotations start with capital letters; and that the terminal punctuation marks (the full stop in the first example and the question mark in the second) fall within the closing quotation mark.

**2. Punctuation between introductory clauses and simple quotations.**
If the quotation consists of one sentence, there are two main punctuation options.

>  **She said,** "It's a fine day."[3]
>
>  **She said**: "It's a fine day."[3]

The comma option is more prosaic and more usual in prose. The colon option gives the quotation a sense of drama. Writers use a colon before a quotation only if the quotation is of some significance.

>  **Caesar said**: "I came, I saw, I conquered."[3]

You can also use a dash instead of the colon.

>  **Caesar said** — "I came, I saw, I conquered."[3]

(For the punctuation of quotations consisting of more than one sentence see number 5 below.)

**3. Introductory clauses and quotations with variable grammatical moods.**
Introductory clauses ("she said", "he asked" and the like) can stand in any of three positions relative to the quotation — before, in the middle, or at the end of the quotation. Here is how we write the sentences in these varying positions.
**a.** Both the introductory clause and the quotation are statements.

---

1 Standard formal: *use this, and you can't go wrong in formal contexts.*
2 Standard formal with consistent options: *choose one and stick to it.*
3 Standard formal with flexible options: *choose any one, any time.*
4 Old-fashioned: *still all right, but fading from modern usage.*
5 Standard informal: *fine in conversation or in personal letters.*
6 Nonstandard: *you jez'gotta be kidding.*

She said, "It's a fine day."[1]
"It is," she said, "a fine day."[1]
"It's a fine day," she said.[1]

**b.** The introductory clause is a statement and the quotation is a question.

He asked, "Is it a fine day?"[1]
"Is it," he asked, "a fine day?"[1]
"Is it a fine day?" he asked.[1]

**c.** Both the introductory clause and the quotation are questions.

Did she ask, "Is it a fine day?"[1]
"Is it," did she ask, "a fine day?"[1]
"Is it a fine day?" did she ask?[1]

In each of the first two examples in **3.c.** a single question mark serves for the whole sentence — introductory question and quoted question. In the last example, because there is a gap between the quotation and the end of the sentence, you use two question marks.

**d.** The introductory clause is a question and the quotation is a statement. This is a hard one: the quotation begs for a full stop, but the introductory clause asks for a question mark. The solution to the problem is this: the question mark takes precedence over the full stop.

Did I hear him say, "It's a fine day"?[1]
"It is," did I hear him say, "a fine day"?[1]
"It's a fine day," did I hear him say?[1]

The unusual feature of this kind of combination is that the question mark falls outside the closing quotation mark. The reason for this is really quite obvious: the quotation itself is not a question, so the question mark cannot be inside the quotation marks; therefore it has to go outside.

**4. Simple quotations embedded in sentences.**
Here we will look at cases in which the quotation comes in the middle of a sentence that begins before, and runs on after, the quotation. Note the punctuation marks (commas, full stops and question marks) and their locations (inside and outside the closing quotation mark).

**Punctuation**

**a.** The surrounding sentence and the quotation are both statements.

She said, "**It's a fine day for a stroll**," and headed for the door.[1]

**b.** The surrounding sentence is a statement and the quotation is a question.

He said, "**Don't you think it's a fine day for a stroll?**" and headed for the door.[1]

**c.** The surrounding sentence is a question and the quotation is a statement.

Did she say, "**It's a fine day for a stroll**," as she headed for the door?[1]

**d.** The surrounding sentence and the quotation are both questions.

Did he say, "**Don't you think it's a fine day for a stroll?**" as he headed for the door?[1]

**5. Multi-sentence simple quotations with introductory clauses.**
**a.** The way to introduce a multi-sentence quotation, when the introductory clause is before the quotation, is to put a colon (rather than a comma) after the introductory clause.

**She said:** "It's a fine day.  Don't you think we ought to go for a stroll?"[1]

**b.** When the introductory clause comes between two quoted sentences, it works like this.

"It's a fine day," **he said**.  "Don't you think we ought to go for a stroll?"[1]

**c.** When the introductory clause comes at the end, the punctuation and capitalisation work as follows.

"It's a fine day.  Don't you think we ought to go for a stroll?" **she suggested**.[1]

---

1 Standard formal: *use this, and you can't go wrong in formal contexts.*
2 Standard formal with consistent options: *choose one and stick to it.*
3 Standard formal with flexible options: *choose any one, any time.*
4 Old-fashioned: *still all right, but fading from modern usage.*
5 Standard informal: *fine in conversation or in personal letters.*
6 Nonstandard: *you jez'gotta be kidding.*

## Quotation marks

**6. Embedded multi-sentence simple quotations.**
We are considering here sentences of the type:

> He said, " . . . ," and headed for the door.

The words enclosed in quotation marks (which we have left out in the above example) constitute two or more sentences. The question that arises is whether it is acceptable to have both of the quoted sentences enclosed by quotation marks within a single surrounding sentence.

**a.** When both quoted sentences are statements, separate them with a full stop; or amalgamate them, using a semicolon.

> He said: "It's a fine day. I think we ought to go for a stroll," and headed for the door.[3]
>
> He said, "It's a fine day; I think we ought to go for a stroll," and headed for the door.[3]

**b.** When the first quoted sentence is a statement and the second is a question, separate them with a full stop; or amalgamate them, using a dash or a colon.

> She said: "It's a fine day. Don't you think we ought to go for a stroll?" and headed for the door.[3]
>
> She said, "It's a fine day — don't you think we ought to go for a stroll?" and headed for the door.[3]
>
> She said, "It's a fine day: don't you think we ought to go for a stroll?" and headed for the door.[3]

**7. Simple quotations consisting of more than one paragraph.**
Start each paragraph with a quotation mark; end only the last paragraph with a quotation mark.

> "Chess probably originated in northern India some time before the sixth century AD. The six kinds of chess pieces originally represented the four arms of the Indian army of the time (foot soldiers, cavalry, chariots and elephants), together with the ruler and the ruler's chief minister or vizier.
>
> "From India, the game spread south and east to other Asian countries, and west to the Middle East. Europeans adopted chess from the Arabs but, around the fifteenth century, altered the rules to a form very similar

**Punctuation**

to the modern western game. In the meantime, various Asian forms of chess developed along independent lines.

"Historians date the first western chess tournament, run along modern lines, to 1851. This tournament was held in conjunction with the great exhibition in London. Since that event, hundreds of international chess contests have been held — including, in recent times, biennial chess team olympiads and matches for the individual world chess championship title."[1]

### B. Quotation marks and complex quotations

Complex quotations are quotations within quotations — somebody saying that someone else has said so-and-so. For complex quotations, you need two sets of quotation marks: an outer (or primary) set of quotation marks for what the somebody has said, and an inner (or secondary) set for what that somebody has quoted someone else as saying. In the overview to this chapter, we noted that it is a matter of indifference whether you use single or double quotation marks as your primary quotation marks. For complex quotations this remains true, but it is important to note that —

**i.** if you use double quotation marks for the primary quotation, you should use single quotation marks for the secondary quotation; or
**ii.** if you use single quotation marks for the primary quotation, you should use double quotation marks for the secondary quotation.

Here is how these options work out in practice.

She said, "Someone has just asked, 'What is the time?'"[2]
She said, 'Someone has just asked, "What is the time?"'[2]

In this section of the chapter, we use double quotation marks as the primary ones, and single quotation marks as the secondary ones. We do this simply to avoid the superfluous repetition of examples. Remember,

---

1 Standard formal: *use this, and you can't go wrong in formal contexts.*
2 Standard formal with consistent options: *choose one and stick to it.*
3 Standard formal with flexible options: *choose any one, any time.*
4 Old-fashioned: *still all right, but fading from modern usage.*
5 Standard informal: *fine in conversation or in personal letters.*
6 Nonstandard: *you jez'gotta be kidding.*

# Quotation marks

though, that the reverse procedure is just as valid — as long as you are consistent in your use of single and double quotation marks for your primary and secondary quotations respectively.

Complex quotations consist of three elements:

   **i.** the introductory clause of the primary quotation (She said, " ... ")
   **ii.** the introductory clause of the secondary quotation ( ... "Someone has just asked, " ... ")
   **iii.** the secondary quotation ( ... 'What is the time?')

The problem that arises with complex quotations is the placement of the terminal punctuation mark — the full stop or the question mark. Is it within the closing secondary quotation mark, within the primary quotation mark, or outside both sets of quotation marks? The answer to that problem is that it all depends on two considerations.

The first of these is that the terminal punctuation mark, whatever it may be, should come as early in the sentence as possible. But this consideration may be overridden by the second one: namely that a question mark takes precedence over a full stop. So the placement of the terminal punctuation mark depends on whether one or more — and which one or more — of the elements of the sentence as a whole (introductory clause and two quotations) are statements or questions.

We now look at how these factors come together in practice.

## 8. All three elements are statements.

No problem. We use a full stop, and the full stop comes at the first possible opportunity — at the end of the secondary quotation, within the closing secondary quotation mark.

   He said, "Someone just said, 'It's a fine day.'"[1]

## 9. All three elements are questions.

Again no problem. We use a question mark, and the question mark comes at the first possible opportunity — at the end of the secondary quotation, within the closing secondary quotation mark.

   Did she say, "Did anyone ask, 'Is it a fine day?'"[1]

## Punctuation

**10. The secondary quotation is a question, and one or both of the other elements are statements.**

Since the question mark takes precedence, and since the secondary quotation is a question, the question mark comes right after the secondary quotation within the closing secondary quotation mark.

> He said, "Someone has just asked, 'Is it a fine day?'"[1]
>
> She said, "Did anyone ask, 'Is it a fine day?'"[1]
>
> Did he say, "Someone has just asked, 'Is it a fine day?'"[1]

**11. The primary quotation is a question, the secondary quotation is a statement, and the introductory clause is whatever you please.**

Since the question mark takes precedence, and since the first opportunity that we can use it is at the end of the primary quotation, the question mark comes between the closing quotation marks of the secondary and of the primary quotations.

> She asked, "**Did anyone remark**, 'It's a fine day'?"[1]
>
> Did he ask, "**Did anyone remark**, 'It's a fine day'?"[1]

**12. The introductory clause is a question, and both quotations are statements.**

Since neither quotation is a question, there can be no question mark within the closing quotation mark of either. In this case, therefore, the question mark stands outside both quotation marks.

> Did she say, "Someone has just remarked, 'It's a fine day'"?[1]

### C. Quotation marks and fragmentary quotations

Fragmentary quotations occur when you don't pause in your own prose to introduce a quotation. Rather, you incorporate some word or words from such a quotation into the structure of your own prose. This often occurs,

---

1 Standard formal: *use this, and you can't go wrong in formal contexts.*
2 Standard formal with consistent options: *choose one and stick to it.*
3 Standard formal with flexible options: *choose any one, any time.*
4 Old-fashioned: *still all right, but fading from modern usage.*
5 Standard informal: *fine in conversation or in personal letters.*
6 Nonstandard: *you jez'gotta be kidding.*

for example, when you are paraphrasing someone else's speech in your own words, but you want to get part of that speech into your sentence, using the original wording.

Compare the following examples. The first gives the full epigram; the second is a paraphrase together with a fragment of the original.

> Oscar Wilde wrote, "The truth is never pure, and rarely simple."

> Writing of the truth, Oscar Wilde declared that it is "never pure, and rarely simple".

Now we look in detail at how we treat fragmentary quotations.

### 13. A fragmentary quotation consisting of a fragment of a statement sentence.

There are three differences between the way in which you treat a full quotation and the way in which you treat a fragmentary quotation. All three differences are illustrated below.

> George Bernard Shaw condemned the English for not respecting their language, and for not being willing to "**teach it to their children**".[1]

(The full sentence as Shaw wrote it reads: "The English have no respect for their language, and will not teach it to their children.")

Note the following about the treatment of the fragmentary quotation.

> **i.** There is no punctuation mark before the opening quotation mark.
>
> **ii.** The fragmentary quotation starts with a lower case letter.
>
> **iii.** The terminal punctuation mark comes outside the closing quotation mark.

### 14. A fragmentary quotation consisting of a fragment of a question.

Here the question mark comes within the closing quotation mark. There is a neat example of this in the 8 April 1991 issue of *Newsweek*. Writing of Rita Marley, the widow of reggae singer Bob Marley, the magazine asserts:

> Rita admitted forging her husband's signature on backdated documents transferring ownership of Marley's companies to her. She did this, she told *Newsweek*, on the advice of her lawyers and in the belief that, since she was the prime heir anyway, "**how can I steal from myself?**"[1]

# Punctuation

(Note, incidentally, that the comma before the fragmentary quotation does not introduce the quotation; it ends the parenthetic clause" . . . that, since she was the prime heir anyway, . . . ".)

**15. A fragmentary quotation hitched to a full quotation.**
You treat the first part as a fragmentary quotation (by not starting it with a capital letter), and the last part as a complete quotation (by putting the terminal punctuation mark inside the closing quotation mark).

> They said that they would be "**too busy for fun and games. After all, the examinations are coming up.**"[1]

> They said that the situation was growing "**more serious. Many of the services in the city have broken down.**"[1]

You often see quotations of this kind in the pages of newspapers and magazines.

## D. Other uses of quotation marks
**16. To enclose the titles of cited short works.**
**a.** The cited titles of short poems.

> Two of my favourite poems are Robert Herrick's "**To Blossoms**" and Siegfried Sassoon's "**Everyone Sang**".[1]

The titles of longer poems (say, ten or more pages in length) are written in italic print.

> I also like William Shakespeare's *Venus and Adonis* and Sir Walter Scott's *The Lay of the Last Minstrel.*[1]

**b.** The cited titles of chapters.

> H.G. Wells wrote about global ecology in a chapter entitled "**Weeding and Conditioning the Planet**" in his book *Phoenix*, first published in 1942.

---

1 Standard formal: *use this, and you can't go wrong in formal contexts.*
2 Standard formal with consistent options: *choose one and stick to it.*
3 Standard formal with flexible options: *choose any one, any time.*
4 Old-fashioned: *still all right, but fading from modern usage.*
5 Standard informal: *fine in conversation or in personal letters.*
6 Nonstandard: *you jez'gotta be kidding.*

## Quotation marks

The title of the book is in italic print.

**c.** A cited encyclopaedia entry.

> There is an interesting article called "**Social Differentiation**" in *The Encyclopaedia Britannica*.[1]

The title of the major work — the encyclopaedia — is in italic print.

**d.** The cited title or headline of an article or news story in a newspaper or journal.

> An issue of *The Economist* in early 1991 carried an article about juvenile street crime under the title "**Dark fears**".[1]

Note that the title of the magazine is in italic print. Note also that, in the magazine itself, the title of the article will not have quotation marks around it. It is only when you are citing the title in your own prose that the quotation marks come in. The same goes for the items under **a. b.** and **c.** above.

**17. To enclose single words, expressions or sentences exemplifying points of language.**
Here the options are to enclose the examples in quotation marks, to underline them, or to cast them in italic print.
**a.** Single words.

> The words "**and**" and "**but**" are conjunctions.[2]
> The words **and** and **but** are conjunctions.[2]
> The words *and* and *but* are conjunctions.[2]

If the words are parts of idiomatic expressions that are integral to the sentence, you don't need quotation marks.

> They were happy from the word **go**.[1]
> They wouldn't say **boo** to a goose.[1]

**b.** Expressions.

> The phrase "**early one morning**" is an adverbial phrase.[2]
> The phrase **early one morning** is an adverbial phrase.[2]
> The phrase *early one morning* is an adverbial phrase.[2]

## Punctuation

**c.** Statement sentences.

If you take a positive sentence such as "**There is a lot to do**", you can change it into a negative sentence by writing "**There is not a lot to do**".[2]

If you take a positive sentence such as **There is a lot to do**, you can change it into a negative sentence by writing **There is not a lot to do**.[2]

If you take a positive sentence such as *There is a lot to do*, you can change it into a negative sentence by writing *There is not a lot to do*.[2]

**d.** Question sentences.

If you take a positive sentence such as "**There is a lot to do**", you can change it into an interrogative sentence by writing "**Is there a lot to do?**"[2]

If you take a positive sentence such as **There is a lot to do**, you can change it into an interrogative sentence by writing **Is there a lot to do?**[2]

If you take a positive sentence such as *There is a lot to do*, you can change it into an interrogative sentence by writing *Is there a lot to do?*[2]

**18. To enclose odd or slang expressions.**

You use quotations marks for such expressions, when you want to dissociate yourself from them as something you yourself wouldn't ordinarily use, or when you want to highlight the fact that the expressions are odd or slang.

There are too many "**nukes**" in the world today.[1]

**19. To enclose words or expressions used ironically.**

You may also opt not to use quotation marks.

What with all their "**help**" we lost everything.[3]
What with all their **help** we lost everything.[3]

---

1 Standard formal: *use this, and you can't go wrong in formal contexts.*
2 Standard formal with consistent options: *choose one and stick to it.*
3 Standard formal with flexible options: *choose any one, any time.*
4 Old-fashioned: *still all right, but fading from modern usage.*
5 Standard informal: *fine in conversation or in personal letters.*
6 Nonstandard: *you jez'gotta be kidding.*

## Quotation marks

**20. To enclose stock expressions used attributively.**
The attributive use of a stock expression is its use as a compound adjective in front of a noun. In this use, hyphens are an alternative to quotation marks.

> I take a "**curse on both their houses**" attitude in this dispute.[2]
> I take a **curse-on-both-their-houses** attitude in this dispute.[2]
> You have this "**devil may care**" air about you.[2]
> You have this **devil-may-care** air about you.[2]

**21. Omit quotation marks from short quotations if the context doesn't require them.**
Typically, this will be with quoted words such as "yes", "no", "hello", "goodbye", "please", "thanks" and a few more. You can still opt to use quotation marks round such expressions, but this usage is becoming old-fashioned.

> I asked them whether they were coming, and they said **yes**.[1]
> I asked them whether they were coming and they said "**Yes**".[4]
> I said **thanks** when they let me in.[1]
> I said "**Thanks**" when they let me in.[4]

If you are writing dialogue, with all the direct speech in quotation marks, you keep them also for such short quotes.

> I asked, "May I come in?"
> They answered, "**Yes**."[1]
> They said, "We'll help you."
> I said, "**Thanks**."[1]

**22. Quotation marks and words on signs.**
**a.** If the sign consists of one or two words you can omit the quotation marks in a continuous passage of prose — or you can put them in, if you don't mind your prose being a little old-fashioned.

> Next to the **stop** sign there was a house with a **for-sale** poster.[1]
> Next to the "**Stop**" sign there was a house with a "**For sale**" poster.[4]

**Punctuation**

**b.** If the sign consists of more words, the quotation marks are standard formal.

Then they saw the "**Wrong way: go back**" sign by the side of the road.[1]

**23. To enclose a nickname used together with the real name.**

Max "**Tangles**" Walker[3]
Max (**Tangles**) Walker[3]

---

1 Standard formal: *use this, and you can't go wrong in formal contexts.*
2 Standard formal with consistent options: *choose one and stick to it.*
3 Standard formal with flexible options: *choose any one, any time.*
4 Old-fashioned: *still all right, but fading from modern usage.*
5 Standard informal: *fine in conversation or in personal letters.*
6 Nonstandard: *you jez'gotta be kidding.*

# CHAPTER 24
# Ellipses

## Overview

The ellipsis ("ellipses" in the plural) is a punctuation mark consisting of three consecutive dots, printed either with intervening spaces ( . . . ) or without intervening spaces ( ... ). Which form you choose to use is entirely a matter of personal preference. Both are equally legitimate for the purposes of punctuation — as long as you use one or the other consistently. In this chapter, except in the overview, we have chosen to give all our examples of ellipses with intervening spaces.

Ellipses are themselves sometimes separated from the associated text with spaces, sometimes not. Here are the guidelines.

**a.** At the beginning of a sentence, separate the ellipsis from the next word with a space.

> . . . Separate the ellipsis from the next word with a space.[2]
> ... Separate the ellipsis from the next word with a space.[2]

**b.** In the middle of a sentence, separate the ellipsis from either flanking word with a space.

> In the middle of a sentence separate the ellipsis . . . with a space.[2]
> In the middle of a sentence separate the ellipsis ... with a space.[2]

**c.** At the end of a sentence, the separation is optional, so take your pick.

> At the end of a sentence, the separation is optional. . .[2]
> At the end of a sentence, the separation is optional . . .[2]
> At the end of a sentence, the separation is optional...[2]
> At the end of a sentence, the separation is optional ...[2]

Ellipses have two different functions.

301

# Punctuation

## A. To mark the omission of one or more words, sentences or letters

To repeat: to mark the omission of . . . words, sentences or letters.

## B. To show hesitant, trailing off or interrupted speech

And that . . . er . . . just about . . . um . . . covers the uses of the ellipsis.

Except that — er — in this use — um — you have the option of using dashes.

## A. To mark the omission of one or more words, sentences or letters

This is the major use of the ellipsis. To illustrate it, we give a short text below and, from that text, we will omit various parts, marking those parts with ellipses. Here, first, is the complete text.

> One day, a big bad wolf met Little Red Riding Hood in the forest. The big bad wolf asked, "Where are you going, my dear?" Little Red Riding Hood said she was going to see her grandmother. Did she then stop to continue her conversation with the big bad wolf? No, she certainly did not stop! Rather, she hurried on and soon arrived at her grandmother's cottage. The big bad wolf had reached the cottage before her and had swallowed the grandmother up. When Little Red Riding Hood reached the cottage the big bad wolf was waiting for her there and swallowed her up too. Thanks, though, to the timely intervention of a woodcutter, the big bad wolf was done in, and grandma and Little Red Riding Hood were saved.

**1. To show the omission of a word or words at the start of a sentence.**
**a.** If the elliptical sentence has the structure of a complete sentence, even though some words are omitted from the beginning of the sentence, there are two options.

---

1 Standard formal: *use this, and you can't go wrong in formal contexts.*
2 Standard formal with consistent options: *choose one and stick to it.*
3 Standard formal with flexible options: *choose any one, any time.*
4 Old-fashioned: *still all right, but fading from modern usage.*
5 Standard informal: *fine in conversation or in personal letters.*
6 Nonstandard: *you jez'gotta be kidding.*

# Ellipses

**i.** Precede the elliptical sentence with an ellipsis and start the sentence with a capital letter — even though, in the original, that segment of the sentence started with a small letter.

... A big bad wolf met Little Red Riding Hood in the forest.[2]

Use this method for all ordinary purposes.

**ii.** Precede the elliptical sentence with an ellipsis and start the sentence with a capital letter in square brackets.

... [A] big bad wolf met Little Red Riding Hood in the forest.[2]

Use this method for all purposes where great precision is necessary: for example, in a legal document or in an official report. The square brackets round the capital letter at the start of the quotation tell the reader that the capital is an editorial intervention. (For a more detailed discussion of the use of square brackets, see chapter 19, section **B**.)

**b.** If the elliptical sentence does not make sense on its own — that is, if you have to add some introductory word or words to it so as to make it a complete sentence — add the word or words in square brackets.

... [In the end] the big bad wolf was done in, and grandma and Little Red Riding Hood were saved.[1]

**2. To show the omission of a word or words in the middle of a sentence.**
Put the ellipsis at that point in the sentence where the word or words are missing.

One day, a ... wolf met Little Red Riding Hood in the forest.[1]

**3. To show the omission of a word or words at the end of a sentence.**
**a.** If the terminal punctuation mark of the elliptical sentence is a full stop, the options are these.

**i.** Use a full stop followed by a three-dot ellipsis. This will give you four dots at the end of the elliptical sentence.

One day, a big bad wolf met Little Red Riding Hood. ...[2]

**ii.** Use a three-dot ellipsis without an additional dot to mark the full

## Punctuation

stop. Here you can choose between separating and not separating the first dot from the end of the elliptical sentence.

One day, a big bad wolf met Little Red Riding Hood...[2]
One day, a big bad wolf met Little Red Riding Hood ...[2]

**b.** If the terminal punctuation mark of the elliptical sentence is a question mark or an exclamation mark, use the usual three-dot ellipsis followed by the question mark or by the exclamation mark, as the case may be.

The big bad wolf asked, "Where are you going ... ?"[1]
No, she certainly did not ... ![1]

**4. To show the omission of a word or words at the end of one sentence and a further omission at the beginning of the next sentence.**
You don't have to have two ellipses cheek to cheek for this one. All you need is one ellipsis between the two sentences.
**a.** If the earlier sentence ends with a full stop, use either —

**i.** a full stop and a three-dot ellipsis, or

**ii.** a three-dot ellipsis alone.

In either case, start the next sentence with a capital letter.

When Little Red Riding Hood reached the cottage the big bad wolf was waiting for her.... The big bad wolf was done in, and grandma and Little Red Riding Hood were saved.[2]
When Little Red Riding Hood reached the cottage the big bad wolf was waiting for her... The big bad wolf was done in, and grandma and Little Red Riding Hood were saved.[2]
When Little Red Riding Hood reached the cottage the big bad wolf was waiting for her ... The big bad wolf was done in, and grandma and Little Red Riding Hood were saved.[2]

---

1 Standard formal: *use this, and you can't go wrong in formal contexts.*
2 Standard formal with consistent options: *choose one and stick to it.*
3 Standard formal with flexible options: *choose any one, any time.*
4 Old-fashioned: *still all right, but fading from modern usage.*
5 Standard informal: *fine in conversation or in personal letters.*
6 Nonstandard: *you jez'gotta be kidding.*

Again, if precision is important, use square brackets at the start of the second sentence to show that the capitalisation is an editorial intervention.

> When Little Red Riding Hood reached the cottage the big bad wolf was waiting for her.... [T]he big bad wolf was done in, and grandma and Little Red Riding Hood were saved.[2]
> When Little Red Riding Hood reached the cottage the big bad wolf was waiting for her... [T]he big bad wolf was done in, and grandma and Little Red Riding Hood were saved.[2]
> When Little Red Riding Hood reached the cottage the big bad wolf was waiting for her ... [T]he big bad wolf was done in, and grandma and Little Red Riding Hood were saved.[2]

**b.** If you can combine the two separate elliptical sentences into a single sentence, then a three-dot ellipsis is enough, and there is no need for a capital letter at the beginning of the second elliptical sentence.

> The big bad wolf had reached the cottage before her and ... was waiting for her there and swallowed her up too.[1]

**c.** If the earlier sentence ends with a question mark or with an exclamation mark, separate the two sentences with an ellipsis followed by a question mark or an exclamation mark, as the case may be, and start the second elliptical sentence with a capital letter.

> Did she then stop ... ?  She certainly did not stop![2]
> Did she then stop ... ?  [S]he certainly did not stop![2]
>
> No, She certainly did not ... !  She hurried on and soon arrived at her grandmother's cottage.[2]
> No, she certainly did not ... !  [S]he hurried on and soon arrived at her grandmother's cottage.[2]

**5. To show the omission of words in several places in a sentence.**
If you don't mind your sentence looking like Swiss cheese — or if you need absolute accuracy, say, for a legal document — you can have more than one ellipsis in any one sentence. As an alternative, you can indicate that you are writing a condensed version of the sentence, and you can then simply write it without ellipses.

> Thanks ... to the ... woodcutter, the ... wolf was done in. ...[2]

## Punctuation

> Thanks ... to the ... woodcutter, the ... wolf was done in... [2]
> Thanks ... to the ... woodcutter, the ... wolf was done in ... [2]

> A condensed version of the original sentence runs as follows: "Thanks to the woodcutter, the wolf was done in."[2]

In such cases, you may vary the punctuation around the ellipses according to the needs of the elliptical sentence. We have shown this in the example above by deleting the comma that appeared in the original after "Thanks".

**6. To show the omission of a whole sentence or sentences after a complete sentence.**

**a.** If the sentence preceding the omission ends with a full stop, mark the omitted sentence or sentences either with a four-dot or a three-dot ellipsis.

> One day, a big bad wolf met Little Red Riding Hood in the forest. ... Little Red Riding Hood said she was going to see her grandmother.[2]
> One day, a big bad wolf met Little Red Riding Hood in the forest. .. Little Red Riding Hood said she was going to see her grandmother.[2]
> One day, a big bad wolf met Little Red Riding Hood in the forest ... Little Red Riding Hood said she was going to see her grandmother.[2]

**b.** If the sentence preceding the omission ends with a question mark or an exclamation mark, show the terminal punctuation mark of the sentence before the ellipsis and follow the punctuation mark with a three-dot ellipsis.

> Did she then stop to continue her conversation with the big bad wolf? ... Rather, she hurried on and soon arrived at her grandmother's cottage.[1]
>
> No, she certainly did not stop! ... The big bad wolf had reached the cottage before her and had swallowed the grandmother up.[1]

---

1 Standard formal: *use this, and you can't go wrong in formal contexts.*
2 Standard formal with consistent options: *choose one and stick to it.*
3 Standard formal with flexible options: *choose any one, any time.*
4 Old-fashioned: *still all right, but fading from modern usage.*
5 Standard informal: *fine in conversation or in personal letters.*
6 Nonstandard: *you jez'gotta be kidding.*

# Ellipses

**7. To show the omission of a longer passage of prose.**
If the omission consists of several sentences or of one or more paragraphs, mark the omission either by putting a three-dot or a four-dot ellipsis at the point of the omission, or by putting a three-dot ellipsis on a separate line.

> One day, a big bad wolf met Little Red Riding Hood in the forest. . . . Thanks, though, to the timely intervention of a woodcutter, the big bad wolf was done in, and grandma and Little Red Riding Hood were saved.[2]
>
> One day, a big bad wolf met Little Red Riding Hood in the forest. . . Thanks, though, to the timely intervention of a woodcutter, the big bad wolf was done in, and grandma and Little Red Riding Hood were saved.[2]
>
> One day, a big bad wolf met Little Red Riding Hood in the forest . . . Thanks, though, to the timely intervention of a woodcutter, the big bad wolf was done in, and grandma and Little Red Riding Hood were saved.[2]
>
> One day, a big bad wolf met Little Red Riding Hood in the forest.
> . . .
> Thanks, though, to the timely intervention of a woodcutter, the big bad wolf was done in, and grandma and Little Red Riding Hood were saved.[2]

**8. To show the omission of a line or lines of a poem.**
Put the ellipses on separate lines.

> I wandered lonely as a cloud
>
> . . .
>
> When all at once I saw a crowd,
> A host, of golden daffodils;
>
> . . .
>
> Fluttering and dancing in the breeze.[1]

(Apologies to William Wordsworth for mangling the first verse of his poem "Daffodils".)

**9. To show the omission of letters from a censored word.**
Use either an ellipsis or a dash.

## Punctuation

"You b ... fool," he swore.[3]
"You b— fool," he swore.[3]

### 10. Omission of ellipses.
If you are condensing a text, and if the condensation involves many omissions in many locations, it can be a nuisance to the writer — and a distraction to the reader — to have many ellipses on the page. In such cases it is best to introduce the passage by saying that the text is a condensation of the original, and to write it without ellipses.

This is a condensed version of the text at the beginning of this chapter.

A big bad wolf met Little Red Riding Hood. She was going to see her grandmother. She soon arrived at her grandmother's cottage. The big bad wolf had swallowed the grandmother up, and swallowed [Little Red Riding Hood] up too. Thanks to a woodcutter, grandma and Little Red Riding Hood were saved.[1]

## B. Interrupted, trailing off or hesitant speech
Choose between a dash and an ellipsis — the latter, with or without an additional dot for a full stop.

### 11. Interrupted speech or trailing off speech.
The dash is perhaps slightly more appropriate where the speech is interrupted by somebody else; the ellipsis, where the speaker herself or himself trails off in midsentence. Really, though, an ellipsis or a dash will do in either case.

**a.** Interrupted speech.

| | |
|---|---|
| JOHN: | I would like to ask you whether... |
| JOAN: | Sorry, I haven't got time for your question now.[2] |
| JOHN: | I would like to ask you whether ... |
| JOAN: | Sorry, I haven't got time for your question now.[2] |

---

1 Standard formal: *use this, and you can't go wrong in formal contexts.*
2 Standard formal with consistent options: *choose one and stick to it.*
3 Standard formal with flexible options: *choose any one, any time.*
4 Old-fashioned: *still all right, but fading from modern usage.*
5 Standard informal: *fine in conversation or in personal letters.*
6 Nonstandard: *you jez'gotta be kidding.*

# Ellipses

JOHN: I would like to ask you whether. . . .
JOAN: Sorry, I haven't got time for your question now.²
JOHN: I would like to ask you whether —
JOAN: Sorry, I haven't got time for your question now.²

**b.** Trailing off speech.

**i.** An incomplete sentence.

If you only knew. . .²
If you only knew . . .²
If you only knew. . . .²
If you only knew —²

**ii.** A complete sentence, hinting at incomplete information.

Here everything is all right. . . And how are things with you?²
Here everything is all right . . . And how are things with you?²
Here everything is all right. . . . And how are things with you?²

## 12. Hesitant speech.

Choose between ellipses and dashes. Ellipses indicate somewhat longer pauses between segments of hesitant speech; dashes, somewhat shorter pauses. Within the same sentence you should use either ellipses or dashes consistently. But within the same text you may opt for ellipses in one sentence and dashes in another.

Well — er — you see — er — I really don't know the answer.³
Well . . . er . . . you see . . . er . . . I really don't know the answer.³

# CHAPTER 25
# Asterisks and allied symbols

## Overview
In this chapter we deal with the following symbols:

the asterisk ( * );
the double or multiple asterisk ( ** or *** );
the dagger, also called the obelisk ( † );
the double dagger, also called the diesis ( ‡ );
other symbols — for example, the dot ( . ).

Nowadays these symbols have a limited range of uses, of which we discuss three.

**1.** The use of symbols for footnoting. In this use, footnote numbers are a modern alternative.
**2.** The use of symbols for articulating a text. In this use numbers or letters are an alternative.
**3.** The use of symbols for decorative effect.

In the past, the multiple asterisk also served as a substitute for the ellipsis. Because this use has gone right out of fashion, we do not discuss it in this chapter. You will find our discussion of the ellipsis in chapter 24.

---

1 Standard formal: *use this, and you can't go wrong in formal contexts.*
2 Standard formal with consistent options: *choose one and stick to it.*
3 Standard formal with flexible options: *choose any one, any time.*
4 Old-fashioned: *still all right, but fading from modern usage.*
5 Standard informal: *fine in conversation or in personal letters.*
6 Nonstandard: *you jez'gotta be kidding.*

## Asterisks and allied symbols

**1. Asterisks, daggers and footnote numbers to draw attention to footnotes.**
The use of asterisks and other symbols to draw the reader's attention to footnotes is rather old-fashioned. The modern method of producing the same effect is to use footnote numbers. Still, if you do want to use asterisks and daggers, the usual practice is as follows.

    **a.** For the first footnote use an asterisk (*).
    **b.** For the second footnote use a double asterisk or a dagger (** or † ).
    **c.** For the third footnote use a triple asterisk or a double dagger (*** or ‡ ).
    **d.** For the fourth footnote use a quadruple asterisk or a dagger and a double dagger (**** or †‡ ).

The text would therefore read as follows:

There is a footnote at the bottom of this page.*
There is a second footnote at the bottom of this page.**
There is a third footnote at the bottom of this page.***
There is a fourth footnote at the bottom of this page.****
There is a footnote at the bottom of this page.*
There is a second footnote at the bottom of this page.†
There is a third footnote at the bottom of this page.‡
There is a fourth footnote at the bottom of this page.†‡
There is a footnote at the bottom of this page.[1]
There is a second footnote at the bottom of this page.[2]
There is a third footnote at the bottom of this page.[3]
There is a fourth footnote at the bottom of this page.[4]

The corresponding footnotes would be:

* This is the first footnote on the page.[4]
[1] This is the first footnote on the page.[1]
** This is the second footnote on the page.[4]
† This is the second footnote on the page.[4]
[2] This is the second footnote on the page.[1]
*** This is the third footnote on the page.[4]
‡ This is the third footnote on the page.[4]

# Punctuation

³This is the third footnote on the page.¹
**** This is the fourth footnote on the page.⁴
†‡ This is the fourth footnote on the page.⁴
⁴This is the fourth footnote on the page.¹

There are two things worth noting about the above examples. One is that, in the text, the symbol or number comes after the item; in the footnote itself, it comes before the item. The other point is that, if you have a need for more than four footnotes on a page, the number of asterisks or daggers and double daggers would become quite unmanageable. Clearly, therefore, footnote numbers are the preferred option.

**2. Asterisks and allied symbols, or numbers and letters, to articulate a text.**

An articulated text is one in which lines or items are preceded by a symbol — for example an asterisk — and indented from the main text. The symbols in front of the articulated lines can be asterisks but they can, of course, be any other symbol you care to choose.

> There were two groups of people at the meeting:
> \* some who favoured immediate change,
> \* others who favoured a gradual approach.²

> There were two groups of people at the meeting:
> . some who favoured immediate change,
> . others who favoured a gradual approach.²

> There were two groups of people at the meeting:
> **i.** some who favoured immediate change,
> **ii.** others who favoured a gradual approach.²

> There were two groups of people at the meeting:
> **a.** some who favoured immediate change,
> **b.** others who favoured a gradual approach.²

There are, of course, other varieties of articulation that you may adopt.

---

1 Standard formal: *use this, and you can't go wrong in formal contexts.*
2 Standard formal with consistent options: *choose one and stick to it.*
3 Standard formal with flexible options: *choose any one, any time.*
4 Old-fashioned: *still all right, but fading from modern usage.*
5 Standard informal: *fine in conversation or in personal letters.*
6 Nonstandard: *you jez'gotta be kidding.*

## Asterisks and allied symbols

3. Asterisks — or any symbols of your choice — make a dandy decorative device.

```
* * * * * * * * * * * *
*                     *
*                     *
*     HAPPY BIRTHDAY! *
*                     *
*                     *
* * * * * * * * * * * *
```

# Glossary of grammatical terms

This is a glossary of the grammatical terms used in the book. The definitions we have given accord with those of traditional grammar. But, since there is no uniform code of English grammar, you may find that the terminology and the definitions in this glossary vary from those in other source books.

**Abbreviation, contraction, fusion**
   a. An abbreviation is a shortened form of a word, in which the first and/or last letters of the shortened word are not the same as those in the full word. ("**Phone**" is an abbreviation of "**telephone**".)

   b. A contraction is a shortened form of a word, in which the first and last letters of the contracted word are the same as those in the full word. ("**Mr**" is a contraction of "**mister**".)

   c. A fusion is the combination of two words into one, with some letter or letters omitted. ("**Isn't**" is a fusion of "**is not**".)

**Absolute construction**   A phrase featuring a present participle that has its own subject. ("**The guests having arrived,** we sat down to dinner" — "having arrived" has a subject different from that of "sat down to dinner". Compare this with PRESENT PARTICIPLE PHRASE.)

**Acronym**   The initial letters of a group of words that stands for the group of words. ("**UN**" stands for "**United Nations**".)

**Active**   One of the two voices of English verbs, the other being passive. (See VOICE.)

**Adjective**   A word that modifies a noun. ("**My big leather-bound** book." Each of the bolded words is an adjective modifying the noun "book". "My" is a possessive adjective; "big", a common adjective;

"leather-bound", a compound adjective.) We distinguish the following uses of adjectives.

   **a.** An adjective used attributively stands before the noun or noun equivalent that it modifies. ("This is a **good** book.")

   **b.** An adjective used predicatively stands somewhere after the noun or noun equivalent that it modifies. ("The book is **good**.")

   **c.** An attached adjective is one that is used either attributively or predicatively. (See the above two example sentences.)

   **d.** A detached adjective is one used separately from the noun or noun equivalent that it modifies, and it is separated from the noun or noun equivalent with a comma. ("**Tired**, they nevertheless continued to work.")

**Adjective clause**  Another expression for relative clause. (See RELATIVE CLAUSE.)

**Adverb**  A word that modifies any word or group of words other than a noun or noun equivalent. ("**Luckily**, they came **early**, but **only** because I had asked them to." "Luckily" modifies the sentence as a whole; "early" modifies the verb "came"; "only" modifies the conjunction "because".) We distinguish two uses of the adverb.

   **a.** A detached adverb modifies a sentence or a clause as a whole and is optionally separated with a comma — in midsentence or midclause, with a pair of commas — from the sentence or clause that it modifies. ("**Fortunately**, they arrived on time.")

   **b.** An attached adverb modifies a specific associated word and is not normally separated from that word with a comma or commas. ("They **usually** arrive on time.")

**Adverb clause**  (See CLAUSE.)

**Adverb of frequency**  A class of adverbs — including words such as "often", "never", "seldom". The following features distinguish them from other adverbs.

   **a.** They usually stand before, rather than after, the verb they modify. (Compare: "I **often** go"; "I go **quickly**".)

**Glossary**

    **b.** They normally stand between the auxiliary and the notional verb. (Compare: "I **have seldom travelled**"; "I **have travelled far**".)

    **c.** When they stand at the beginning of a sentence, they skew the word order of the sentence. (Compare: "**I have seen** . . . "; "**Never have I seen** such a thing".)

**Affix** Another term for a prefix or a suffix. (See PREFIX and SUFFIX.)

**Agreement** The concord of singular and plural between a nominative and a finite verb. (In "**It is** . . . " and "**They are** . . . ", the singular "it" agrees with the singular "is"; the plural "they", with the plural "are".

**Anomalous finite** Any one of the twenty-four finite verbs that normally stands before the subject of a question sentence: am, is, are, was, were, have, has, had, can, could, shall, should, will, would, may, might, must, ought, need, dare, used, do, does, did. ("**Are** they coming?" "**Did** they come?")

**Antecedent** The word or words to which a pronoun refers. ("I took the **book** and read it." "Book" is the antecedent of the pronoun "it".)

**Antecedent clause** In the case of a sentence featuring a relative pronoun, the antecedent clause is the clause in which the antecedent occurs. ("**I returned the book** that she lent me." "I returned the book" is the antecedent clause of the relative pronoun "that".)

**Anticipatory question** A question to which the answer is anticipated, and which is characterised by a question-tag ending. ("**They aren't here yet, are they?**" See also QUESTION TAG.)

**Apostrophe** A punctuation mark ( ' ) used, among other things, to indicate the location of an omitted letter or letters in a fused word. ("**Isn't**".)

**Apposition** The relationship to each other of two nouns, or noun equivalents, when they refer to the same entity. ("**My wife, Deborah,** is here." "My wife" and "Deborah" refer to the same person — as the singular verb "is" attests.)

**Aspect**   One of four variations of a tense. (See TENSE AND ASPECT.)

**Asterisk**   A punctuation mark that looks like a star ( * ) and that serves, among other things, as an old-fashioned alternative to a footnote number.

**Attached and detached adjective**   (See ADJECTIVE.)

**Attached and detached adverb**   (See ADVERB.)

**Attributive adjective**   An adjective positioned before the noun or noun equivalent it modifies. ("She is a **fine** person." See also ADJECTIVE.)

**Auxiliary verb**   (See NOTIONAL AND AUXILIARY VERBS.)

**Base form of the verb**   The infinitive form of the verb without "to". (See VERB FORMS.)

**Brackets**   A punctuation mark consisting — usually — of two related signs turned towards each other. In prose, as distinct for example from mathematics, brackets are either round, ( ), or square, [ ].
    **a.** Round brackets serve to enclose part of a text.
    **b.** Square brackets serve to enclose an editorial addition to a text.

**Capital letters and small letters**   Capital letters are also called capitals or upper case letters; small letters are also called lower case letters. The former have the appearance "A", "B", "C" . . . ; the latter, "a", "b", "c" . . .

**Cardinal number**   (See NUMBER.)

**Clause**   A coherent group of words, ordinarily part of a sentence, that contains a nominative and a finite verb, either but not both of which may be implied by way of an ellipsis. ("**I came** home and **I showered**" has two full clauses. "**I came** home and **showered**" has one full and one elliptical clause.) Clauses divide into five functional types.

## Glossary

**a.** An independent clause, also called a main clause, is one that — except when a noun clause binds to it — can stand as a sentence on its own. ("**I want a book**...")

**b.** A coordinate clause is one that binds to an independent clause with a coordinating conjunction — though the conjunction may be implicit rather than explicit. ("They came home **and they had dinner**"; "They came home; **they had dinner**".)

**c.** A noun clause binds to an associated clause in a noun function — a subject, for example. ("**What I want** is a book.")

**d.** An adjective clause, also called a relative clause, modifies a noun or a noun equivalent in an associated clause. ("I want a book **that will interest me**.")

**e.** An adverb clause modifies an element other than a noun or noun equivalent in an associated clause. ("I want a book **when I go to bed**.")

Noun clauses, adjective clauses and adverb clauses are called subordinate clauses, to distinguish them from independent and coordinate clauses. (See also COORDINATING CONJUNCTION, SUBORDINATING CONJUNCTION and PARALLEL CLAUSES.)

**Collective noun**   A noun that is singular in form but plural in connotation. The usage problem associated with such a noun, when it functions as a nominative, is whether it associates with a singular or a plural finite verb. (Is it "The **jury has** come to a decision" or "The **jury have** come to a decision"?)

**Colon**   A punctuation mark consisting of two dots one above the other ( : ). It is used, among other things, as an alternative punctuation for a dash. ("They were few in number: still they battled on." A dash could substitute for the colon.)

**Comma**   A punctuation mark ( , ) with many and varied uses, discussed in chapter 16.

**Common fraction**   (See NUMBER.)

**Common gender**  (See GENDER.)

**Common noun**  (See NOUN.)

**Comparative degree**  (See DEGREES OF THE ADJECTIVE.)

**Compound adjective**  An adjective consisting of more than one word, often hyphenated or amalgamated. ("A **leather-bound** volume"; "a **breathtaking** view". See also ADJECTIVE.)

**Compound noun**  A noun consisting of more than one word, often hyphenated or amalgamated. ("A **Johnny-come-lately**"; "a **necktie**". See also NOUN.)

**Compound subject**  A subject consisting of more than one noun. A usage problem arises if one noun in the compound is singular and another is plural. (Is it "A **bag of coins** was . . . " or "A **bag of coins** were . . . "?)

**Compound verb**  A verb consisting of one or more auxiliary verbs and a notional verb. ("They **have been resting**" — consists of the auxiliary verbs "have been" and the notional verb "resting". See also NOTIONAL AND AUXILIARY VERBS.)

**Conditional**  A conditional, also called a conditional sentence, is a sentence that consists of a condition clause and a consequence clause. ("**If I were not so busy, I would help you.**") The condition clause is characterised by having some such conjunction as "if", "unless", "in case" at its start. Conditionals often involve the use of subjunctive verbs. (See also "subjunctive" under MOOD.)

**Conjunction**  A joining word used to join words, phrases, clauses or sentences. ("Jack **and** Jill"; "My place **or** your place"; "They came **as** we were leaving"; "It's early. **But** we'll start anyway." See also COORDINATING CONJUNCTION and SUBORDINATING CONJUNCTION.)

**Continuous**  An aspect of the tenses. (See TENSE AND ASPECT.)

**Contraction**  (See ABBREVIATION, CONTRACTION AND FUSION.)

## Glossary

**Coordinate clause**  (See CLAUSE.)

**Coordinating conjunction**  A conjunction that joins words, phrases, clauses or sentences in a coordinate — that is, a coequal — relationship. ("A table **and** a chair"; "We came **but** no one was there".) The most common coordinating conjunctions are "and", "but", "or". These conjunctions are characterised by their fixed position between the elements that they join. In this they differ from subordinating adverbial conjunctions, which can stand — together with their associated word or words — either before or after the element with which they are joined. ("We rested **when we had finished**"; "**When we had finished** we rested". See also SUBORDINATING CONJUNCTION and CLAUSE.)

**Dagger**  A punctuation mark that has two different forms: a single dagger ( † ) and a double dagger ( ‡ ). It is used, among other things, as an old-fashioned substitute for a footnote number.

**Dangling hyphen**  (See HYPHEN.)

**Dash**  A punctuation mark consisting of a horizontal stroke — either longer than a hyphen or the same length as a hyphen, but with a space on either side of it. It is used, among other things, as an alternative punctuation mark for a colon. ("They were few in number — still they battled on." A colon could substitute for the dash.)

**Decimal fraction**  (See NUMBER.)

**Decimal point**  A full stop used to separate a whole number from a fraction, when the latter is expressed as a decimal number. ("A half is the same as 0.5.")

**Defining relative clause**  (See RELATIVE CLAUSE.)

**Degrees of the adjective**  Qualitative attributes of the adjective, marked in the comparative and superlative degrees by characteristic suffixes or additional words. The three degrees of adjectives are the following:
- **a.** Positive:     big;     luminous.
- **b.** Comparative:     bigg**er**;     **more** luminous.
- **c.** Superlative:     bigg**est**;     **most** luminous.

# Glossary

**Descriptive adjective** (See ADJECTIVE.)

**Detached adjective** (See ADJECTIVE.)

**Detached adverb** (See ADVERB.)

**Direct question** (See QUESTION.)

**Direct speech**  The actual words used by the cited source ("**We need this tomorrow**") as distinct from reported speech ("They said that **they needed that the next day**". See also REPORTED SPEECH.)

**Double-barrelled adjective**  A hyphenated adjective pair. ("She attended a **north-south** conference".)

**Double-barrelled noun**  A hyphenated noun pair. ("He is the **director-producer** of the film.")

**Double dagger** (See DAGGER.)

**Ellipsis**  A punctuation mark ( . . . ) used, among other things, to indicate the omission of a word or words in a text. ("What the . . . do you mean?")

**Elliptical and full clauses**  An elliptical clause is one in which either the subject or the verb is implied but not stated. ("They came home **and freshened up**" — the subject "they" is implied in the second clause. "She went to Minorca; **he, to Majorca**" — the verb "went" is implied in the second clause.) A full clause is one in which both the subject and the verb are stated. (" . . . **and they freshened up**"; " . . . **he went to Majorca**".)

**Elliptical and full sentences**  An elliptical sentence is one in which either the subject or the verb — in some cases both — is implied but not stated. ("Do you feel like tennis?" "**Yes**." In the answer sentence, both the subject "I" and the verb "do" are implied.) A full sentence is one in which both the subject and the verb are stated. ("**Yes, I do**.")

**Emphatic** (See MOOD.)

## Glossary

**Emphatic pronoun**  (See REFLEXIVE AND EMPHATIC PRONOUNS.)

**Exclamation and interjection**  The former is a word or words, other than an interjection, used in an exclamatory way and terminating in an exclamation mark. ("**Out!**" "**Well done!**") The latter is any of a specialised class of words. ("**Wow!**" "**Ouch!**")

**Exclamation mark**  A punctuation mark (!) used, among other things, to terminate an exclamation or interjection. ("**What a sight!**" "**Oh!**")

**Feminine**  (See GENDER.)

**Finite verb**  (See VERB FORMS.)

**Fragmentary quotation**  (See QUOTATION.)

**Full clause**  (See ELLIPTICAL AND FULL CLAUSES.)

**Full quotation**  (See QUOTATION.)

**Full sentence**  (See ELLIPTICAL AND FULL SENTENCES.)

**Full stop**  A punctuation mark consisting of a dot or point (.). It is used, among other things, to terminate a sentence other than a sentence that needs a question mark or an exclamation mark at its end. ("**I'll do it now.**")

**Future in the past tense**  (See TENSE AND ASPECT.)

**Future tense**  (See TENSE AND ASPECT.)

**Gender**  A feature of nouns, pronouns and personal adjectives that correlates roughly — but not entirely — with sex or sexlessness. English recognises four genders.

| | | | | | |
|---|---|---|---|---|---|
| a. | Masculine: | man | boy | he | his |
| b. | Feminine: | woman | girl | she | her |
| c. | Neuter: | table | chair | it | its |
| d. | Common: | person | lawyer | they | their |

# Glossary

**Genitive**   Also called the possessive, the genitive is a feature of nouns, pronouns and personal adjectives, indicating a particular relationship between the genitive word and another word or words in the sentence. ("This is **Elizabeth's** work, that is **your** work, and the other is **mine**" — "Elizabeth's" is a genitive noun; "your", a genitive personal adjective; "mine", a genitive personal pronoun. Each of the genitives relates to "work". See also POSSESSIVE PRONOUN AND ADJECTIVE.)

**Hyphen**   A punctuation mark that consists of a short horizontal stroke ( - ). It is used, among other things, to show the syllabic division of a word ("**hy-phen**") or to join the two parts of a compound word. ("**Two-way** traffic.") A dangling hyphen is one that does not immediately connect to another word or element. ("My **father-** and mother-in-law.")

**Imperative**   (See MOOD.)

**Independent clause**   (See CLAUSE.)

**Indicative**   (See MOOD.)

**Indirect question**   (See QUESTION.)

**Infinitive**   The base form of the verb with "to" in front of it — "**to be**", "**to see**". (See also VERB FORMS.)

**Inflection**   A feature of certain words, namely their ability to change or vary their forms in varying grammatical contexts. ("They **go**"; "She **goes**" — the verb inflects to accommodate a variation of subject from "they" to "she".)

**Interjection**   A specialised word class, including words such as "Yoohoo" and "Hello". (See EXCLAMATION AND INTERJECTION.)

**Interrogative**   (See MOOD.)

**Introductory clause**   A clause that functions, among other things, to introduce direct speech. ("**He said,** 'I didn't know that.'")

## Glossary

**Introductory verb** The verb that occurs in an introductory clause. ("She **asked**, 'What are you doing?'" See INTRODUCTORY CLAUSE.)

**Inverted commas** Another expression for quotation marks. (See QUOTATION MARKS.)

**Italic and roman prints** Italic print features sloping letters — *as with the letters in these words* — distinguished from the **upright letters in roman print**.

**Lower case** Another expression for small letters. (See CAPITAL LETTERS AND SMALL LETTERS.)

**Main clause** An alternative expression for independent clause. (See CLAUSE.)

**Masculine** One of the four genders in English. (See GENDER.)

**Mobile conjunction** A conjunction that can occupy various places in a clause. ("**Therefore** it is time to start"; "It is **therefore** time to start"; "It is time to start, **therefore**".) The two most common mobile conjunctions are "however" and "therefore".

**Modal auxiliary** Any of the verbs "would", "should", "could", "may", "might", "must", "ought" — when they are used in a subjunctive, as distinct from an indicative, function. "**Would** that it were dawn." Compare the subjunctive use of "would" in the foregoing example with the indicative use of "would" in the following example: "He said that he **would** come later." (See also MOOD.)

**Modifier** An adjective or an adverb — so called because an adjective modifies a noun or noun equivalent ("It was a **good** supper"), while an adverb modifies a word or a group of words other than a noun or noun equivalent ("They came **quickly**").

**Mood** A mode of expression denoted by the verb. The term "mood" is applicable also to the clause or sentence in which the verb occurs. The following are the moods in English.

324

| INDICATIVE | (the mood of reality or matter-of-factness) |
|---|---|
| **I go.** | (Positive) |
| **I don't go.** | (Negative) |
| **Do I go?** | (Interrogative) |
| **Don't I go?** | (Negative-interrogative) |
| **I do go.** | (Emphatic) |

| IMPERATIVE | (the mood of command) |
|---|---|
| **Go!** | (Positive) |
| **Don't go!** | (Negative) |
| **Do go!** | (Emphatic) |

SUBJUNCTIVE  (the mood of hypothesis, wishful thinking or just-suppose)

| | |
|---|---|
| If he **took** my advice it **would be** good. | (Positive) |
| If he **didn't take** my advice it **wouldn't be** good. | (Negative) |
| If he took my advice, **would it be** good? | (Interrogative) |
| If he took my advice, **wouldn't it be** good? | (Negative-interrogative) |
| If he **did take** my advice it would be good. | (Emphatic) |

**Negative**   (See MOOD.)

**Negative-interrogative**   (See MOOD.)

**Neuter**   (See GENDER.)

**Nominative**   That part of a subject, if a subject consists of more than one word, that determines the number — singular or plural — of the associated finite verb. ("Their **sister** with all her friends **is** now overseas" — only the nominative "sister" determines the number of the finite verb "is". "**Bags** of flour **are** stacked to the ceiling" — only the nominative "bags" determines the number of the finite verb "are".) If a subject consists of one word it also constitutes the nominative. ("**It** is good.")

**Nondefining relative clause**   (See RELATIVE CLAUSE.)

## Glossary

**Notional and auxiliary verbs**   A notional verb is one that carries a meaning, as well as having a grammatical function, in a sentence — as distinct from an auxiliary verb, which has only a grammatical function. (The sentence "They **were being entertained**" has one notional and two auxiliary verbs. "Entertained" is notional; "were" and "being" are auxiliary, acting to indicate the tense-aspect and the passive voice of the whole of the compound "were being entertained". See also COMPOUND VERB, VERB FORMS and VOICE.)

**Noun**   A word used as a name to denote a person or thing. The sentence "**Margaret** did a **drawing** of the **cross-section** of a **flower**" contains four nouns of different kinds or structures — a proper noun ("Margaret"); a gerundial noun ("drawing"); a compound noun ("cross-section"); a common noun ("flower"). (See also COLLECTIVE NOUN.)

**Noun clause**   (See CLAUSE.)

**Number**   A sign or a word denoting quantity. The main kinds of numbers appearing in prose are the following.

    **a.** Cardinal numbers:   1, 2, . . . ; one, two . . .
    **b.** Ordinal numbers:   1st, 2nd . . . ; first, second . . .
    **c.** Decimal numbers:   0.1, 0.2 . . . ; point one, point two . . .
    **d.** Common fractions:   1/2, 1/3 . . . ; a half, a third . . .

**Object**   A word or words that stand after a verb and that relate to it as the target of the action that the verb denotes. ("They saw **it**.") Also a word or words that stand after a preposition and that relate to the preposition as its object. ("We were rewarded for **what we had done**.")

**Ordinal number**   (See NUMBER.)

**Parallel clauses**   Two or more clauses that relate to an associated clause in the same manner. ("I came **because I wanted to** and **because you called for me**." The two bolded clauses are parallel adverb clauses, both functioning as modifiers of the independent clause "I came . . . ".)

**Parenthesis**   Another term for a parenthetic element. (See PARENTHETIC ELEMENT.)

# Glossary

**Parenthetic element**   A group of words or a word — usually marked off from the surrounding text with a comma, a pair of commas, a dash, a pair of dashes, or a pair of brackets — that functions as an amplifying aside and that is not essential to the structure of the surrounding text. ("We were glad, **as you might well expect,** that the job was over." For the pair of commas in the foregoing example you might equally well substitute a pair of dashes or a pair of round brackets.)

**Passive**   One of the two voices of English verbs, the other being active. (See VOICE.)

**Past participle phrase**   A phrase featuring a past participle that implicitly takes its subject from the accompanying text. ("**Tired but happy,** they headed for home" — the bolded phrase implicitly takes the subject "they".)

**Past tense**   (See TENSE AND ASPECT.)

**Perfect**   An aspect of the tenses. (See TENSE AND ASPECT.)

**Perfect continuous**   An aspect of the tenses. (See TENSE AND ASPECT.)

**Period**   Another word for a full stop. (See FULL STOP.)

**Person**   A feature of pronouns and of genitive personal adjectives. There are three persons. The first person is the person or persons speaking; the second, the person or persons being spoken to; the third, the person or persons being spoken about.

   **a.** First person: I, me, my, mine, myself, we, us, our, ours, ourselves.

   **b.** Second person: you, your, yours, yourself, yourselves.

   **c.** Third person: she, he, it, they, her, him, them, hers, his, its, their, theirs, herself, himself, itself, themselves.

**Personal pronouns and adjectives**   The pronouns and adjectives listed under PERSON above make up the complete tally of personal pronouns and adjectives.

**Phrasal verb**   A combination of a verb and a word such as "in", "on", "with" or "by", such that the added word changes the meaning of the verb.

327

## Glossary

(Compare the meaning of the verb "got" in "I got a letter", with the meanings of "got" as a phrasal verb in "I **got by** without help", "I **got on** with them", "I **got through** all right", "I **got back** at them", "I **got up**".)

**Phrase** A coherent group of words — ordinarily part of a clause or a sentence — that does not have a finite verb, either stated or implied, and that does the job of a single identifiable word class. There are at least a dozen classes of phrases.

| | |
|---|---|
| Noun phrase: | **An old friend** called me up. |
| Pronoun phrase: | **I myself** saw them do it. |
| Adjective phrase: | The view **from the window** is lovely. |
| Preposition phrase: | They stood **in front of** the door. |
| Conjunction phrase: | She was there **as well as** he. |
| Verb phrase: | I realised what needed **to be done**. |
| Present participle phrase: | **Wanting a break**, I stopped work. |
| Past participle phrase: | They found the paper **torn into bits**. |
| Infinitive phrase: | **To run a marathon** you need to be fit. |
| Gerund phrase: | I thanked them for **coming to my aid**. |
| Adverb phrase: | They worked **with a will**. |
| Interjection phrase: | **Goodness gracious**! |

(See also separate entries under PRESENT PARTICIPLE PHRASE, PAST PARTICIPLE PHRASE and ABSOLUTE CONSTRUCTION.)

**Plural** (See SINGULAR AND PLURAL.)

**Positive** (See MOOD.)

**Positive degree** (See DEGREES OF THE ADJECTIVE.)

**Possessive** Another word for genitive. (See GENITIVE.)

**Possessive pronoun and adjective** Any of the pronouns and adjectives in the possessive — that is, genitive — form. The complete tally of these words is as follows.

    a. Possessive pronouns: mine, yours, his, hers, its, ours, theirs.
    b. Possessive adjectives: my, your, his, her, its, our, their.

# Glossary

**Predicate**  One of the two major divisions of a simple sentence. (See SUBJECT AND PREDICATE. For a third division of some sentences, see SENTENCE ANCILLARY.)

**Predicative adjective**  An adjective positioned somewhere after the noun or noun equivalent that it modifies ("That person is **fine**." See also ADJECTIVE.)

**Prefix**  A dependent element that you can add to the beginning of a word and that changes its meaning or function. ("**Un**necessary", "**de**stablise". See also SUFFIX and AFFIX.)

**Preposition**  A relational word such as "in", "on", "with", "by", "for". The second member of the relational pair that flanks the preposition is called the prepositional object — see immediately below.

**Prepositional object**  The object of a preposition. ("They were with **me**"; "They were in **the room**"; "They were rewarded for **what they had done**".)

**Preposition-prefixed verb**  A verb with a preposition-like prefix. ("**Under**pay", "**over**whelm".)

**Present participle**  (See VERB FORMS.)

**Present participle phrase**  A phrase featuring a present participle that implicitly takes its subject from the accompanying text. ("**Having the means**, I offered to help them." The bolded phrase implicitly takes the subject "I". See also PAST PARTICIPLE PHRASE and ABSOLUTE CONSTRUCTION.)

**Present tense**  (See TENSE AND ASPECT.)

**Pronoun**  A word that substitutes for a noun. ("I poured a drink and stirred **it**." The pronoun "it" substitutes for "drink".) Among other classes of pronouns, we distinguish personal pronouns and relative pronouns. (See PERSONAL PRONOUN and RELATIVE PRONOUN.)

**Proper adjective**  An adjective derived from a proper noun, and usually distinguished by being written with an initial capital letter. ("They travelled in an **Australian** airline to a **European** destination.")

## Glossary

**Proper noun** The particular name of a person or thing, usually distinguished by being written with an initial capital letter. ("I travelled to **Rome** with **Jane** in a **Boeing**.")

**Question** An inquiry intended to elicit a reply. ("**Where are you going?**") We distinguish two types of questions.

    **a.** A direct question, which is stated in the interrogative, and which ends with a question mark. ("**What is your name?**")

    **b.** A reported question, which is stated in the positive, and which does not end with a question mark. ("I asked him **what his name was**.")

**Question mark** A punctuation mark (?) that terminates a direct question. ("**How do you do?**")

**Question tag** The combination of a verb (with, in some cases, "not") plus a pronoun at the end of an anticipatory question. ("They haven't arrived, **have they**?" "We're going, **aren't we**?" See also ANTICIPATORY QUESTION.)

**Quotation** A word or words cited from speech or from writing, and normally enclosed in quotation marks. We distinguish two kinds of quotations.

    **a.** A full quotation is one that is self-contained and, normally, separated by a punctuation mark from the words of the person quoting it. (He said, "**It's a lovely morning**.")

    **b.** A fragmentary quotation is one that incorporates a part of the full quotation in the speech of the person quoting it. (It was indeed what he called a "**lovely morning**".)

**Quotation marks** A punctuation mark — also called inverted commas — consisting of single or double signs above line-level, and serving to enclose a quotation. ('Hello' or "Hello".)

**Reflexive or emphatic pronouns** The pronouns: myself, yourself, himself, herself, itself, oneself, ourselves, yourselves, themselves. In their reflexive function, these pronouns indicate that the subject and the object of the verb refer to the same person/s or thing/s. ("The **children** washed **themselves**.") In their emphatic function, they emphasise a cognate noun or pronoun. ("**They themselves** could not have done better.")

**Relative clause**   A relative clause, also called an adjective clause, is one that relates adjectivally — that is, in a modifying relationship — to some noun or noun equivalent in, and sometimes to the whole of, an associated clause. ("I have something **that I want to show you**" — "that I want to show you" modifies "something" in the antecedent clause.) There are three classes of relative clauses.

> **a.** A situational relative clause relates to the situation denoted by the whole of the associated clause. ("They rang me up, **which is what I had hoped for**.")
>
> **b.** A defining relative clause tells us which one, or what kind of, noun or noun equivalent it is that it relates to. ("I want a pen **that has a fine point**.")
>
> **c.** A nondefining relative clause adds some incidental detail to, but does not define, the noun or noun equivalent that it relates to. ("My father, **who has just returned from overseas**, brought me a present.")

The distinction between these classes is important, since it can affect the choice of the relative pronoun for, and the punctuation of, the relative clause.

**Relative pronoun**   A pronoun that stands at or near the beginning of a relative clause. Chapter 8 deals with the four major relative pronouns "who", "whom", "which" and "that". Some of the others not dealt with are "whose", "where" and "when". ("This is the person **whose** job I got"; "I'll meet you at the place **where** we met before"; "I'll meet you at any time **when** you are free".) The relative pronoun — like the relative clause in which it occurs — relates to a noun or noun equivalent, called the antecedent, in an associated clause. In the bracketed examples, "person" is the antecedent of "whose"; "place", of "where"; "time", of "when".

**Reported question**   (See QUESTION.)

**Reported speech**   Speech transformed into the words of the person

## Glossary

reporting it ("I told them **not to do that**") — as distinct from direct speech, which gives the words actually used by the person whose words we cite. ("**Don't do this**." See also DIRECT SPEECH.)

**Roman print**  (See ITALIC AND ROMAN PRINTS.)

**Round brackets**  (See BRACKETS.)

**Semicolon**  A punctuation mark consisting of a comma topped by a dot ( ; ). It serves, among other things, to separate elements that contain internal commas. ("I would like you to meet Kitty, my sister; Daphne, my daughter; and Renata, my granddaughter.")

**Sentence ancillary**  Any word or group of words that you can add to, or omit from, a sentence without affecting the essential structure of the sentence. The characteristics of a sentence ancillary are that —

    **a.** you can optionally separate it from the rest of the sentence with a comma or a pair of commas;

    **b.** it can usually occupy different positions in the sentence with which it is associated.

("**Once upon a time**, there was a magic flute"; "There was, **once upon a time**, a magic flute"; "There was a magic flute, **once upon a time**".)

**Sibilant**  A letter or letters, alone or in a word, that — when pronounced — produce a hissing or a buzzing sound. The words "**ice**", "**is**", "**axe**", "**doze**" — though variously spelled — all end in sibilant sounds. We distinguish two kinds of sibilants.

    **a.** Voiceless, or hissing, sibilants that produce only the sound of expelled air without involving a humming sound of the voice ("**ice**" and "**axe**").

    **b.** Voiced, or buzzing, sibilants that produce both the sound of expelled air and a humming sound of the voice ("**as**" and "**doze**").

The distinction is important to the spelling and punctuation of genitive proper nouns that end in sibilant sounds. ("I have read both **Knox's** and **Hopkins'** books.")

# Glossary

**Simple**  An aspect of the tenses. (See TENSE AND ASPECT.)

**Singular and plural**  A feature of nouns, personal pronouns, genitive personal adjectives, and verbs — where the singular denotes one, and the plural more than one. ("**My doctor is** examining **a friend** of **hers**" exemplifies the singular; "**Our doctors are** examining **friends of theirs**" exemplifies the plural.)

**Situational relative clause**  (See RELATIVE CLAUSE.)

**Slash**  A punctuation mark that is also called diagonal, oblique stroke, solidus, slope bar and virgule. It consists of a diagonal bar ( / ) and is used, among other things, to indicate alternatives. ("An adult should be responsible for **her/his** actions.")

**Small letter**  (See CAPITAL LETTERS AND SMALL LETTERS.)

**Split infinitive**  An infinitive verb that has a word or words interposed between the element "to" and the base form of the verb. ("To **quickly** go".)

**Square brackets**  (See BRACKETS.)

**Subject and predicate**  The two natural major divisions of a sentence. Loosely defined, the subject is the part of a sentence that expresses who or what the sentence is about; the predicate is the part that expresses something about the subject. The following examples show the division of simple sentences into subject and predicate.

| SUBJECT | PREDICATE |
|---|---|
| They | were going about their daily business. |
| My first night out | proved to be a great success. |
| A friend of my parents' | came visiting from abroad. |
| The family living next door to us | is friendly. |

Distinct and apart from the subject and the predicate are sentence ancillaries. (See also NOMINATIVE, FINITE VERB and SENTENCE ANCILLARY.)

# Glossary

**Subjunctive** (See MOOD.)

**Subordinating conjunction** A conjunction that binds or joins a subordinate clause to an associated clause.

    **a.** They took **what** they wanted. ("What" binds the noun clause "what they wanted" to the independent clause "they took".)

    **b.** These are the books **that** I want. ("That" binds the adjective clause "that I want" to the independent clause "these are the books".)

    **c.** They came **as** we were leaving. ("As" binds the adverb clause "as we were leaving" to the independent clause "they came".)

(See also COORDINATING CONJUNCTION and CLAUSE.)

**Suffix** A dependent element that you can add to the end of a word and that changes the meaning or the function of the word. ("Quick**ness**", "Quick**ly**". See also PREFIX and AFFIX.)

**Superlative degree** (See DEGREES OF THE ADJECTIVE.)

**Tense and aspect** Tense is an indicator of time or mood in verbs; aspect is a variation of tense. There are four tenses in English: present, past, future, future in the past. Each tense has four aspects: simple, continuous, perfect, perfect continuous.

TABLE OF TENSES AND ASPECTS

|  | *Present* | *Past* | *Future* | *Future in the past* |
|---|---|---|---|---|
| *Simple* | I go | I went | I will go | I would go |
| *Continuous* | I am going | I was going | I will be going | I would be going |
| *Perfect* | I have gone | I had gone | I will have gone | I would have gone |
| *Perfect continuous* | I have been going | I had been going | I will have been going | I would have been going |

(See also COMPOUND VERB and NOTIONAL AND AUXILIARY VERBS.)

**Underlining**  A line drawn under a word or words — <u>as with these words</u>.

**Upper case**  (See CAPITAL LETTERS AND SMALL LETTERS.)

**Verb forms**  The forms that a verb can take to reflect the way that it functions in various contexts. The verbs "to be" and "to go" display the following forms.

| | | |
|---|---|---|
| **a.** Base: | be | go |
| **b.** Infinitive: | to be | to go |
| **c.** Finites: | am / is / are / was / were | go / goes / went |
| **d.** Present participle: | being | going |
| **e.** Past participle: | been | gone |
| **f.** Gerund: | being | going |

The present participle and the gerund look identical but function differently. The former is a verbal adjective ("a **running** stream"); the latter, a verbal noun ("**running** is fun").

**Verbal adjective**  Another expression for a present participle. (See PRESENT PARTICIPLE and VERB FORMS.)

**Vocative**  The form of address, using a noun or a pronoun. Characteristically, the vocative is separated by a comma or commas from the associated text. ("Won't you come with me, **darling**?" "**You**, what are you doing?")

**Voice**  A feature of a verb, by which the relation of the subject to the verb is indicated. English has two voices.

    **a.** Active voice, in which the subject is the agent — or "doer" — of the state or action denoted by the verb. ("I **saw** it.")

    **b.** Passive voice, in which the subject is the target of the state or action denoted by the verb. ("It **was seen** by me.")

**Glossary**

**Voiced sibilant** One of two kinds of sibilants, the other being voiceless. (See SIBILANT.)

**Voiceless sibilant** One of two kinds of sibilants, the other being voiced. (See SIBILANT.)

# Index

abbreviation 176, 181, 314
    and apostrophe 250f, 253ff
absolute construction 207, 314
acronym 314
    and apostrophe 263
    and brackets 247
    and capital letters 151, 171f
    and full stops 176, 179ff
active (See **voice**)
address, punctuation of 219, 283
adjective 15, 199, 205ff, 314f
    attached and detached 204, 315
    attributive and predicative 269ff, 315, 317, 329
    clause (See **relative clause**)
    common gender personal 25
    compound 266, 268ff, 319
    degrees of the 15, 215, 320
    double-barrelled 272, 321
    personal 327, 333
    possessive 328
    proper 160ff, 329f
    used as a noun 36
    verbal 335
adverb 50f, 315f
    attached and detached 202f, 315
    clause (See **clause**)
    of frequency 50, 315f
    phrase 50f, 203f
affix 316, 329, 334
"agendum" and "agenda" 35
agreement, defined 30
agreement of nominative and finite verb 30ff, 316
"along with" 40

"am", "ain't", "aren't" 33
ambiguity 225
"and" 38f
    "and not" 40
    at the start of a sentence 2f
    "both . . . and" 38
    in mathematics 39
    with apostrophes 253
    with commas 198ff
    with numbers 75ff
anomalous finite (See **verb**)
antecedent 101ff, 316
antecedent clause 101ff, 316
anticipatory question 195, 316
apostrophe 250ff, 316
    and abbreviation 250f, 253ff
    and contraction 250f, 253ff
    and fusion 250ff
    with genitive common noun 250f, 256ff
    with genitive proper noun 251, 258ff
    omission of 251, 260ff
apposition 220f, 248, 316f
archaism, archaic x, 3
"as" 9, 11ff
"as if", "as though" 60f
"as well as" 40
"asked"
    and quotation marks 284ff
    in direct and reported speech 127ff
    usage of 8, 10ff
asterisk and allied symbols 317, 320
    articulating a text 310, 312
    decorative effect 310, 313
    footnoting 310f

# Index

Austen, Jane 5
auxiliary verb (See **verb**)

"billion" and "milliard" (See under **numbers**)
"both . . . and" 38
brackets, round 187f, 246ff, 317
    acronyms 247
    appositions 248
    dashes 244
    dates or places 247
    list markers 247f
    nicknames 248
    numbers 247f
    optional addition of a letter to a word 247
    parenthetic elements 116ff, 327
    publication details 247
    single bracket 248
brackets, square 246, 248f, 317
    editorial correction 249
    editorial comment 249f
    editorial explanation or amplification 249
    "*sic*" 249
    with ellipses 303ff
*Bulletin with Newsweek* quoted 3ff, 295
"but"
    "but not" 40
    at the start of a sentence 2, 3f

Caesar, Julius quoted 288
capital letters and small letters 150ff, 317
    acronyms and abbreviations 151, 171f
    address blocks, salutations and signature blocks 216f
    after a colon 170, 237
    after an exclamation mark 183, 187f
    chapters 168
    cosmic objects 164
    deities 164f
    descriptive place names 163

    geographic features 163
    headings 166ff
    hyphenated 266, 278ff
    names of organisations and titles of office bearers 151, 152ff
    newspapers, journals, etc 169
    poetry 170f
    points of the compass 163f
    proper nouns and their derivatives 159ff, 330
    proprietary names 160f
    prose 153ff, 169f
    quotations 170, 287ff
    religions and associated words 165
    reports 168
    Roman numerals 93ff
    settlements 162
    subtitles 243
    time and historical events 166
    titles of written and artistic works etc 151, 166ff, 243
    town features 161
    various uses of 171f
    vehicles 145f, 161
    with ellipses 303ff
Caxton, William 5
*Chambers' Dictionary* quoted 12, 265
Chaucer, Geoffrey 5
Chesterton, G K quoted 249
city and state, punctuation of 222
clause 208ff, 226ff, 317f, 319, 324
    (See also **introductory clause**)
    adjective (See **relative clause**)
    adverb 210f, 212, 215ff, 318, 334
    coordinate 212ff, 228, 231ff, 318
    defined 209
    full and elliptical 231ff, 244f, 321
    independent 210ff, 227f, 231ff, 238, 242f, 318, 324, 334
    noun 212, 218f, 318, 334
    parallel 216ff, 229, 233ff, 326
    relative (See **relative clause**)
    subordinate 227f, 318, 334
    types of 209ff, 317f

# Index

coinage (of words) 23f
colon and dash 236ff, 318, 320
   (See also **dash**)
   and capital letters 170, 237
   and introductory clauses 237ff
   and lists of items 237ff
   and quotations 237, 240ff, 288
   and sentence parts 237, 242f
comma 197ff, 318
   and clauses 198, 208ff
   and dashes 244f
   and numbers 74ff
   and parenthetic element 117ff, 327
   and quotations 288ff
   and semicolon 226ff, 332
   and sentence ancillaries 198, 201ff
   and word or phrase series 197, 198ff
   before "and" 199ff
   in addresses and correspondence 198, 219
   miscellaneous uses of 198, 220ff
common gender (See **gender**)
comparative (See **degrees of the adjective**)
condition clause and consequence clause 63ff, 319
conditional sentences (See under **mood**)
conjunction 2ff, 11ff, 38f, 213ff, 318, 319
   coordinating 228f, 231ff, 320
   in direct and reported speech 129ff
   "like" as a 11f
   mobile 224, 232, 324
   subordinating 320, 334
continuous (See **tense and aspect**)
contraction 176, 181f, 314
   and apostrophe 250f, 253ff, 264
correspondence (letters) gender identification in 20, 21ff
"could" 55f, 324
counterfactual in conditional sentences 63ff
"couple of" 43

"criterion", "criteria" 35
"Crown" 159

dagger (See **asterisk and allied symbols**)
dangling participle 206f
dash 175 (See also **colon and dash**)
   and parenthetic element 117ff, 327
   and semicolon 233
   as alternative to brackets 237, 244
   as alternative to commas, semicolons and ellipses 237, 244ff, 307f
   unique uses of 237, 245
"datum", "data" 35
denominator 91f, 282
diagonal (See **slash**)
dialogue, transcript, question–answer 242, 299
Dickens, Charles quoted 3ff
"different" with a preposition 8, 9f
digits (See **numbers**)
direct and reported speech 127ff, 177, 321, 331f
   changes to tenses in 132ff
   changes to words in 131ff
   introductory clause and 127, 128ff
   introductory verb and 130ff
   mood and 128ff
   quotation marks 284ff
dot (See **asterisk and allied symbols**)
double dagger (See **asterisk and allied symbols**)
double genitive (See **genitive**)
double punctuation 285f

"eg", "for example" 223
"either . . . or" 41
ellipsis 175, 301ff, 321
   and capital or small letters 303ff
   and dashes 245
   in poetry 307
   omission of 305, 308
   to mark interruptions etc 302, 308f

# Index

to mark omissions 302ff
emphasis 148f
emphatic (See **mood**)
*Encyclopaedia Britannica* quoted 7
"etc", "et cetera" 199
exclamation 175ff, 183ff, 322
    punctuation of 183ff, 233
exclamation mark 175ff, 183ff, 322
    and capitalisation 183, 187
    and elliptical sentences 304
    and imperative sentences 185
    and indicative sentences 186f
    and question sentences 182f
    and semicolon 226, 233
    and subjunctive sentences 186
    in brackets 188
    multiple 183, 188f
    with a question mark 188

failed past in conditional sentences 68ff
feminine (See **gender**)
"fewer" or "less" 9, 15f
finite verb (See **verb**)
"first", "firstly" 205
foreign words and expressions 147f, 266, 275
Fowler, H W quoted 13
"frequently" 50
full stop 175ff, 197, 322
    and abbreviations 176, 181
    and acronyms 176, 179ff
    and contractions 176, 181f
    and ellipses 301ff
    and indicative sentences 176
    and question sentences 192
    and reported questions 177
    and semicolon 226ff
    as decimal point 89ff, 320
    artificial 179
    double 181f
    omission of 177f
    substituting for an exclamation mark 178
    substituting for a question mark 178

fusion 250ff, 314
future (See **tense and aspect**)
future in the past (See **tense and aspect**)

gender 19ff, 322
    gender-specific and gender-free terms 28f
    relationship to sex 19, 322
genitive 251, 323
    and apostrophes 251, 256ff
    double 261
"get" 2, 5f
grammar viiff
Greek word endings 35f
greetings ("hello" etc) 136f, 299

Herrick, Robert quoted 170f, 283
honorifics 221f
"hopefully" 203
"however" 224
hyphen 265ff, 323
    dangling 265f, 266f, 323
    with numbers 75ff
    word division 265f, 266f

"I move that" 61f
"I wish" 59ff
"-ics", words ending in 34
idiom 17
"ie", "that is" 223f
"if" 65ff
    and other words with a similar function 65
    as a substitute for "whether" 10f
    "if . . . then" 2, 6f
"if only" 59f
imperative (See **mood**)
"in addition to" 40
indentation 238ff
indicative (See **mood**)
indirect questions 193
inflection 30f, 323
"inquired" (See "**asked**")
interjection 322, 323

# Index

"like" as a 12
punctuation of 183ff
interrogative (See **mood**)
introductory clause 127, 128ff, 194, 229, 233ff, 323, 324
   incomplete 239f
   independent 238ff
   with quotations 287ff
inverted commas (See **quotation marks**)
inverted names 222
irony 298
italic and roman print 142ff, 297f, 324
   reverse italics 142, 149
"its", "it's" 262

Kant, Immanuel quoted 284
Kennan, George F quoted 138ff

Latin word endings 35
"let alone" 40
letter
   addition of, to a word 247
   and apostrophe 263f
   and slash 282
letters (See **correspondence**)
"like" 9, 11ff
list markers 247f
*Listener, The* quoted 20
"lot of" 43

*Macquarie Dictionary* 12
masculine (See **gender**)
"may" 55f, 324
"medium", "media", "mediums" 35
"might" 55f, 324
Miller, Henry 5
mobile conjunction (See **conjunction**)
modal auxiliaries 55ff, 324
mode (See **mood**)
modifier 324
monosyllabic (See **syllable**)
mood 52ff, 117, 121ff, 128ff, 175ff, 183ff, 189ff, 324f, 334

and conditional sentences 52ff, 319
and direct and reported speech 128ff
and introductory clauses 287
and punctuation 121ff, 233
emphatic 325
imperative 53, 135, 183, 189
indicative (statement) 52, 58ff, 134, 175f, 176, 186f, 189f, 242, 287ff, 325
interrogative (question) 50, 135, 186, 189, 242f, 287ff, 325
negative 50, 134f, 175, 186, 189, 287ff, 325
negative-interrogative 50, 135, 187, 189, 325
positive 134, 175, 186, 189, 325
subjunctive 33f, 52ff, 186, 319, 325
uses of 58ff
   stock expressions in 62f
multisyllabic (See **syllable**)
"must" 55f, 324
"myself" and other "-self" forms 9, 13ff, 327, 330f

"namely" 223f
names and titles (See **titles and names**)
negative (See **mood**)
negative-interrogative (See **mood**)
"neither . . . nor" 41
neuter (See **gender**)
"never" 50
"news" 34
"no" (See "**yes**", "**no**")
nominative 30ff, 325
"none" 37f
nonstandard (*passim*)
   defined xi
"nor" 41
"not to mention" 40
noun viii, 43, 326
   antecedent 101ff
   apposition 220f, 248, 316f
   clause (See **clause**)

# Index

collective 36f, 318
common gender 26f
compound 266, 272ff, 319
  double-barrelled 273, 321
  genitive common 256ff
  genitive proper 258ff
  proper, and derivatives 159ff, 251, 258ff, 330
  singular and plural 15f, 31ff, 333
number, grammatical (See **singular and plural**)
numbers 71ff, 326 (See also **singular and plural**)
  and clock times 72, 98f
  and dates 72, 96ff, 247, 283
  and money sums 72, 99f
  and sporting scores 72, 100
  and standard units of weights and measures 73f
  and stock expressions 73
  Arabic (as alternatives to Roman) 95f
  as digits 71ff
  as words 71ff
  at the beginning of a sentence 73
  avoiding ambiguity with 74
  "billion" and "milliard" 80ff
  bracketed 247f
  cardinal 71, 74ff, 326
  footnote 310ff, 317, 320 (See also **asterisks and allied symbols**)
  fractions 71, 89ff, 326
  hyphenated 75ff, 266, 272ff
  mathematical 39
  ordinal 71, 83ff, 326
  punctuation of 74ff
  Roman 71, 93ff
  slash 91f, 281, 282f
  "zero" and its synonyms 76, 89f
numerator 91ff, 282

object viii, 47ff, 326
  relative pronoun as 103ff
oblique stroke (See **slash**)

"of" 41ff
"often" 50
old-fashioned (*passim*)
  defined xf
"ones", "one's" 262
"only" 8, 11ff
"or" 41
"others", "other's", "others'" 262f
"ought" 55ff, 324
*Oxford English Dictionary* quoted 12, 265

paragraph 3
parenthesis (See **parenthetic element**)
parenthetic element 49ff, 232, 246ff, 327
  multiple 117ff
  position of 118ff
  punctuation of 117ff, 223f, 246ff
  uses of 116ff
"parliament" 159
passive (See **voice**)
past (See **tense and aspect**)
past participle (See **verb**)
perfect (See **tense and aspect**)
perfect continuous (See **tense and aspect**)
period (See **full stop**)
person of pronoun and of genitive personal adjective 327
"phenomenon", "phenomena" 35
phrases (and *passim*) x, 226ff, 243, 314, 319, 320, 327, 328, 329
  series of 197, 198ff
"please", "thanks" 135f, 299
plural (See **singular and plural**)
"plus" 39f
poetry (verse) 170f, 281, 283, 307
Pope, Alexander 5
positive (See **mood**)
positive degree (See **degrees of the adjective**)
possessive (See **genitive**)
predicate 329, 333

342

# Index

prefix (See **affix**)
preliminary clause 61f
preposition 103ff, 222f, 272f, 326, 329
   at the end of a sentence 2, 4f, 108ff
   "plus" as a 39f
   "like" as a 11f
   object of 329
present (See **tense and aspect**)
present participle (See **verb**)
pronoun 43f, 101, 329 (See also
   **relative pronoun**)
   common gender personal 25ff
   in direct and reported speech 131
   personal 22ff, 101ff, 327, 333
   person of 31, 58f, 327
   possessive 328
   reflexive and emphatic 14f, 330f
prose
   capitals in, and poetry 153ff
   numbers in 71ff
   sexist language in 20, 22ff
publication details and brackets 247
punctuation (*passim*)
   and avoiding ambiguity 225
   determines meaning 197
   of direct speech 127ff
   of elliptical sentences 305f
   of introductory clauses 287ff
   of numbers 74ff
   of parenthetic elements 117ff
   of relative clauses 101ff
   problems in vii

"Queen" 159
question 175, 176f, 178f, 183, 189ff,
   316, 330 (See also **interrogative**
   under **mood**)
   and introductory clause of a
     quotation 287ff
   and semicolon 233
   and statement in the same sentence
     191, 195f
   multiple 191, 194
   single 191ff

question mark 175ff, 189ff, 330
   and ellipses 304ff
   and multiple questions 191, 194
   and semicolon 226, 233
   and single questions 191ff
question tag 195, 223, 316, 330
question word 191
quotation x, 237, 240ff, 284ff, 330
   (See also **quotation marks**)
   complex 286, 292ff
   consisting of more than one
     paragraph 291f
   embedded in a sentence 291f
   fragmentary 286f, 294ff, 330
   fragmentary with full 296
   full 286, 330
   multi-sentence 290f
   primary 292ff
   punctuation of 285ff
   secondary 292ff
   short 299
   simple 286, 287ff
   single-sentence 284ff
quotation marks x, 284ff, 330
   (See also **quotation**)
   and dialogue 299
   and direct speech (quotations)
     127ff, 284ff
   and introductory clauses 286ff
   and ironical expressions 298
   and odd or slang expressions 298
   and related punctuation 285ff
   and stock expressions 299
   and titles of cited short works 296f
   and words, expressions, sentences
     297f
   and words on signs 299f
   omission of 299
   other uses of 286, 296ff
   single and double 284, 292ff

*Random House Dictionary of the*
   *English Language* 12
"rather than" 40

# Index

relative clause 101ff, 211f, 218, 315, 318, 331, 334
   defining 101ff, 331
   nondefining 101ff, 331
   punctuation of 101ff, 331
   situational 101ff, 331
relative pronoun 101ff, 331
   omission of 109ff
   with a singular or a plural verb 43f
reported speech (See **direct and reported speech**)
roman print (See **italic print and roman print**)
rule of proximity 8

"said", "said that" 8, 10
   and quotation marks 287ff
   in direct and reported speech 127ff
salutation and complimentary closing line 219
paraphrase 294ff
"seldom" 50
"-self", "-selves", pronouns ending in 9, 13ff, 327, 330f
semicolon 226ff, 332
   and appositional pairs 230f
   and titles 230
   as a substitute for a comma 200f
sentence (and *passim*) 209f, 213ff, 319f, 333
   ancillary 198, 201ff, 332, 333
   capital letters and 150ff
   colon or dash in a 237, 242ff
   comma in a 197ff
   conditional 52ff
   direct and reported 127ff
   exclamation 175, 183ff
   full and elliptical 321
   full stop and 175ff, 322
   incomplete 175
   indicative 175ff, 189ff
   in quotation marks 297f
   parenthetic 119f
   position of "only" in a 8, 11
   punctuation of a 213ff
   question 175ff, 189ff
   quotation embedded in a 289ff
   semicolon in 226ff
   sudden turn in a 245
   with an object 48f
"series" 34f
sexist language 19f, 22ff
Shakespeare, William quoted 3ff, 249
"shall", "will" 9, 16ff, 252
Shaw, George Bernard 5, quoted 295
"should" 55, 324
sibilant 258ff, 332, 336
simple (See **tense and aspect**)
singular and plural viii, 15f, 208f, 318, 325, 333
   agreement of nominative and finite verb 30ff
   genitive common nouns 256ff
   separated by "of" 41ff
   sexist language 22ff
slang 298
slash 281ff, 333
   addresses 283
   and acronyms 282
   and numbers 91f, 281, 282f
   and units of measurement 282
   and verse 281, 283
   indicating alternatives 281f
   indicating separation 281, 282
slope bar (See **slash**)
solidus (See **slash**)
"species" 35
spelling vii
split infinitive (See **verb**)
sporting events 37
standard formal (*passim*)
   defined ixf
standard formal with consistent options (*passim*)
   defined x
standard formal with flexible options (*passim*)
   defined x

# Index

standard informal (*passim*)
    defined  xi
statement (See "indicative" under
    **mood**)
stock expression  62f, 73, 299
Strunk, William Jr and White E B
    quoted  13
subject  viii, 58, 190f, 191, 213ff,
    231f, 314, 321, 325, 327, 329, 333
    defined  31f
        relative pronoun as  103ff
        scattered  245
        simple and compound  31ff, 319
subjunctive (See **mood**)
suffix (See **affix**)
superlative (See **degrees of the adjective**)
syllable  259ff

Tennyson, Alfred Lord  5
tense and aspect  317, 334
    in direct and reported speech  132ff
    present  59f, 132f
    past  59f, 133f
    continuous  67f, 319
    past simple  59ff
    past perfect  60f, 133f
    past perfect continuous  68f
    future  16ff, 59ff, 132, 134
    future in the past  134
    future in the past simple  133f
    future in the past perfect  134f
"thanks", "thank you"  136f, 299
"that" (conjunction)  8, 10f, 61ff
    (See also **relative pronoun**)
    and reported speech  129ff
"that" (relative pronoun)  101ff
    (See also **relative pronoun**)
*TIME International* quoted  37
titles or names
    and subtitles  243
    artistic works  145
    books etc  166ff, 296
    chapters  143, 168, 296

cosmic objects  164
deities  164f
ending in "s"  261
geographic features  163
headings  166ff
journals  143, 169
legislation and law reports  143f
musical works  144f
nicknames  248, 300
organisations and office bearers  151ff
people  160
poetic works  144, 170f, 296
premises  261
proprietary names  160f
punctuation of  230, 296f
religions  165
reports  143, 168
seasons and festivals  165f
settlements  162
town features  161
vehicles  145f, 161
written works  143, 151, 166ff
"together with"  40
"told"  10 (See also "**said**")
"Treasury"  159
Treble, H and Vallins, G H quoted  12
Twain, Mark  5

underlining  142ff, 297f, 335
    (See also **italic and roman print**)
units of measure  37
usage (*passim*)
    problems of  vii, 8ff
    dogmatic myths about  1ff
    "good", defined  1, 2

verb  viii, 103, 321, 326 (See also **mood** and **tense and aspect**)
    auxiliary  46, 317, 326
        modal  55ff, 324
    base form  57, 317, 335
    compound  31, 45ff, 319
        split  45ff

# Index

finite 30ff, 189ff, 208ff, 213ff, 226f, 231f, 325, 335
   anomalous 191ff, 316
   gerund 335
   infinitive 45ff, 135, 205, 323, 328, 335
      phrase 205
      split 45ff, 333
   introductory, in reported speech 129ff, 324
   "like" as a 12
   moods of 52ff
   nonfinite 209
   notional 46, 326
   past participle 207f, 270f, 335
      phrase 207f, 327, 328
   past perfect form 57f
   past simple form 57f
   phrasal 274, 327f
   preposition-prefixed 266, 274, 329
   present participle 205f, 269f, 314, 329, 335
      phrase 206f, 328, 329
verse (poetry) 170f, 281, 283, 307
virgule (See **slash**)
"viz" 223f
vocative 156ff, 221, 244, 335
voice, active and passive 270, 314, 327, 335
voiced and voiceless sibilants (See **sibilant**)

Warnock, Dame Mary quoted 20
"were" in the subjunctive 33f, 54f, 63ff
"what" as a question word 192
"whether" 193
   and "if" 8, 10f
   and reported speech 129ff
"which" 101ff (See also **relative pronoun**)
   as a question word 192
White, Patrick quoted 3ff
"who" 101ff (See also **relative pronoun**)
   as a question word 192
   relating to a compound subject 43f
"whom" 101ff (See also **relative pronoun**)
Wilde, Oscar quoted 6
"with" 40
word (*passim*)
   additional, with ellipsis 303
   censored, punctuation of 245, 307f
   syllabic division of 265f, 266f
   in quotation marks 297, 298
   omission of, in ellipsis 301ff
   on a sign 299f
Wordsworth, William quoted 307
"would" 55, 324
"would that" 59ff

"yes", "no" 137, 176, 299
"you" 33

# Summary of common applications

# Summary of common applications

# Summary of common applications

# Summary of common applications

# Summary of common applications

# Summary of common applications

# Summary of common applications

# Summary of common applications